Community Performance

'This is an excellently structured and written book which clearly gives a context for Community Performance whilst invigorating this theory and history with illustrations of practice which are engaging and informing. The book allows the reader to feel guided as they reflect on their own work or imagine and plan work for the future. It covers a vast amount of ground, connects distinct areas of practice, doesn't assume a particular knowledge and places faith in the reader to develop their own knowledge through the practice of the exercises outlined in the book. It is a very useful, engaging book that could be returned to time and again, as people reflect and develop their own practice.'

Caoimhe McAvinchey, *Goldsmiths College, University of London*

Community Performance: An Introduction is a comprehensive and accessible practice-based primer for students and practitioners of community arts, dance and theatre. This book is both a classroom-friendly textbook and a handbook for the practitioner, perfectly answering the needs of a field where teaching is orientated around practice.

Offering a toolkit for students interested in running community arts groups, this book includes:

- international case studies and first-person stories by practitioners and participants
- sample exercises, both practical and reflective
- study questions
- excerpts of illustrative material from theorists and practitioners.

This book can be used as a stand-alone text or together with its companion volume, *The Community Performance Reader*, to provide an excellent introduction to the field of community arts practice.

Petra Kuppers has drawn on her vast personal experience and a wealth of inspiring case studies to create a book that will engage and help to develop the reflective community arts practitioner.

Petra Kuppers is a community artist, a disability culture activist and Associate Professor of English, Theatre and Women's Studies, University of Michigan. She is the author of *Disability and Contemporary Performance: Bodies on Edge* (2003), *The Scar of Visibility: Medical Performance and Contemporary Art* (2007) and co-editor of *The Community Performance Reader* (2007).

Community Performance

An Introduction

Petra Kuppers

Routledge
Taylor & Francis Group

LONDON AND NEW YORK

First published 2007
by Routledge
2 Park Square, Milton Park, Abingdon, Oxon OX14 4RN

Simultaneously published in the USA and Canada
by Routledge
270 Madison Ave, New York, NY 10016

Routledge is an imprint of the Taylor & Francis Group, an informa business

© 2007 Petra Kuppers

Typeset in Helvetica and Avant Garde by
Florence Production Ltd, Stoodleigh, Devon
Printed and bound in Great Britain by
MPG Books Ltd, Bodmin

British Library Cataloguing in Publication Data
A catalogue record for this book is available from the British Library

Library of Congress Cataloging in Publication Data
Kuppers, Petra.
    Community performance: an introduction / Petra Kuppers.
        p. cm.
    Includes bibliographical references and index.
    1. Performing arts – Social aspects.   I. Title.
    PN1590.S6K87 2007
    306.4′84 – dc22   2006029155

ISBN10: 0–415–39228–4 (hbk)
ISBN10: 0–415–39229–2 (pbk)
ISBN10: 0–203–96400–4 (ebk)

ISBN13: 978–0–415–39228–0 (hbk)
ISBN13: 978–0–415–39229–7 (pbk)
ISBN13: 978–0–203–96400–2 (ebk)

Contents

Illustrations

Preface

This book emerges from two decades of community arts practice, collaboration, transmission, workshopping, performance, discussion and ongoing learning. During these twenty years, I learned so much from so many people, there is no way to mention them all here.

First of all, to all Olimpias participants, all my love to all of you – this book is my gift back.

Thanks to the many workshop leaders and directors in Germany who taught me the fundamentals of dance theatre, devised theatre and community arts. Thanks to the Laban Guild, and the fantastic teachers on the Powys Dance Leaders in the Community course; thanks to Bev Stevens and the students at the Manchester Metropolitan University Community Dance course for the three years I taught on it; thanks to Anna Marie Taylor and the University of Wales, Swansea for making much of my experimentation possible; thanks to Community Dance Wales for being a lovely and sustaining network; thanks to the Community Dance Foundation as our national networking body; thanks to the various disability arts organizations in the UK. Thanks go to Jeannine Chartier for making Olimpias' work in the USA possible; thanks to all my community performance students at Bryant University; and thanks to Bryant University and the Rhode Island Foundation for funding the Community/Performance Conference and the Community Performance Network that emerged from it. Thanks to the trustees of the Caroline Plummer Fellowship in Community Dance, which gave me time to write this book as well as create community arts work, and to the teachers and students on the Community Dance course at the University of Otago, New Zealand. Thanks also to New Pacific Studio, Masterton, New Zealand, The Mesa Refuge, California, USA and the Institute of Medical Humanities, Galveston, Texas, USA, who offered me space and time to concentrate on developing my practice and writing.

Thanks to Joan Schirle for inviting me to see her students working in community settings, and thanks to the many, many people who have invited me over the years to work with different communities: they include Ramsey Loft at the University of New Mexico, USA, Kim Dunphy at Community Cultural Development, Melbourne, Australia, Fiona Campbell at Griffith University, Brisbane, Australia, Gisela Hermes in Germany, Tania Kopytko at DANZ New Zealand, Ruth Gould at North West Disability Arts Forum, UK, and many more. Thanks also to the collaborators who worked with the Olimpias over the years: Margaret Sharrow, Sophia Lycouris, Ana Flores, Kanta Kochhar-Lindgren, Derek McCormack, Sara Domville-Maguire, Agnieszka Woznicka and many others. A great big thanks to the participants at the Community/Performance Conference, and to my editors at Routledge who asked me to write this book. And at the conference I met my editorial buddy and organization queen, Gwen Robertson – thank you!

A note about images in this book: as you will quickly notice, I am not involved or interested in star-making, or in creating a 'canon' of 'good practice'. Instead, I try to present many everyday practices in community performance, and the photos represent this attempt – many of them are not glossy, high-res, professionally shot images. And many of the images in this book chart parts of my own workshops in recent years. There is a reason for this: community performance images are hard to come by. Documentation is not necessarily first and foremost in many practitioners' and groups' minds. Once I knew that this book was happening, I started to snap away furiously with my camera – even though there are still many private workshop experiences where the camera remained out of sight. Not everything is meant to be shared this way. The Olimpias workshop photos presented here were, as far as possible, taken with the express permission of the participants, and again, as far as possible, I ascertained that similar ethical engagements ruled the work of the other photographers in this book. I also invited many other community performance practitioners to send in photos, and many responded – but often to say, sorry, we have no images. Issues of digital divides, access and dissemination also stand in the way of a fuller representation. There are many more great community performance examples out there: experience them.

CHAPTER 1

Introduction

Experiencing myself and others dare to tell stories usually hidden, dare to face one another, via theatrical expression, via the power, the danger and the safety of theatrical process, about our differences, our unequal opportunities, our unequal privilege. And to stay in the room together, via the theatre image, and tell the truth, listen and hear each other as we hadn't before.

Jan Selman on popular theatre as social transform-ation, Prentki and Selman, 2000: 2

Our collective experience after 23 years of writing shows based on people's direct experience of resistance is that every interview reveals a new reality for us, as well as hopefully for our audiences. Each new project involves a continual process of digging beneath the media representations of reality to find out what is really happening in people's daily lives. This reality is frequently revealing, often shocking and always an education for us. It is after all a privilege to be able to reflect on these concrete experiences, and to take these experiences, combined with our own reflections, to a wider audience. If, as part of this process, we can help to make connections between people and ideas, that's one thing; if we can clarify issues along the way, that's something else; if we can boost morale and help to develop solidarity and mutual support as well, then we're really getting somewhere. We don't pretend to provide cog wheels for the great machinery of progressive change, merely a few drops of lubrication oil.

David Rogers of the UK-based Banner Theatre Company, 1997

Figure 1.1 The Olimpias Community video still: *Lady of the Lake* circle.   Photo: Petra Kuppers

Do you want to change the world through performance? Do you want to facilitate people so that more voices are heard, more moving bodies seen, more experiences felt? If so, this book can go on a journey with you. No-one can give you an answer about how to change the world, but many different voices here can show you that there is value in acting creatively and communally in our lives.

Here, I offer you ways of thinking about and engaging with community performance. I think of this book as a **toolbox**: it offers different materials, voices, wisdoms, practices and experiences that hope to provide inspiration and ideas to people engaged in, or hoping to find out more about, community performance work.

This book focuses on practices that involve different people, facilitate communication and encourage new thinking and experiencing. An important design feature of this book is **openness and dialogue**. Many community artists, theorists and historians speak in these pages, and share their experiences. Their voices mix with my own to weave a sustaining web, a snapshot of ways of working and thinking that go beyond one single person's imagination and ways of doing things.

This book's emphasis is on **questions** rather than answers and on inspiration rather than prescription. I try to guide you through significant stories about and issues in the historical development, practical application and aesthetic practice of different community performance approaches. But this book offers a partnership, a joint journey: I ask you to become involved and think about the issues from your own perspective, your own grounding in your local environment and personal history.

The aim of this book is to be a developing ground for the **reflexive practitioner**: an artist and facilitator who is grounded in thoughtful and ethical practice, aware of the direction of current debates in community performance issues, and able to be flexible, engaged and empowering. Clearly, this is a large agenda for a book. Ultimately, you are the one who enables yourself, embedded within your local framework, and this book is only a tool in the process.

How to use this book

This book works as a continuous text as well as a resource to be dipped in and out of. Throughout it you will find exercises: some are reflection exercises, some involve external research, some are practical. Some exercises address you as an individual, some encourage you to work with a partner or a group. Often, these exercises draw you to problematic areas in thought about community work. They are points of departure, and offer moments of reflection. Therefore, there is never a right or wrong way to go about working with them.

Some exercises later in the book point back to work you have done earlier: you might therefore find it useful to hold onto the notes you make to yourself.

Beyond the specific exercises, you might find it useful to create a file or box with material you have gathered or worked with. In my own practice as a community performance facilitator, I have a large box full of files with session ideas, impetus material, chalk for street drawing, scarves for dancing, small musical instruments, beautiful stones or leaves, music CDs and postcards. The box also contains my contact files for professional associations, fellow local artists, and local agencies, collaborating organizations, art providers and so on. When I am on the road for a multiple-day workshop, I add books such as Boal's *Games for Actors and Non-Actors* and *Dagyaw: A Manual*, Laban dance charts and other inspirations to the box. This box traveled with me in my car every day when I was working as a community dance artist in Wales, covering large distances to get from one group to the next. It is now in my home, and acts as a mini-filing cabinet from which I draw material for the Olimpias interdisciplinary arts workshops.

If you do not already have a box like this, you might find it useful to create the beginnings of a file system like it while working with this book. Whether you are a dancer, theatre artist, musician, visual artist or interdisciplinary practitioner, you will have resources that are particularly useful to you, and that stem from your base disciplines. They can provide the basis of the box, and the kind of exercises offered here can build on these original disciplines. For many of the exercises, I invite you to use your specific performance skills in order to address ways in which they can work in community settings. You will quickly notice that my own background emerges from dance and storytelling traditions – but throughout this book, I try to model how to reach out across disciplines, adapting forms in order to bring out voices, bodies, presences and memories.

What is community performance?

There are many different definitions of community performance, and many practices that relate to it, such as Applied Theatre, New Genre Public Art, Community-Based Performance, Participatory Arts, Community Dance, Theatre for Social Change and Engaged Art. This book presents a spectrum of different practices, with many differently nuanced and weighted ways of thinking about communal practice and community performance. 'To nail it down', to define, is an act that opposes many of the principles of community performance work itself, at least in my understanding of it. Thus, I invite you to approach definitions as journeys, different paths, ways of moving. In the following, I will share some way-marks in my journey of understanding the concept. Through a range of reflection exercises, I invite you to create the coordinates of your own provisional map of community performance.

I understand community performance to be work that facilitates creative expression of a diverse group of people, for aims of self expression and political change. Community

Definitions, decisions, power

Definitions are necessary if we are to have a clear sense of what we mean when we speak of artist and community collaborations. Delineating the terms provides direction that is critical to setting intentions, contextualizing commitment, and understanding the ethical, affective and aesthetic processes and the results that emerge from such projects.

Whether we opt for categories such as community-based, community advocacy and community-derived, or we choose to understand the practices of engagement based on a question of how collaborative specific projects are, we must address the issue of consensus. To speak of consensus (which by definition means agreement in opinion, testimony or belief), implies a decision-making process and an inherent power. Who gets to decide?

Devora Neumark, the *Reader* (eds Kuppers and Robertson, 2007)

1 Reflection exercise

What do *you* think – what are potential definitions of community performance? Write a list. As you continue reading, do you see relationships between your definitions and the ones I am presenting here?

performances are **communally created**. They are not individually authored: the end product, if it comes into existence, is not predetermined by an artist who directs people towards this goal. Instead, the outcome is (relatively) open, maybe within a thematic field opened up by the facilitator, but full of spaces and times for people to create their own expressive material. With this approach, community performances challenge conventional performance aesthetics.

Equally importantly, in my definition, community performance rests in **process rather than product**: in the act of working together, allowing different voices, bodies and experiences to emerge. Terry Galloway, Donna Maria Nudd and Carrie Sandahl name the assumptions of this way of working 'an ethic of accommodation' (see the *Reader*): a way of working that proactively challenges existing ways of working in order to allow wider participation, expression for everyone, and not just the majority. A new way of understanding 'art making' can emerge from this: an aesthetic of access that redefines who makes art, what art is, the nature of beauty and pleasure, and appropriate ways of appreciating art. These expanded concepts of art making can impact community performance in many ways. For instance, many community performance practitioners work through workshops or a series of meetings, rather than through rehearsal periods and pre-set performance dates. Many find new ways of

Figure 1.2 Spanish–British artist Carlos Cortes (far right in image) leads a workshop at the Community/Performance Conference at Bryant University, 2004. Photo: Petra Kuppers

sharing the excitement of performance, bringing creative experiments into communities.

If one conceptualizes community performance as process-based, many traditional performance issues are challenged. The following box shows what UK dance professional Anthony Peppiatt writes about community dance.

Since community performances feed from different traditions, and utilize techniques from other fields, it is not possible to distinguish them decisively from developments in theatre, dance, music and some visual art practices. Other fields also impact: art therapists, for instance, often use similar methodologies. Expressive art therapies usually aim to enable change within an individual, so that this individual can function better within the already given social world. Community performance, on the other hand, often aims to enable change both within individuals and

---

2 Reflection exercise

Discuss with a colleague the implications of this aesthetic of access. Is a performance of a Shakespeare play by a non-professional cast a community performance? If yes or no, in what ways? By what kind of definitions? Then explore the issue from the other perspective.

---

1 **Territory**

The territory of community dance activity is everywhere except professional dance performance. The driving forces in the world of professional dance performance are essentially different from those in community dance. Community dance involves all dance activities at every level but not professional dance performance. Professional dance performance has important links with community dance activities but is essentially focused on professional performance itself (training, creation, performance and touring).

This distinction can be summarized as:

Professional dance = Everything FOR performance
performance   (training, creation and touring)

Community dance = Everything AND performance (activities that do not always lead
                 to performance and performances that are not professional)

2 **Purpose**

The essential purpose of community dance activity is to increase access to dance – through experience and participation – for the benefits of all kinds of people.

3 **Process**

The main 'product' of community dance is the process in which participants are involved.

4 **Diversity**

Community dance embraces diversity, involving every dance style and everyone in the whole community (inclusive of class, age, ability, gender, sexuality and race).

5 **Economy**

Community dance broadens the arts economy through partnership with a greater range of funders, without the commercial motif of profit.

Peppiatt, 1996: 2–3

3 Reflection exercise

Can you see connections between your lists of definitions and Peppiatt's points?

within wider social structures. In some form or other, many community performance practitioners understand their work to be a form of **political labor**: facilitating creative expression as a means to newly analyze and understand life situations, and to empower people to value themselves and shape a more egalitarian and diverse future.

Freire, 1998: 14

Paolo Freire: *Pedagogy of the Oppressed*

- Man's ontological vocation is to be a Subject who acts upon and transforms his world, and in so doing moves toward ever new possibilities of fuller and richer life individually and collectively.
- Every human being, no matter how 'ignorant' or submerged in the culture of silence he or she may be, is capable of looking critically at the world in a dialogical encounter with others.
- Provided with proper tools for this encounter, the individual can gradually perceive personal and social reality as well as the contradictions in it, become conscious of his or her own perception of that reality, and deal critically with it.

Even if workshops are closed and outside the public eye, they can be political: people work together to understand their situation, and to rehearse new forms of being together and working towards a more diverse world. With this understanding of political action, many community performance practitioners point to Brazilian education theorist Paolo Freire, who writes: *'consciousness of and action upon* reality are . . . inseparable constituents of the transforming act' (Freire, 1998: 502). An analysis of reality can be achieved through different means, appropriate to the group. Formal discussion and communal analysis of local and historical patterns of oppression is one way to raise consciousness. But community performance offers a much richer view of analytical exploration that can avoid 'preaching' or purely educational approaches. Community performers can use Augusto Boal's games, explore modalities and reactions of bodies in interaction, manipulate the sounds of their environment, or listen and work with local legends, developing a poetic understanding of life. Action upon reality can also take many different forms: a different public visibility in a parade, a stage action or similar event reminiscent of traditional theatre, a video, a participatory performance that brings the audience into the circle of performers, or a communal dreaming.

Figure 1.3 Teatro Lucha actors show children all about Type 2 diabetes at a San Felipe parish fair. Teatre Lucha/de Madres a Madres & Colonial Cameron Park, Brownville, TX, 2005.   Photo: John Sullivan

Action can mean many things, including reaching out and entering into dialogue with an audience. Following theatre theorist Bertolt Brecht and his theorization of epic theatre, many community performance practitioners try to find connections with their audiences, and to instigate social change by combining the pleasures of performance with aesthetic forms that link the performance situation and the wider social world.

The following box is a chart created by Brecht to highlight aspects of his theatre politics, contrasting his approaches with 'dramatic theatre', that is, a theatre of illusion where people are entertained, and leave the theatre without feeling the need to change the world. Brecht's aesthetics have been criticized, but they still have significant impact on community performance practitioners, in modified form. As you read through this list, can you see connections with your understanding of community performance?

This Brechtian sense of breaking out of the conventional roles of theatre perfomer and theatre audience provides an important inspiration for many community performance practitioners.

Bertolt Brecht

'Certain changes of emphasis as between the dramatic and the epic theatre'

Brecht, 1964: 37

Dramatic Theatre	Epic Theatre
Plot	Narrative
Implicates the spectator in a stage situation	Turns the spectator into an observer
Wears down his capacity for action	Arouses his capacity for action
Provides him with sensations	Forces him to take decisions
Experience	Picture of the world
The spectator is involved in something	He is made to face something
Suggestion	Argument
Instinctive feelings are preserved	Brought to the point of recognition
The spectator is in the thick of it, shares the experience	The spectator stands outside, studies
The human being is taken for granted	The human being is the object of the enquiry
He is unalterable	He is alterable and able to alter
Eyes on the finish	Eyes on the course
One scene makes another	Each scene for itself
Growth	Montage
Linear development	In curves
Evolutionary determinism	Jumps
Man as a fixed point	Man as a process
Thought determines being	Social being determines thought
Feeling	Reason

Gatti, 1994: 112

French theatre director Armand Gatti

The theatre must enable people who have been deprived of a chance to express themselves to do so. We said: we have to get out of the ghetto of the theatre world and away from the language of commercial production. We had to try to develop a multiplied language that resembled the language of the street.

Haedicke, 1998: 132

Susan Chandler Haedicke on community-based devised performance

[It is] an activist form of dramaturgy which aims to influence and alter the actual world, not just reflect it. It provides an avenue to individual empowerment and community development as it moves the audience into a new role: an artist, a maker of culture who can create a community.

Every community performance practitioner has to define for her- or himself what 'changing the world' means, what 'connection' means, and what 'community' means *for them*. And any answer that you might find for yourself will probably be provisional: open to change, open to be challenged, open to be improvised through theatre, dance, music and visual art practice. We all learn, change and grow as we practice.

One significant influence on the development of community performance was the opening of the term 'performance' in the 1960s and 1970s, following on from sociological thoughts that discussed the working of everyday behavior in the shaping of social reality. Erving Goffman was a sociologist who investigated the function of roles and performances in everyday life. In the following quote, he draws attention to the interactive component of performance: a feature that is important for community performance.

Goffman, 1959: 15–16

Erving Goffman on performance

A 'performance' may be defined as all the activity of a given participant on a given occasion which serves to influence in any way any of the other participants.

Taking a particular participant and his performance as a basic point of reference, we may refer to those who contribute to the other performances as the audience, observers, or co-participants. The pre-established pattern of action which is unfolded during a performance and which may be presented or played through on other occasions may be called a 'part' or a 'routine.' These situational terms can easily be related to conventional structural ones. When an individual or performer plays the same part to the same audience on different occasions, a social relationship is likely to arise. Defining social role as the enactment of rights and duties attached to a given status, we can say that a social role will involve one or more parts and that each of these different parts may be presented by the performer on a series of occasions to the same kinds of audiences or to an audience of the same persons.

4 Reflection exercise

How can this definition of performance become resonant for community performance work? Above, I discussed community performance as a way to analyze reality, and to impact it. Using this as a starting point, how can you apply Goffman's definition to the interactions in a community performance group? Find ways to answer for yourself, and then discuss these answers with a colleague.

Figure 1.4 Performance still from *Get a Real Job*, a play about working in call centres, written and performed by telemarketers, Vancouver, Canada. Front: Cheryl Whynott as the boss; Rear: Judy Searson, Wendy Johns, Alan Asher, Linda Dickerson, Cheryl Way as the telemarketers.   Photo: Laurie McGauley

5 Reflection exercise

(Begin to) define 'community' for yourself, and give five examples of communities. Now find two colleagues, and compare your definitions and examples. What themes emerge? Are there differences? Of what kind?

What is community?

'Community' is a complex concept: how can one understand the tension between people as individuals, and people as members of a group? What are the dynamics of inclusion and exclusion that emerge in community-building? There are multiple definitions of community, and analyses of how communities emerge, regulate themselves, and act.

Warm and fuzzy

Williams, 1973: 76

Community can be the warmly persuasive word to describe an existing set of relationships, or the warmly persuasive word to describe an alternative set of relationships. What is most important, perhaps, is that unlike all other terms of social organization . . . it never seems to be used unfavorably, and never to be given any positive opposing or distinguishing term.

In his definition of community, British cultural critic Raymond Williams offers a way to think about the ubiquitous nature of the word 'community'. In the light of the Williams quote, look again at your own definitions. Do you see a problem with the 'warmly persuasive' nature of the word 'community'? How can someone from a very different political persuasion from yours utilize the world 'community'?

Iris Marion Young presents a reading of longings for community that are based on a form of illusion, a willful mis-recognition of the world we live in.

Young, 1990: 300

Us vs. them: communities of exclusion

The ideal of community . . . privileges unity over difference, immediacy over mediation, sympathy over recognition of one's understanding of others from their point of view. Community is an understandable dream, expressing a desire for selves that are transparent to one another, relationships of mutual identification, social closeness and comfort. The dream is understandable, but politically problematic . . . because those motivated by it will tend to suppress differences among themselves or implicitly exclude from their political groups persons with whom they do not identify.

Community performance practitioners face the challenge of filling the concept of community with meaning: they have to facilitate an exchange, bring people together, enable ways for the group to find its ways of working, and allow a group to value all its members. The 'warmly persuasive' nature of the concept can stand in the way of rigorous and effective exchange and exploration. Who is included, who excludes, through which explicit and implicit means? It is easy to be caught up in the warmth of communal celebration, and to uncritically stop exploration and development too early. And yet, even issues of 'too early' are problematic: who makes these decisions?

To understand 'community' as a fluid process rather than a fixed identity helps to move community arts practice forward.

Jellicoe, 1987: 46

Uniting communities

This opportunity for friendly cooperation over a long period stimulates and helps to unite a community. . . . Communities need community events to continually refresh them. Community plays can't draw everyone in and can't change everyone, but they are one of the most successful and all-embracing community events.

And within this process, problems can be addressed and change improvised – if there is space given for reconsideration, and an articulation of even small disagreements and different perspectives. But the 'warmly persuasive' nature of community is similar to the great affective power of performance: when caught up in a communal song, a movement sequence or a production number, it is hard to assess the material critically. How can the excitement of difference and plurality become the driving force for the power of performance?

Haedicke and Nellhaus, 2001: 19

Experiment

[T]here is no guarantee that the community's 'voice' will be at all univocal; more likely, in fact, it will be decisively plural, conflicted, even contradictory. That reality brings us to the second major function of community-based theatre: to experiment with strategies for solving problems affecting a particular community.

As a community performer, one difficult question concerns how this approach to improvised and rehearsed solutions can come to effect the wider social world, beyond the process of community initiated in a specific group of people. And how can products (such as staged performances) show the processes of decision-making that lead to them?

Equally important, 'community' as a process, moving towards a future, can be an important aspect of understanding the dynamics within a community group. Instead of creating a snap-shot of existing life (as individuals, as a group), community performance participants might decide that their goals lie elsewhere. Amanda Stuart Fisher found this, as she describes processes during the creation of a community performance at the Camden's Youth People's Theatre (CYPT).

Towards a different world

Fisher, 2004: 145

We had presumed that CYPT shared a coherent identity and expected the young people to create a production that reflected this.

However the play that emerged revealed a shifting and fluctuating relationship to theatre-making and lived experience. In retrospect it seems that each young person negotiated a self-defined level of identification with the characters they created. For some young people it was an aspirational process: these were characters they wanted to be like. For others, it was an escape from their own lives into a fantasy version of adult life or a make-believe world of theatre.

The final production could perhaps be best understood as a playful experiment in living a different sort of life.

This is the conundrum of community performance: how political change can be made imaginable, become tangible, and finally happen through aesthetic practice. Personal empowerment and enjoyment (such as when donning a mask in a carnival procession) is not the same as moving towards political change on a structural level. As you work through this book, return to this question: how do politics intersect community performance?

Community performance: definitions in practice

Art workers and art agencies have to negotiate these issues of community, as they relate their practices and politics to themselves, to their audiences and to their constituencies. In this example, a theatre group used different perspectives on community as the organizing principle for a performance series (for more on Cornerstone, see Kuftinec, 2003).

There follows an example of a definition of community used by a community performance agency. As you read through it, keep in mind that it is vital for community performance practitioners who wish to access these government funds to find a fit – how does the definition offer multiple fits?

Cornerstone Theater

A US-based group, created a community performance project that focused on different definitions of community

THREE DEFINITIONS OF COMMUNITY (Los Angeles, CA) 1992–4

By age: The Angelus Plaza, Los Angeles (residents: 1,200) – *THE TOY TRUCK:* adapted from a Sanskrit epic and performed in English, Spanish, Mandarin, and Korean with residents of the nation's largest low-income housing complex for seniors.

By geography: Pacoima, Los Angeles (population: 93,358) – *RUSHING WATERS*: an original musical fantasy by Migdalia Cruz about racism, justice, and a search for spiritual healing; based on 400 years of history in this community in LA's northeast San Fernando Valley.

By culture and language: Arab-Americans, Los Angeles (population: 250,000) – *GHURBA*: a play by Shishir Kurup based on stories of the Arab experience in Los Angeles, told through interviews with local residents citywide; an event of the Los Angeles Festival.

From publicity material

6 Research exercise

Research community performance examples on the Internet, if you have access to it. As you go about your research, note what is required for you to find material about these companies and artists. What resources are necessary, what language skills (on their and your part), what access to news outlets, digital resources etc.?

If you are working in a group, research each one group/artist/project, and share it with the others. With each example, discuss the appropriateness of aspects of community performance definitions.

Figure 1.5 Community participant John Graber in Cornerstone Theater Company's production of *Crossings*, journeys of Catholic immigrants, performed at St Vibiana's Cathedral in downtown Los Angeles (June/July 2002).   Photo: Craig Schwartz

Australia Council

Community Cultural Development definition

What is the Australia Council's definition of a community?

The Australia Council for the Arts does not prescribe what constitutes a community. A community can define itself by such things as geographic location, cultural background, religious belief, gender, disability or a myriad of other common factors.

Generally the Australia Council sees a community as a group of people who wish to express artistically, something about their shared experience as individuals. Through the CCD Grants Program applicants are encouraged to identify who the community is in a project. The applicant must present the arguments as to why the project is important to those communities.

Australia Council website, FAQs

---

7 Reflection exercise

With a colleague, discuss this statement: What kind of projects fall within its scope? Invent three different examples of projects one could develop with this as guidance.

Can you conceive of community performance projects that would not be within the definition given? Why would they not be within it?

You have now worked through different definitions of community performance, and hopefully the list you assembled at the beginning of this chapter is growing and changing. The provisional definitions will win even more nuance as you link the abstract concepts to creative endeavors out in the world, and as you participate in community performances yourself.

Some examples to get you going (and since it is in the nature of much community performance

Figure 1.6 Suzy Mitchell and Peter Taylor performing *Peter's Hands*. Choreographed by Peter Taylor. Magpie is an inclusive community dance company for adults with and without learning disabilities and has been based in Bromley, UK, for over ten years.   Photo: Phil Polglaze

Figure 1.7 Performance shot of refugee performers in *Pericles*, Cardboard Citizens/Royal Shakespeare Company co-production in 2003. Cardboard Citizens is a London, UK based performance group, who run free, weekly, open access, workshops for homeless and ex-homeless people led by professional artists.
Photo: Robert Day

work to fall outside the radar of many critics and art publications, remember that 'fame' is not necessarily an important consideration):

Teatro Trono, Bolivia
Natya Chetana, India
Sistren Theatre Collective, Jamaica
Philippine Educational Theater Association
    (PETA), Philippines
7:84 Theatre Company, Scotland, UK
Cardboard Citizens, UK
David Glass Ensemble, UK/Vietnam
Gravity, UK
San Francisco Mime Troupe, USA
Liz Lerman Dance Exchange, USA
Barefoot Artists, Rwanda/USA
Appalachia's Roadside Theater, USA
Chikwakwa Theatre, Zambia

Add the definitions of community performance that you find in this way to your growing list. Is your map changing?

Community arts have moved on from early conceptions. In particular, many contemporary community performance practitioners recognize that there are no 'basic' and given communities: most community projects will emerge through self-selection, through provisional and temporary identification with a specific group's aims. Everybody has multiple identities, and works through different roles. In community performance projects, the aim of inclusion, openness and movement towards a mutually agreed goal can only ever be improvisational. To me, the point in community performance is in this improvisation, this balance: in allowing oneself to be part of something, giving up some autonomy in order to win a different kind of self-expression and empowerment.

CHAPTER 2

Remembering histories

Writer and theorist N'Gugi Wa Thiong'o is a major influence on community performance practitioners in Africa and beyond. He has a vision of performance and art as a humanizing influence, celebrating local creativity in a post-colonial world:

> In an age where science and technology have developed to a level where it is possible to outlaw poverty, we see the return of the Dickensian world on a global level. More and more people feel themselves confined to mega-ghettos. And the state, far from being subject to social control of the majority, becomes even more beholden to financiers. [. . .] In such a world, art, with its embodiment of notions of creativity and freedom, needs to assert itself. It needs to be active, engaged, the embodiment of dreams for a truly human world where the progress of any one person is not dependent on the downfall of another, [. . .] where millionaires are not created on the backs of a million poor. [. . .] The goal of human society is the reign of art on earth.

N'Gugi Wa Thiong'o, 1998: 6

The story of community performance can be told in many different ways. The practices that come together under the label 'community performance' are diverse and varied, and so are the histories through which practitioners arrive at their work. For the purposes of this book, I will open up a small number of historical narratives that all feed what can be identified as community performances in (predominantly) Western performance practices. As you will see, these stories are just that – they are ways of making sense, not firm, exclusionary 'facts' that attempt to pinpoint specific ways in which history unfolded. I will trace a number of storylines:

- the re-discovery of folk practices;
- avant-garde practices;
- 'art of the everyday' movements;
- animator movements;
- arts in service.

Many of these movements came into being as oppositional movements: as ways to counteract certain tendencies their proponents identified in the dominant art forms. With this, I am identifying community performance not with age-old, uninterrupted folk traditions, ritual cultures or the many spiritual and secular performance routines that nourish cultural life in all cultures. Instead, I place community performance within the counter-movements that emerged in twentieth- and twenty-first-century Western performance work, although many of these forms are informed and shaped by vernacular older performance practices, and impact these practices as we move into the future. Oftentimes, the boundaries between vernacular performative practices and community performance are fluid, and therefore these lines through the history of community performance need to be supplemented by the many histories assembled in areas such as theatre, art, dance, anthropological research, sociocultural research, theology and sport studies.

Given the scope of this book, and the breadth of different practices and histories, I will not provide specific histories for the development of community performance practices in different countries. But this book attempts to engage you, and make you an active participant. One exercise in Chapter 3 (p. 58) focuses on exploring your network, placing your own ambitions for projects and art practice into your local context. As a preparation for this exercise, begin some initial research into the community performance ecology of your country, region or locality. Look out for terms such as Applied Theatre, Community Dance, Community-Based Theatre, Engaged Art, New Genre Public Art, Theatre for Social Change, Theatre for Development, Community Cultural Development, or whatever terms might be in use where you live. What are the conditions in which community performance work exists and grows in your area? Some of the histories and stories I am presenting will be nearer to you than others, but many of the connections between different accounts, practices and narratives will hopefully have resonance for you.

Figure 2.1 The author's early community performance experiences. With sister and friends, getting ready to join the village's carnival parade, in the early 1970s.
Photo: most likely my mum

Processions: Mardi Gras

Mardi Gras, Shrove Tuesday or Fat Tuesday is a celebration that merges Christian ritual with other historic, 'Pagan' origins: within the Christian calendar, Fat Tuesday is a celebration of excess leading up to Lent, the fasting days before Easter (hence 'carnevale': goodbye to meat). The rites hold memories of the Lupercalia, a Roman celebration. The Mardi Gras processions are a firmly established part of life in many areas of the world, from the New Orleans Mardi Gras to the Sydney Lesbian and Gay Mardi Gras, from the Rosenmontags-Parades I grew up with in Germany to the stylized masks of Venice. Many of these celebrations go back hundreds of years, and have sub-rituals and traditions.

2.1 Remembering folk practices

Part of modern thought in Western cultures included a critique of the economic practices that made modernity possible. Many attacked the industrial revolution and its tendency to standardize features of life across large swathes of the population, its reinforcement of class distinctions, and its general disruptions of older patterns of life. From early on in the eighteenth century, thinkers rebelled against the sameness and soullessness that they identified with modernity. Romanticism as a way of thinking about the world emerged in many different cultural circles. As a movement it was not unified by a specific style of art, but by a rebellious attitude towards authority, modernity and industrial life. Many romantics turned to nature as the source of spiritual and aesthetic rescue from the mundane and predictable rhythms of the factory and the machine. And just as 'nature' was cast as the other to 'culture' (and the usefulness of this distinction and binary has spurned on thought ever since), so the everyday emerged as a realm of wonder and beauty. Many romantic artists rejected classical training as a prerequisite for art making, and instead they valued the complexities inherent in human minds per se – dreams, visions, madness became recognized as places

> ## 8 Research exercise
>
> Research three different Mardi Gras/Carneval/Fasching practices, or a similar events meaningful to you, and discuss in what way these can be seen as traditional ritual, as contemporary recreation, as a community intervention, as a one-off performance event, as culture 'from below' or 'from above', as spectacle, economic event, civic affirmation, religious practice. Create a chart, and assemble arguments. Most likely, you will see that all events have aspects of most of these categories, and can be discussed in myriad ways.

where mystery and interest intersected. They turned away from art productions in workshops, taught as a craft by masters, which were dominant features of art production until the eighteenth century. Instead, these artists embraced art practices that seemed to them more closely in touch with 'the natural': folk art, half-forgotten rituals, often pre-Christian pagan rituals. And this new interest in folk art led to scholarly activity, and to attempts to hold on to half-forgotten and half-recreated histories. Much of the knowledge of earlier European folk practices of various kinds come to us today through the efforts of antiquarians and researchers, artists and connoisseurs active in the eighteenth and

Figure 2.2 *Longline – The Carnival Opera*. Welfare State International's last event after 38 years, March 2006.
Photo: Ged Murray

Remembering carnival

Carnival celebrated temporary liberation from the prevailing truth of the established order: it marked the suspension of all hierarchical rank, privileges, norms and prohibitions.

Bakhtin, 1968: 10

nineteenth centuries. They worked at the meeting points of classicism and romanticism with their dual interests in archiving and cataloging, and the widening of the archive to its explosive limits. In the early nineteenth century, the brothers Grimm in Germany researched fairy tales, and laid down a huge store of storylines and myth elements that might have been lost without this labor, or might be even harder to trace than they are now. In 'collecting' these works, often through oral history methods, people like the Grimms listened to the stories in their many forms, since everybody told them a bit

differently. The researchers by necessity overlaid the 'originals' with the language, concepts and values of their time and production constraints, and in many cases, the act of archiving became an act of reinvention. To capture a fairy tale in a book intervenes in the mechanism of oral tradition – but it also enables the dissemination and re-invention of the oral traditions at moments where the conventional methods for dissemination are disrupted (through population movements, labor practices, changes in the way that people live together).

Figure 2.3 Ake Ake Theatre Company, a circus theatre performance group, presents stilt-walkers, roller-skaters and clowns at an interactive public performance of *Our Secret Garden* in the Te Papa museum, Wellington, New Zealand 2006.
Photo: Petra Kuppers

Welfare State International and vernacular art

Vernacular is a Latin term that we use in English only for the language that we have acquired without paid teachers. In Rome, it was used from 500 BC to AD 600 to designate any value that was homebred, homemade, derived from the commons, and that a person could protect and defend though he neither bought nor sold it on the market. I suggest that we restore this simple term 'vernacular' to oppose commodities and their shadow.

Illich, 1981

In his impassioned plea for poetry, Welfare State International (WSI) founder John Fox describes how WSI's practices are based on notions of vernacular art. He gives an example that shows the wide-reaching and large-scale effects of WSI's performance work:

With this concept of Vernacular Art mind WSI began, in 1979, to create a series of Lantern Processions in Ulverston, Cumbria. The idea came after we had performed a carnival King Lear at a 'big art' theatre festival in north Japan. On holiday afterwards we visited a small village to observe a Shinto Lantern Festival. Here large and heavy wooden constructions with lantern sails, each carried by fifty men and fifty drummers, were duly floated out to sea in a 'blessing of the boats'. Later we wondered: could anything of this be transferred to Anglo-Saxon rainy Cumbria in autumn?

Well, in fact the transfer has been extraordinary. Nine years ago we started with a procession of three hundred people with one hundred lanterns. Simply made from dried willow sticks and white tissue paper and candles, the lanterns were truly homemade and certainly vernacular. Now the procession has grown to many thousands and the lanterns have become large and wonderful sculptures of every shape and form. People who had probably never made anything in their lives are now accomplished artists.

If it were relevant this work would look elegant in any large art gallery, but it would be without the context of purpose and sharing which readily draw the community together in a great glow-worm river of light. It is unspoken but there is a sense of this being a secular religious festival staged at the time of migration filling 'the gaps between words and thoughts'.

Ulverston is a comfortable market town of 12,000 population and we had thought that this kind of event might only work in a rural environment.

But we tried it in Glasgow as well. Here, using the 'City of Culture' resources (and the shop window) of Glasgow 1990, we demonstrated that it is possible to make a symbolic community based around the making and parading of art objects. Over a period of 18 months we organised workshops throughout Strathclyde and Glasgow so that on the 6th October 1990, 10,000 people gathered with over 8,000 lanterns in four simultaneous processions. At the end of the parade a large percentage of these lanterns were hung on five wooden towers. The towers were constructed of hexagonal sections which could be raised steadily by large cranes. As they rose in the air the participants hung their lanterns on three rising pagodas so that before the final firework display they and we had constructed together five complex, celebratory sculptures.

John Fox, 1991

Invented tradition

'Invented tradition' is taken to mean a set of practices, normally governed by overtly or tacitly accepted rules and of a ritual or symbolic nature, which seek to inculcate certain values and norms of behaviour by repetition, which automatically implies continuity with the past. In fact, where possible, they normally attempt to establish continuity with a suitable historic past. . . . However, insofar as there is such reference to a historic past, the peculiarity of 'invented' traditions is that the continuity with it is largely fictitious. In short, they are responses to novel situations which take the form of reference to old situations, or which establish their own past by quasi-obligatory repetition

Hobsbawm and Ranger, 1983: 1f.

One example of these 'invented traditions' born out of a romantic interest in the past is the Druidic circle (gorsedd) in Wales, where druids meet in stone circles for ritual work. The man credited with the revival/invention, Morganwg (1747–1826), was a contemporary of the Grimm brothers mentioned earlier. His actions were partly spurned as a form of resistance to the ongoing colonialization of Welsh land, language and customs by the English:

The Gorsedd of Bards . . . was born of the imagination of a humble, but scholarly, country stonemason, Iolo Morganwg, who came under the influence of the antiquarian revival that turned men's minds towards Stonehenge and 'druidical altars', and of the radical romanticism that was stimulated by the French Revolution. He had a dream in which he saw the land of his fathers as a haven of culture as it was, according to Caesar, in the time of the Druids . . . He linked the Welsh bardic tradition with ancient beliefs and created 'an arcana of neo-druidism', and set out to 're-establish' the Gorsedd of Bards of the Isle of Britain.

Miles, 1992: 7

Community performances can tap into the pleasures of traditions – invented, reimagined, re-born. There can be many sources of a given community performance's power, and a reflective practitioner can find ways of finding connection in multiple ways. How can performances consciously reveal their use/remake/change of tradition?

Clearly, the dominant vision of 'invented traditions' is negative: they are somehow 'less valuable' because they are 'newly' invented. But, from a different perspective, any form of transmission is a form of re-invention. And when this re-invention is bodily based (as in much performance work), conventional notions of the relative superiority of the word can stand in the way of acknowledging the legitimacy and power of these alternatives to book-based knowledge.

At Culture Moves!, a Pacifica dance conference in Wellington, New Zealand (2005), I witnessed a very moving and powerful re-invention. A group of people from the Pacific island of Guam presented *Inetnon Gef Pa'go* as an attempt to re-invent a dance form lost after hundreds of years of colonial contact and after missionaries suppressed Islander dance traditions. The performance gave rise to much discussion with the audience: 'Who created this dance?', 'In what way is it validated by the Islander community?', 'In which ways and why does it matter that there is no "legitimized" transmission?', 'What is at stake here in our attempts to discuss legitimization in the face of these dancers' pleasure and pride?'.

One of the pleasures of tradition is the focus on ritual, and on the dual moments of suspension and affirmation that can occur in rituals.

Victor Turner and communitas

The anthropologist Victor Turner created highly influential definitions of the relationships between ritual, community and the potential for change inherent in ritual action. He focuses this through the complex term 'communitas': a state in which social distinctions are in (problematic) suspension in the joint experience, a liminal or edge-state outside normal structures:

> I have used the term 'anti-structure,' . . . to describe both liminality and what I have called 'communitas.' I meant by it not a structural reversal . . . but the liberation of human capacities of cognition, affect, volition, creativity, etc., from the normative constraints incumbent upon occupying a sequence of social statuses
>
> Turner, 1982: 44

9 Reflection exercise

Discuss with a colleague your experiences (or imaginings) of ritual. What experiences come near? Think of events such as religious services, raves and club events, or protest marches. Do you have a sense of what Turner means when he speaks of a 'liberation of human capacities from normative constraints'? What is so problematic about this place of 'liminality': of being in suspension? Are rituals radical, or do they affirm existing structures?

European countries know colonial histories: areas of land were constantly fought over, territorialized and reclaimed – parts of kingdoms, feudal holdings, Roman principalities and war annexes. These lands changed their names, languages, religions and cultural practices over time. In Britain, processions, parades, masques and other ritual-based performance forms, and Anglo-Saxon and Germanic traditions mixed with Norman court practices and Christian ritual, creating material for contemporary forms that wish to honor the memory of land and people. In the more colonial context of nations such as the USA or Australia, the encounter with traditions works by necessity along different lines.

Jan Cohen-Cruz has provided an in-depth history of the development of community-based performance in the USA in *Local Acts*. She writes about sources of the development of the form:

> Evidence of precursors to community-based performance establish it as a field with a rich past, providing models, variations, and legitimizations. Community-based art in this country extends back to Native American forms that expressed and preserved the collective identity of the original inhabitants of this land. As other cultural groups came, by force or by choice, each brought traditions that they continued to practice, often with innovations, in the 'new world'. At some relatively recent point – writer/director John Reed and designer Robert Edmond Jones's collaboration with 1500 immigrant workers on the Paterson Strike Pageant in 1913 comes to mind (see Nochlin 1985) – professional artists began working with collectively identified groups, providing craft and receiving, in turn, meaning-rich performance content. The intended audiences were primarily of the same community as the performers.
>
> Cohen-Cruz, 2005: 9

Later, Cohen-Cruz discusses some of the critical issues that can pertain to the use of ritualized large-scale performances:

> Assimilation was . . . a goal of MacKaye's pageant to accompany naturalization ceremonies. Undertaken on a massive scale – a St. Louis one was performed by a cast of 7500 before an audience of a half million – patriotic songs and dances helped to transform foreigners into American citizens. My critique is not the celebration of Americana, a totally appropriate focus of a naturalization ceremony, but the implicit message that one could not have dual allegiances to one's place of birth and one's new home. Pageants are problematic in their unequal power dynamic and the overly simplified message they often projected concerning 'Who is "us"'?
>
> Cohen-Cruz, 2005: 18

10 Reflection exercise

Look at the various ritual/pageant performances mentioned in the previous pages. Research some of them in more detail, and think about examples in your own community (carnivals, parades). In what ways are voices and visibility controlled? Who makes the decisions?

Commedia dell'Arte

Commedia is exaggerated acting, but it should be the exaggeration of a truth. Its parallel in illustration is caricature, which takes a politician's bulbous nose, or a royal prince's large ears (facts, truths) and 'exaggerates' them for our amusement. Its target is often the same as that of Commedia – an attack on the foibles of human vanity and pomposity.

Grantham, 2000: 36

Beyond the pageant and the procession, many other early performance forms impact on community performance. A beloved European tradition is Commedia dell'Arte, a form that uses a number of specific characters, such as Pantalone, the Doctor, Arlecchino, Pierrot, Pulcinella, Colombina, the Lovers, all (relatively) easily adopted by community performers who are familiar with the form, to satirize issues and events.

Cultural contact through colonialist practices, warfare and trade is a part of many peoples' history. For Western European and later North American cultural development, and to some extent for other colonial societies, the exotic Other

Figure 2.4 Mask workshop with students at Bryant University, Rhode Island, USA, 2004.
Photo: Petra Kuppers

has functioned as a significant draw and point of fascination. Thus, artists did not only look towards their own hidden folk practices, but also to art forms from elsewhere. Picasso sought inspiration among African masks in museums, and many performance artists likewise looked for 'the primitive' and 'the exotic' in other peoples' art practice. But again, the alignment of other peoples' art with notions of primitivism obscures art's own significant social and cultural roles, its own complexities and its own historical trajectory. In contemporary community performance work, practitioners strive to be respectful to all art practices, and to understand them as complex parts of complex societies, not as ideas that can be picked up, recycled and easily incorporated.

Issues in intercultural performance: energy

Energy and tension are two much discussed principles of performance – and many practitioners have identified these elements in various cultural forms of this work. In response, much performance training aims to focus, bundle and strengthen energy, allowing the performer's presence to be a conduit through which forces flow in and out. This way of thinking about performance also shapes much intercultural work. John Martin writes:

> When we see actors from Kathakali, Noh Theatre or the Beijing Opera we sense that they have an inner energy supporting the role they are playing. We often sense that this energy is much greater than that which is being used in performance, but which has huge latent potential. In Noh there is a tenet: feel in the heart ten, but show in the body only seven. It implies that the audience should always feel that much more is possible at any moment, giving a sense of potentiality, almost of danger.
>
> Martin, 2004: 12

What are the equivalents to this kind of 'extra' charge or energy in Western performance methodologies?

It would be easy to see a redemptive Other to Western (or European) supposed 'stiffness' or 'lethargy' in non-Western cultural forms, and the charge of exoticism and Orientalism has indeed been made against many Western-based performance companies who aim to use non-Western performance methodologies. The dualisms that underpin such problems might be Western/non-Western (already a problematic distinction), 'high art'/folk (a distinction that had particular currency in modernist discussions of art practice), commercial/authentic, stiff/natural, aesthete/direct, secular/ritual. All of these dualisms are themselves suspect, and mobilize all kinds of stereotypes about selves and Others, and different kinds of cultural contact.

11 Research exercise

Research three of these: Kathakali, Noh Theatre, the Beijing Opera, Wagnerian opera practice, or romantic ballet. How does energy and the withholding of it feature in these forms? Think about these concepts in relation to non-dramatical forms: how does energy feature in a Catholic mass, in yoga practice, in boardroom discussions?

Antonin Artaud

The key to throwing the audience into a magical trance is to know in advance what pressure points must be affected in the body. . . . To be familiar with the points of localisation in the body is to reforge the magical skills. Using breathing's hieroglyphics, I can rediscover a concept of divine theatre.

Artaud, 1970: 101–2

Figure 2.5 Uncle Sam, Bremen Bilder Theatre, Germany 1977.   Photo: Joan Merwyn

Contemporary intercultural theatre emerges from three themes:

- the ongoing tensions surrounding a romanticizing of the 'Other';
- a need for a self-critical examination of one's own stance and background;
- the requirement to clarify one's own goals and the cultural basis for one's politics.

Many of the issues have strong resonance for community performers. Rustom Bharucha used theatre work to confront the life of *dalits* (landless laborers in India), and to open up a space of contact between castes. He acknowledges the significant problems with working within these debates.

How does one intervene in any intracultural encounter without becoming coercive or violent through the force of an assumed enlightenment? Not to intervene, however, could only perpetuate the 'primitivization' of Third World actors, whose 'instinct' and 'spontaneity' have been valorized for so long (and particularly by interculturalists) at the expense of acknowledging their consciousness. . . .

I would suggest that in any work with actors from 'other' cultures, and, more specifically, from deprived socio-economic contexts, the point is not to use their 'indigenous' skills or resources in order to authenticate them, but, in a catalytic process, to ignite what has been submerged so that the critical consciousness of the actors can be heightened.

Bharucha, 2000: 107

2.2 Questioning the boundaries

Avant-garde practices and their oppositional stance to 'traditional' Western art practices provide a related important and fruitful reservoir for community arts development. In this history story, practitioners find themselves unhappy with existing aesthetic forms and their rules and conventions. Surrealism was one of the first modernist art movements that emerged from this frustration with existing practice, that responded by enlarging the potential sources for creative endeavor. Surrealist artists are often concerned with bringing unconscious impulses to expression: dreams, automatic writing and doodling were important sources for surrealist art. One such source of 'unadulterated', 'raw' expression was outsider art, which was understood to mean art created by people outside the conventional art system, and in particular art created in psychiatric institutions, by children and by folk artist. Surrealist artists and writers were fascinated with this supposed 'direct' art, the authenticity of art without aesthetic frame, structure or focus on markets.

---

12 Reflection exercise

Discuss with a colleague the meaning of Bharucha's 'critical consciousness'. Is this an undoing of 'authentic' forms? What are the costs for performers who approach their communities and traditional frameworks from a critical perspective?

Outsider art

We understand by this term works produced by persons unscathed by artistic culture, where mimicry plays little or no part. . . . These artists derive everything – subjects, choice of materials, means of transposition, rhythms, styles of writing, etc. – from their own depths, and not from the convention of classical or fashionable art. We are witness here to the completely pure artistic operation, raw, brute, and entirely reinvented in all of its phases solely by means of the artists' own impulses. It is thus an art that manifests an unparalleled inventiveness.

Jean Dubuffet, 1949, quoted in Rhodes, 2000: 24

Of course, there are significant problems with the label 'outsider art', and with the practices that have emerged from this labeling. The term solidifies social disjunction; it keeps people in their places. It is not concerned with widening access to artistic expression, training, funding and networking. It does not recognize the kind of non-formalized training that occurs in social settings (for instance, in folk practices) and assumes a kind of 'non-cultured' innocence of both children, mental patients and 'primitives'.

But issues of self and Other, and a need to undo the certainties of the 'individual', continue to influence contemporary art practice. Many community arts practitioners use avant-garde practices to rehearse alternative forms of understanding agency, selfhood, interconnection and interdependence.

Suzi Gablik on art, values, egos

As artists learn to integrate their own needs and talents with the needs of others, the environment and the community, a new foundation for a non-self conscious individualism may emerge – and we will have, not necessarily better art, perhaps, but better values, aims, beliefs. But the ego must pass through its death first, as Levin points out, before it can be reborn in its other vision of community and intersubjective coexistence; and the 'ego' in question is not just the individual ego, it is the social and historical ego as well, whose thinking is still under the spell of narcissism as a model for the self's development.

Gablik, 1991: 144

**C
A
S
E
S
T
U
D
Y**

Anna Halprin

Anna Halprin is an experimental dance artist and ritualist, creating participatory events for social change and community healing. She is, together with Daria Halprin-Khalighi, co-founder of the Tamalpa Institute in California, a study center where psychology, community arts, ritual practice and dance intersect. In *Moving Towards Life*, Halprin shares elements of her transformational dance practice. She writes about two elements of her contemporary dance rituals, trance dancing (a form of movement practice found in many cultures) and myth making:

The motivation in (this) trance dance is to experience the process of the journey from the self to the many and back to the self again; to move with collective energies and flow with them, discovering where they will take up without knowing anything before it happens. . . .

Trance dance

Objective: To create a communal rhythm to flow between everyone, performers and audience. Abolition of resistance through moving into trance-like state. Separating the 'mind' (intellect, attention) from the 'body' (feeling, awareness).

Score: Adopt and repeat basic step with up-down rhythm. Use drumming as unifying element. Flow with other movements . . . vocalize breath. . . . merge with other sounds. . . . Allow 'myth' to happen through the creation of this moving community.

As we do this dance, outside stimulus fades out, the drum correlates and unifies the dancing, the collective energy and group consciousness gather, and a *Myth* (tribal happening) emerges. A *Myth* is a formalized even that emerges spontaneously from the group. The *Myth* is unique to that moment in time and space. It is a tribal event that has never happened before, with only one life. This *Myth* symbolizes the spirit of the collective psyche of the group. . . . It could be anything, and whatever the event is, it is unpredictable. As you read this, you may wonder, what is a *Myth*? It will happen, and when it does, you will know.

Halprin, quoted in Kaplan, 1995: 128

In 1967, as part of an ongoing exploration of audience participation and community building, Halprin led dancers and audiences in ten weeks of weekly 'performances'. In these participatory events, audiences and performers together tested out ideas of 'community', release of creativity, meaningful encounter, environmental exploration, ritual and play. Each event was different, and the weekly 'myths' had themes such as creation, atonement, trails, totem, maze, dream – concepts that emerged from many different cultures' mythical heritage. For each event, about fifty people gathered at the Dancers' Workshop studios in San Francisco. Here are two examples of these myths: week eight, Masks, and week nine, Storytelling.

Figure 2.6 *The Planetary Dance*, Marin County, California.   Photo: Marguerite Lorimer

Myth eight: Masks

After a briefing, everyone was given an apple. The audience sat in pairs opposite each other eating their apples, and were told to look at each other's faces while eating. They were asked, in partners, to mold each other's faces. They began to respond to their faces and the way the altered face made them feel and behave, to react to people around them with their faces. Groups moved their chairs to the center space facing the platform and we took photographs of groups of people reacting to each other with their altered faces frozen. Small groups performed, supposedly for the camera, but actually for the rest of the people who were watching. There was rapt attention given to the performers, and much humor, laughing and tremendous enjoyment with one another.

Myth nine: Storytelling

This *Myth* was devoted to storytelling, and placed great stress on an individual statement to the group. Each person walked around the interior of a large circle of people. He was asked to tell a story he had never told to anyone before, something that happened when he was a child. A lighted candle was given to him, illuminating his features, and he was told to pass it to another person when he completed the story. As it was passed, the musicians improvised and the mover and the musicians were doing something together. The storytelling was woven into the moving and passing of the candle.

Each person revealed the intimacy of himself, his deepest feelings, in a story that had been so personal that he had never told it before. His use of the candle, the place he chose to tell the story, and the gestures he used, all contributed to the inner qualities of his story. The audience then broke into smaller groups and those who had not had a chance to tell stories began to tell theirs to a person sitting next to them. The evening concluded with everyone moving and dancing a very soft and ceremonious dance with his own candle lit.

Halprin, quoted in Kaplan, 1995: 138

Part of a challenge to mainstream aesthetics emerges from an understanding that the agreement between audiences, performers and the social field that surrounds them is exclusionary, and prohibits some people from participation. If participation is valued higher than the existing aesthetic, new forms of encounter and performance can emerge.

Figure 2.7 Fremantle Parade, Australia, 2005.
Photo: Petra Kuppers

Study questions

- What do you imagine could be the potential effects of a ten-week happenings cycle like this on participants? What kind of transformations might be part of the experience?
- These myths are powerfully composed of many traditional ritual, myth and storytelling traditions. Example: apples hold mythical meaning. In Christian-inspired mythological universes, the apple signifies forbidden knowledge (as the apple was the object of desire offered to Eve by the Serpent). In Greek mythology, the apple of Paris was an object that initiated discord between goddesses who tried to discern which of them was the most beautiful, and it started the Trojan War. Knowledge, truth, beauty: these are themes connected with the apple. Other cultural traditions also award special narrative status to the apple. Try to identify four different such elements in the two sample sessions. In what way does using these mythologically loaded elements influence the ritual/performance/happening? Does it matter that not all people will know these stories?

2.3 Valuing the everyday

Social sculpture: Joseph Beuys

My objects are to be seen as stimulants for the transformation of the idea of sculpture . . . or of art in general. They should provoke thoughts about what sculpture can be and how the concept of sculpting can be extended to the invisible materials used by everyone.

> THINKING FORMS – how we mold our thoughts or
> SPOKEN FORMS – how we shape our thoughts into words or
> SOCIAL SCULPTURE – how we mold and shape the world in which we live:
> SCULPTURE AS AN EVOLUTIONARY PROCESS; EVERYONE IS AN ARTIST.

That is why the nature of my sculpture is not fixed and finished, processes continue in most of them: chemical reactions, fermentations, color changes, decay, drying up. Everything is in a state of change.

Beuys, in Kuoni, 1990: 19

Artists who are interested in practices of the everyday recognize its importance in the inscription of social and cultural values and concepts. We are acculturated by what we do: every time a young girl puts on a skirt and plays with dolls, she re-inscribes herself and her body into a gendered order.

If performance merely repeats existing genres, existing experiences, it becomes stale, and loses its power – that is the belief of many practitioners who place their work at the borderline of art and everyday life.

Allen Kaprow on happenings

The line between art and life should be kept as fluid, and perhaps as indistinct as possible. . . . Something will always happen at this juncture, which, if it is not revelatory, will not be merely bad art – for no one can easily compare it with this or that accepted masterpiece.

Kaprow, 1966: 188

For many artists, audience participation, happenings that blurred the boundaries between stages, public and private spaces, and installations in public environments became important new principles in creating art experiences. The lure of these activities rested in their perceived transgression – they shocked audiences, threw people off balance, created curiosity and excitement. Richard Schechner sums up some aspects of this alluring potential for new forms in the following box.

Richard Schechner on the power of participation in theatre

What is it about participation that gives it such seductive and dangerous charm? Theatre is traditionally the interplay of destinies, the actualization of stories already completed by the author and rehearsed by the performers. The performance is less dangerous than the processes that lead up to it. The logic of the play-in-performance is the 'destiny' of tragedy and the 'fortune' of comedy. Participation voids destiny and fortune, throwing drama back into its original theatrical uncertainty: re-introducing elements of the unrehearsed into the smooth ground of the performance. . . . The audience is invited to put aside the role of witness and assume other, more active roles. . . . Participation doesn't eliminate the formalities of theatre – it goes behind them to fetch private elements into the play.

Schechner, 1994: 78

Community performance owes some of its international practices to this re-evaluation of the everyday as a significant place of political action and of community development. Contact improvisation has become a significant tool in community dance (see Novak, in the *Reader*), and the practices at Judson Church and other historical coalescing points for contemporary artists have allowed many contemporary community performers to explore experimental practices.

Ping Chong, an Asian-American artist, also explores community-based methods in some of his work, which often focuses on intercultural issues and fields of contact. In *Undesirable Elements*, Chong works with immigrant actors (some with, some without previous theatrical experience) local to the performance site, and gives a form to the multiple and varied stories that make up people's lives and their family's journeys. Using the power of speaking from one's own life, a strong and simple stage lighting scheme, and ritualized actions that frame the often moving biographical material,

Contact improvisation

Steve Paxton is one of the instigators of contact improvisation, a form of dance that emerges in 1970s New York. In contact improvisation, the focus is on flow, engagement with the moment, and attention to the specifics of bodies as agents in gravity:

> Contact improvisation is an activity related to familiar duet forms such as the embrace, wrestling, martial arts, and the jitterburg, encompassing the range of movement from stillness to highly athletic. The exigencies of the form dictate a mode of movement which is relaxed, constantly aware and prepared, and on-flowing. As a basic focus, the dancers remain in physical touch, mutually supportive and innovative, meditating upon the physical laws relating to their masses: gravity, momentum, inertia and friction. They do not strive to achieve results, but rather, to meet the constantly changing physical reality with appropriate placement and energy.
>
> Paxton, 1978: 1

Undesirable Elements celebrates the strength of its actors and uses a recognizable and familiar Western format to allow these everyday stories to be heard. The publicity material posits: 'Since each individual's experience encompasses that of his or her ancestors and culture, the piece is a journey through the turbulent history of the 20th century from a global perspective' (program notes).

Engagement, and a reaching out from separate aesthetic spheres into other public spaces, is the core concern of 'new genre public art', a form of thinking about art practice that builds from the push towards redefining monumentality and the place of art on plazas, streets or other public environments.

Many contemporary artists who explore work on the boundaries of community performance are influenced by Nicolas Bourriaud (see also Nordbye, Robertson and Shaw in the *Reader*).

Most of the artists discussed in these pages can be discussed through a lens of relational aesthetics – their work relies first and foremost on the engagement engendered by their activity. What 'engagement' means, though, changes in different contexts.

Figure 2.8 Magpie Dance Youth Group; Hannah Dempsey and David Nurse. Magpie is an inclusive community dance company for adults with and without learning disabilities and has been based in Bromley, UK, for over ten years.   Photo: Phil Polglaze

Figure 2.9 *Secret History*, a Ping Chong & Company production, produced in NYC, 2000.
Photo: Jonathan Staff

13 Research exercise

Research one of the following from the list of artists/projects who are part of new genre public art's history, and find one more new genre public art/environmental art artist through research on the Internet and beyond. How specifically do these projects engage and interact with their audiences?

– Vito Acconci's architectural work;
– Judith F. Baca's mural projects;
– Joseph Beuys's tree planting campaign;
– Mel Chin's *Revival Fields, plantings to clean contaminated soil*;
– The Christo's *The Gates*;
– Guerilla Grrls public actions;
– Hachivi Edgar Heap of Birds' work on Native American stereotyping;
– Viet Ngo's *Devils Lake Lemna*;
– Bonnie Sherk's *Crossroads Community, a farm environment*;
– William Pope.L's use of space.

Suzanne Lacy on New Genre Public Art

Dealing with some of the most profound issues of our time – toxic waste, race relations, homelessness, aging, gang welfare, and cultural identity – a group of visual artists has developed distinct models for an art whose public strategies of engagement are an important part of its aesthetic language. . . . We might describe this as 'new genre public art,' to distinguish it in both form and intention from what has been called 'public art', new genre public art – a term used for the past twenty-five years to describe sculpture and installations in public places. Unlike much of what has heretofore been called public art, new genre public art – visual art that uses both traditional and nontraditional media to communicate and interact with a broad and diversified audience about issues directly relevant to their lives – is based on engagement.

Lacy, 1995: 19

14 Reflection exercise

As you read through these chapters, try to trace relationships between these concepts and the art work you have read about. How is engagement defined? How is it achieved? Can you see tensions between the artist's concepts and the potential reaction of participants or audiences?

2.4 Community building and cultural diversity

The nation state and nationhood are important categories for cultural studies, and these concepts often provide frameworks for community performance work. The concepts continue to deeply influence thoughts on social organization and symbolical self-images, and they have a profound influence on thoughts on community. Nationality provides one important lens through which people see themselves, and make sense of their affiliations and behaviors. 'Imagined communities' is a term explored in detail by sociologist Benedict Anderson, and it refers to the symbolic power of national affiliation.

Nations as imagined communities, then, speak to the powers of desire and hope. At the heart of national identity is a certain amount of exclusion: only some strands of the general population, some values, identities and ways of life make it into the national picture.

Community performances are an important part of the symbolic and real actions that define nationhood and cultural affiliation: from American Independence Day July 4 parades to the National Sorry Day in Australia to commemorate atrocities against the aboriginal population, from remembrances of the Treaty of Waitangi in New Zealand to the carnivalesque parties at the Queen's Birthday in the Netherlands. These national performances are open to change and reinvention: both the Sorry Day and the celebration of the Treaty are post-colonial acknowledgements of national development, historic change and moral responsibility. In these performances, rituals enact and create the certainties at the heart of 'nationhood': the embrace of people not personally known, its limited and specific nature, its privileged position apropos leading one's own destiny, and its longing embrace of communality. As performances of the everyday, these events reinforce ways of thinking about self and community.

Figure 2.10 Hundertwasser public toilets, New Zealand: This public art project, now a tourist attraction, was funded by the Kawakawa Community Board and designed by Austrian artist and local resident Frederick Hundertwasser. It incorporates ceramic tiles by students from the Bay of Islands College.   Photo: Petra Kuppers

---

French art critic Nicolas Bourriaud: relational aesthetics

Relational aesthetics
Aesthetic theory consisting in judging art works on the basis of the inter-human relations which they represent, produce or prompt. . . .

Relational (art)
A set of artistic practices which take as their theoretical and practical point of departure the whole of human relations and their social context, rather than an independent and private space.

Semionaut
The contemporary artist is a semionaut, he invents trajectories between signs.

Bourriaud, 1998: 112–13

15 Reflection exercise

Think about spectator and sportspeople rituals at major sport events. In what ways are imagined communities played out in these environments? How does nationhood intersect with these events, how is cohesion created, in what way are boundaries drawn?

As these kinds of celebration diversify and shift in time, many countries attempt to embrace the responsibilities of their colonial pasts. Colonizer and colonized countries (often having accepted 'nationhood' as part of the colonial experience) reinvent their communities in ways that seem more in tune with the make-up of the actual population.

One important concept in this ongoing struggle to reinvent national life is multiculturalism. How can cultural values, performances, life and actions reflect the diverse make-up of these entities, 'nations', that by definition forged one unified identity out of what at all times where multiple local, temporal and diverse populations?

Benedict Anderson: the imagined community

In an anthropological spirit, then, I propose the following definition of the nation: it is an imagined political community – and imagined as both inherently limited and sovereign.

It is *imagined* because the members of even the smallest nation will never know most of their fellow-members, or even hear of them, yet in the minds of each lives the image of their communion. . . . The national is imagined as *limited* because even the largest of them encompassing perhaps a billion living human beings, has finite, it elastic boundaries, beyond which lie other nations. . . . It is imagined as *sovereign* because the concept was born in an age in which Enlightenment and Revolution were destroying the legitimacy of the divinely-ordained, hierarchical dynastic realm. Coming to maturity at a stage of human history when even the most devout adherents of any universal religion were inescapably confronted with the living pluralism of such religions, and the allomorphism between each faith's ontological claims and territorial stretch, nations dream of being free, and, if under God, directly so. The gage and emblem of this freedom is the sovereign state. Finally, it is imagined as a *community*, because, regardless of the actual inequality and exploitation that may prevail in each, the nation is always conceived as a deep, horizontal comradeship.

Anderson, 1991: 5–7

Cross-cultural cultural memories

This ability to recount the founding events of our national history in different ways is reinforced by the exchange of cultural memories. . . . In this exchange of memories it is a matter not only of subjecting the founding events of both cultures to a crossed reading, but of helping one another to set free that part of life and of renewal which is found captive in rigid, embalmed and dead traditions.

Ricoeur, 1996: 8

16 Reflection exercise

For a society to be 'multicultural' rather than just culturally diverse, certain criteria need to define the cultural life. Here is one set of criteria:

> (1) Cultural diversity, in the form of a number of groups – be they political, racial, ethnic, religious, economic, or age – is exhibited in a society; (2) the coexisting groups approximate equal political, economic and educational opportunity; and (3) there is a behavioral commitment to the values of CP [cultural pluralism] as a basis for a viable system of social organization.
>
> Pratte, 1979: 6

Apply these criteria to the society you live in. Do all or any of these criteria apply? Do you find any problems applying them? Could you extend or modify the list of criteria? How do important aspects of cultural identity such as aesthetic practice, art making, ritual and the symbolic component of cultural identity find their way into these criteria?

Guillermo Gomez-Pena

I physically live between two cultures and two epochs. . . . When I am on the US side, I have access to high-technology and to specialized information. When I cross back to Mexico, I get immersed in a rich political culture. . . . When I return to California, I am part of the multicultural thinking emerging from the interstices of the US's ethnic milieus. . . . I walk the fibre of this transition in my everyday life, and I make art about it.

Gomez-Pena, 1991: 22–3

17 Reflection exercise

Focus on the ability of 'communitas' in performance to conceal difference. From your personal experiences of community performances, can you identify moments where this overshadowing can occur? What are its positive and negative effects?

Figure 2.11 'Looking for Bosnia'. Performance workshop led by Sonja Kuftinec.   Photo: Scot McElvany

Community performance can provide a ground to test, rearrange and re-think identities, and, as Gomez-Pena shows, the fluidities of identity can provide rich fields for both everyday and stage performances.

But performance's power as agent for social change can be overshadowed by other aspects of the experiences associated with performing, with being on stage. Sometimes, the euphoria of the stage is only that: momentary, fleeting, 'out of this world'. Can it nevertheless have effects *in* this world? Community performance artists need to negotiate these issues of fantasy, stage world and political impact in their work. Theatre writer and artist Sonia Kuftinec analyses these complexities in her experiences of working in a refugee camp in Croatia.

Community, identity, performance

The concept of community remains difficult to pin down, but depends in large part on borders of inclusion and exclusion. Community members define these borders in both perceptual and material ways, noting shared values, interests, and territories, while differentiating themselves from others who don't share these defining features. Yet even within seemingly bounded communities, differences exist, and individuals continuously cross and renegotiate borders of difference. In *The Symbolic Construction of Community* sociologist Anthony Cohen suggests that while boundaries of identity hold great meaning for the individual, these borders are more perceptual than actual, and can thus be redrawn. As a site of re-presentation, performance becomes a medium through which this redrawing can occur. The performance process reinforces commonalities, illuminates difference, and alters boundaries of identity, bringing together, for a time, those who perceive themselves as belonging to different communities.

Before beginning work on the Varazdin project, Peck, Chornesky, and I had presumed a commonality of background and experience among the refugees, mostly Muslims from Bosnia. Engagement in the performance process revealed internal divisions characterized by differences in education, ethnicity, and age, among other factors. These differences suggest the difficulty of drawing clear boundaries within and between groups and categories in the Balkans. Early stages of rehearsal revealed how the semiotics of space and language inscribed difference among refugee teenagers in Varazdin.

[. . .]

Boundaries between IRSA and camp youths, volunteers and residents, town and camp residents, IRSA and Suncokret workers, and audience and performers seemed to dissolve in the moment of performance. Status structures did seem to dissipate, resulting in a feeling of 'oneness.' This moment of *communitas* is extremely powerful in the way that it dissolves as well as potentially conceals difference. As Cohen points out, and as Turner himself underlines, *communitas* is an essential though temporary enactment of community, and can thus veil difference as much as it seemingly enacts commonality. Theatre can edit and exclude, concealing its dissonances and limitations in the momentary unity of performance; it is important to maintain an awareness of these limitations in analyzing the impact of community-based productions.

Kuftinec, 1997: 178, 181

2.5 Animator movements

Animation

Animation is that stimulus to the mental, physical, and emotional life of people in a given area which moves them to undertake a wider range of experiences through which they find a higher degree of self-realization, self expression, and awareness of belonging to a community which they can influence.

From a report of the European Cultural Foundation

Animation is 'a process in which individuals, small groups or larger communities are activated or animated to create for themselves and their neighbours improved social, physical, cultural or emotional settings'.

Berrigan, 1974

In many countries, community performance has been recognized as a significant influence on community development, the fostering of social ties and stability, and the wellbeing of people and places. Because of this recognition, community performance practitioners can be employed by local councils to 'animate' communities, to provide and organize events around which people can come together, to help integration of immigrant communities, youth communities, disabled people, and many other social goals. In different countries, these positions have different names: animators, cultural workers, arts development officers etc.

Paulo Freire

The pedagogy of the oppressed, animated by authentic, humanist (not humanitarian) generosity, presents itself as a pedagogy of man. Pedagogy which begins with the egoistic interests of the oppressors (an egoism cloaked in the false generosity of paternalism) and makes of the oppressed the objects of its humanitarianism, itself maintains and embodies oppression.

[. . .]

The pedagogy of the oppressed, as a humanist and libertarian pedagogy, has two distinct stages. In the first, the oppressed unveil the world of oppression and through the praxis commit themselves to its transformation. In the second stage, in which the reality of oppression has already been transformed, this pedagogy ceases to belong to the oppressed and becomes a pedagogy of all men in the process of permanent liberation.

[. . .]

Libertarian education consists in acts of cognition, not transferals of information.

Freire, 1983: 39, 40, 67

In Europe, the roots of much of this activity are in the social changes following the student revolts of 1968. Community animators rejected paternalistic modes of 'top-down' education, and embraced instead a mode of working towards social change that rested in notions of community, and of a closeness between worker and target group. Indeed, the vocabulary change towards 'worker' shows a socialist understanding of arts labor as a worker's activity within a larger society (see also material on workers' theatre, street theatre and other movements, such as Filewood and Watts, 2001; Hyman, 1997; Kershaw, 1997; Mason, 1992; Sainer, 1997; and many articles on international radical theatre in the journals such as The Drama Review (TDR).

In France, Italy and other countries, art workers engaged with the thoughts of Paulo Freire and others, and challenged segregationist institutions such as mental health asylums, prisons and others areas of social exclusion. Art workers drew from the experiences of de-colonialization, and the growing recognition of the problems of post-colonial life. Cultural contact and intercultural experimentation laid the groundwork for many community performances today.

One of the challenges to animators is to find ways to connect with communities, and to find forms of expression that are specific to a particular group – in other words, not to become 'specialists' who use a specific set of techniques. Christine Lomas, who worked for a long time with UK group Jabadeo, sums up some of these challenges:

> For some of the safe forms, techniques in the broadest sense, are an end in themselves, whether the activities are based on aerobics, fitness, physical/social therapy, or person-centered dance techniques. Technique itself is adaptive, and it has been adapted by the animateur, requiring adaptive behaviors from participants. The dance worker is more 'at risk' in emphasizing the authentic: how will people respond? What do I do? How do I handle it? Teaching technique is safe. Although teaching technique offers a challenge, is it truly a dance challenge? . . . Why do animateurs focus on adaptive forms of art when the capacity exists to celebrate authenticity? We must shake off the shackles of conventional aesthetics with its focus on technique that consigns the 'unskilled' dancer to being a nondancer and subliminally emphasizes the second-rate in terms of those involved in community dance.
>
> Lomas, 1998: 157, also in the Reader

---

18 Research exercise

Research the history of the use of performance, and especially community arts/community performance in one of these or other liberatory movements:

– Women's Movement

– Gay and Lesbian Movement

– Ethnic Minority Culture Movements

– Harlem Renaissance

– Disability Culture

– Maori Renaissance

– Aboriginal Movement.

Augusto Boal

Augusto Boal has a deep and rich influence on the field of community performance. His origins are in theatre and political activism – he began creating participatory theater in the 1950s and 1960s in Rio de Janeiro while he was artistic director for the Arena Theater, and he was also a Worker's Party Activist. He took the theatre troupe's work outside the stage and organized performances in churches, factories, streets and other places where they could reach people living in the slums of Rio (see also material in the *Reader*). His political work within these environments led to his torture and exile.

For Boal, theatre is a form of communication. His most significant point of departure from traditional theatre is his insistence on the importance of dialogue. Monologue is a tool of oppression: one speaks, and the other can't reply. Boal created means that allowed an interaction between audience and actor that blurs the boundaries between the two beyond the conception of epic theatre associated with Bertolt Brecht, where audiences are challenged to be active in their reception of a theatre performance, but do not actively change the course of the play.

Spect-actor

In this **Theatre of the Oppressed**, Boal developed methods that allowed audience members to engage actively with the performance. Audiences suggest courses of action to the actors on stage. One night, a woman in the audience was so frustrated by an actor who couldn't grasp her suggestion that she came on stage and began to play the role herself. For Boal, she was the first spect-actor.

A Theatre of the Oppressed workshop

The 'typical' Theatre of the Oppressed [TO] workshop comprises three kinds of activity. The first is background **information** on TO and the various exercises provided by the workshop facilitator (or 'difficultator,' as Boal prefers to describe it). Such information begins the workshop, but is also interspersed throughout the games and exercises. Moreover, the group is brought together periodically to discuss responses to games and to ask questions of the various processes.

The second kind of activity is the **games**. These are invariably highly physical interactions designed to challenge us to truly listen to what we are hearing, feel what we are touching, and see what we are looking at. The 'arsenal' of the Theatre of the Oppressed is extensive with more than 200 games and exercises listed in Boal's *Games for Actors and Non-Actors* alone. Several years ago Boal's Center for the Theatre of the Oppressed in Paris (CTO – Paris) proceeded methodically through all the TO activities; the inventory took two years to cover. Ultimately, these games serve to heighten our senses and demechanize the body, to get us out of habitual behavior, as a prelude to moving beyond habitual thinking and interacting. We also become actively engaged with other participants, developing relationships and trust, and having a very good time.

Finally, the third area of activity involves the **structured exercises**. Although there is a kind of gray area at times when one might call an activity a game or an exercise, the exercises are formulated so as to infuse a given structure with genuine content.

These activities are designed to highlight a particular area of TO practice such as Image Theatre, Forum Theatre, Rainbow of Desire, etc. Thus we are invited not only to imagine new possibilities and solutions, but to actively participate in them, Forum style. Group problem solving, highly interactive imagining, physical involvement, trust and fun combine to create vigorous interpersonal dynamics. As a result, we learn that we are, if not the source of our difficulties, at least the reason for their maintenance. More importantly, we are clearly the source of our mutual liberations.

Douglas Paterson, 1996

Approaches to Boal's Theatre of the Oppressed can come out of specific questions, specific sets of circumstances in which it becomes important to find ways to engage community voices, and bring the expressions and concerns gathered in this way to governments, non-governmental organizations (NGOs) and other bodies. John Sullivan works in this framework, and he writes on the background to his Theatre of the Oppressed work on projects such as COAL (Communities Organized against Asthma and Lead/Comunidades Organizadas contro la Asma y el Plomo) in Texas, US:

In 2001, the National Institute of Environmental Health Sciences (NIEHS) Center in Environmental Toxicology at the University of Texas Medical Branch in Galveston, Texas, launched a unique project to supplement its Community Outreach & Education Program (COEP). The center's former director, Stephen R. Lloyd, is a genetic scientist who truly appreciates the power of live theater to shed light on difficult ideas with plain speech and compelling images. He hired me to create a TO-based Image Theatre educational curriculum in toxicology and risk assessment, and produce Forum Theatre workshops and performances. He wanted to engage citizens, scientists, health care providers, regulatory personnel and public policy-makers in dialogue on the health effects of toxic exposures, and the possibilities of improved environmental health through more effective coalition-building and policy action. As these Community Environmental Forum Theater projects developed, this new outreach methodology began to narrow the 'gap of Otherness' that normally separates environmental-health specialists from 'communities of interest.' Terms like interaction, dialogue, participatory research, iterative processes, collaboration and project sustainability came to populate our discussions of how citizens and scientists could reconfigure our former, mostly utilitarian relationships. We began to see new ways of infusing respect and mutual regard into the process of doing public health.

Community Arts Network, 2005

Sullivan facilitates theatre work with the ongoing group that formed out of this project: El Teatro Lucha por la Salud del Barrio.

Brief definitions of Theatre of the Oppressed terms

Forum Theatre is a TO technique that begins with the enactment of a scene (or anti-model) in which a protagonist tries, unsuccessfully, to overcome an oppression relevant to that particular audience. The joker then invites the spectators to replace the protagonist at any point in the scene that they can imagine an alternative action that could lead to a solution. The scene is replayed numerous times with different interventions. This results in a dialogue about the oppression, an examination of alternatives, and a 'rehearsal' for real situations.

Image Theatre is a series of wordless exercises in which participants create embodiments of their feelings and experiences. Beginning with a selected theme, participants 'sculpt' images onto their own and others' bodies. These frozen images are then 'dynamized,' or brought to life, through a sequence of movement-based and interactive exercises.

Invisible Theatre is a rehearsed sequence of events that is enacted in a public, nontheatrical space, capturing the attention of people who do not know they are watching a planned performance. It is at once theater and real life, for although rehearsed, it happens in real time and space and the 'actors' must take responsibility for the consequences of the 'show.' The goal is to bring attention to a social problem for the purpose of stimulating public dialogue.

Rainbow of Desire is the name of a specific TO exercise in Boal's therapeutic repertoire and, for a while, referred to his whole body of therapeutic techniques. Boal recently stated that neither Cop-in-the Head nor Rainbow of Desire was the right name for that series but he had not yet determined a name he found more suitable.

Schutzman and Cohen-Cruz, 1994

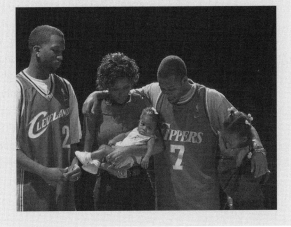

Figure 2.12 A 'fence-line' (i.e. near a toxic dump or facility) family confronts the health effects of benzene emissions from a nearby refinery head on when their son is diagnosed with leukemia. Citizens In-Power & Development Association, Port Arthur, TX, 2004.   Photo: Bryan Parras

Transcript of interview

This interview is by Tom Magill with Augusto Boal, from Northern Vision Media Center, Belfast, an Ireland-based organization that runs community television journalism courses. The interview is published on their website, www.northernvisions.org. I am quoting this interview here to allow Boal's voice to speak in his own English: words do not mean the same everywhere, and his location and thoughts on Brazil are important to his aesthetics and politics. To use his methods means to pay careful attention to the locality and specificity of the work. We need to listen carefully to people's language, meanings and context.

Tom: Augusto, in your latest book *Legislative Theatre* you used a term community theatre. Could you define this term and tell us how it's different from conventional theatre.

Augusto Boal: The word community, **communitage** in Portuguese, we use to define sometimes a region of the city, e.g., a slum. In this state there is a communitage within that slum. Sometimes we can talk about also the communitage of psychiatric hospitals or we can talk about the communitage of a trade union for instance, so the word communitage/community has not the same meaning as it has in English, and of course they don't have theatre inside those communities. In slums there is no theatre only one slum which is an area called Digegow in Rio has a community and curiously, Cicerly Berry, who is the great teacher or a voice of the Royal Shakespeare Company when she went to Brazil twice she went to that community in the slums to teach the people how to pronounce better, how to free their voices and so community means that. It means a group of people who can be located geographically or because they have the same interests and they don't have specialities so there is not a difference between that community theatre and the other forms because they don't have other forms. And then we worked with those communities to make them produce theatre.

Criticism

Theatre critic and practitioner Mady Schutzman points out some of the problems with bringing Boal's methodologies into societies where issues of oppression are not easily mappable. She analyses how a US citizen occupies multiple roles with the oppressor/oppressed paradigm (1994: 144). John Fletcher discusses the implication of this inability to map clear political action (2003: 192). The fact that we can't share a 'common enemy' and 'common identity' creates a central problem for people who work in communities: there is no stable ground, no ultimate aim, no shared utopia we can all work towards.

Information and emotion are held in many different ways, and community performance work can excavate some of these hidden areas of experience, and make them expressive. When you work with bodies, voices and spaces, powerful experiences can come to the fore, and you need to be open and attentive to the processes your group is going through.

When I first began working with people in mental health contexts, I found that what I regarded as preparatory performance exercises, just being in space and finding a balance, was a real problem for people whose sense of self was significantly under pressure through forced incarceration, injections and their rejection in most social situations. I had to learn quickly to think about what political action would mean for us in our situation. For us, this meant asserting the breath as the first political action: taking space, claiming a place to be, for our lungs to expand into, finding a balance for our bodies, feeling good about being seen.

Native American arts practitioner Qwo-Li Driskill had similar experiences when ze used Theatre of the Oppressed methodologies with fellow Native people.

19 Reflection exercise

What do you think? What is useful about polarization – creating a relatively clear narrative of us/them? What is problematic about it? Is there a way to embrace the positive aspects without falling into an easy binarization?

As you read through and work through the three Boal exercises in Chapter 4 (p. 112), pay attention to issues of multiplicity, complex narratives, and strategies used to access them.

Boal and Native American theatre work

In my own experiences, I find that facilitating TO (Theatre of the Oppressed) with other Native people tends to be more intense, more emotional and more transformative than when facilitating TO with people not sharing a common oppression. This is not only because TO was created for communities facing a common oppression, but also because Native people are survivors of intense tribal and personal histories under colonial governments and TO sparks powerful feelings and reactions to these histories. I had a fairly surprising experience the first time I facilitated TO with an all-Native group. There is a fairly standard warm-up exercise often called 'Cover the Space,' in which participants are asked to walk around the space fairly briskly and try to make sure no space is left uncovered while remaining equidistant from other participants (Boal, 1992, p. 116). . . . I asked participants to be aware of their own bodies, and to notice how they felt within them as they walked around the room. I then asked participants to create a vocalization on how they were feeling at that moment and to exaggerate their emotions through their bodies. The result caught me off guard: All of the participants began to moan or

PRACTICE EXAMPLE

scream, and their movements became heavy and slow, as if they were carrying huge weights on their limbs. . . ., I . . . found we needed to have a discussion to process the first exercise, which is usually considered low impact. Some of the participants, I found out later, began crying as soon as I asked them to be aware of themselves in their bodies. I believe that collectively Native people suffer from severe Post Traumatic Stress Disorder, which is further impacted by our personal experiences with trauma. Simply asking us to be present in our own bodies can be a frightening, and also healing, experience. Many of us were taught that we have no right to our own bodies, which directly relates to being taught that we have no right to our homelands, languages, or lifeways. For me, this experience was further evidence of how important TO work is within Native communities. In the case of language restoration, for example, how can we hope for our peoples to learn our languages if we are not able to be present within our bodies?

How can we heal these deep wounds so we can embrace our Mothertongues? Conversely, how can our Mothertongues be used as medicinals on our journey toward personal, community and cultural restoration?

Driskill, 2003: 157, 158

Theatre of Oppression and Boal's methodologies are based in and thus are themselves open to change, adaptation, reinvention and creative play. Many people adapt the exercises, and use the basic fundaments of Boal's methods to develop their own style, appropriate to the groups they are working in.

Here is a short example from a Tawainese production, where Chung Chiao, a director/facilitator, uses techniques from magic realism and Theatre of the Oppressed in a production based on workshops in the aftermath of the 1999 Taiwanese earthquake, created by a Hakka women's group of farmers, the Shigang Mamas, who have been working together for many years.

Figure 2.13 Shigang Mamas: dreaming of traveling abroad during *River in the Heart*.
Photo: Ron Smith

Shigang Mamas

In the 2003 production of *River in the Heart,* issues of oppression relevant to the women's livelihoods as farmers were explored and then discussed with the audience afterward in an open forum setting. These issues, which came out of the safe and protected 'rehearsal reality' of their workshops, were later edited and scripted by Chung Chiao into play form. Given the ultraconservative nature of Hakka culture regarding the outspokenness of women, it's highly unlikely that the Mamas would have ever felt secure or confident enough to broach these issues publicly had they not experienced the nonthreatening and safe environment of Chung Chiao's theatre workshops. Later, during an improvisational rehearsal for *River in the Heart,* aspects of Magical Realism and Theatre of the Oppressed became identifiable. Chung Chiao explained that this coexistence was intended to create a magically charged liminal space empowering the Mamas to rehearse alternative solutions to oppression that could 'right the wrongs,' thereby moving them closer to improving their realities.

[. . .]

Staged at the Huashan Arts District in Taipei, *River in the Heart* opened with the women slowly entering the space from all directions, even from the audience, crossing through a river of real water that I as the set designer created for the piece and that separated the stage from the audience. The opening scene is dreamlike. In a cloud of memory, with the women spreading seeds for planting (symbolic of their roles as mothers), they say, 'There is a river that flows through my heart . . .'

Smith, 2005: 110, 111

Animation and institutionalization

What happens with the radical potential of animation once it finds a wider social acceptance of animation as a cultural good? When animation artists, cultural workers and community artists are integrated into political and governance systems, and are employed by local governments, they have to carefully negotiate their dual roles as community members and institution affiliates. Today, workers in the field need to think about questions such as:

- Do you do something to people? Or do you work with them to find and foster their own goals?
- How do you define 'community', and whose goals come to prominence?
- Are you a member of this community?
- Who has mobility and the power to identify 'community' and its participants?

- What happens if your or your employer's value scheme contradicts those of people in the community?
- How do issues of confidentiality intersect with your reporting duties?

Here Shulamith Lev-Aladgem writes about what happened to the Community Theatre of Katamon, Israel, and the outreach worker Michael Pharan, from the Municipal Department for the Advancement of Youth, who was working with street gangs. Lev-Aladgem also describes the conflicts that emerged as the show was ready to be performed.

Community Theatre of Katamon: *Joseph Goes Down to Katamon* (1972–3)

Pharan was indeed a rare establishment person whose personal social vision was in fact anti-establishment. However, he was unable to prevent the censorship by the municipal delegates of *Joseph Goes Down to Katamon*; they had expected a grateful celebration, not a fierce social critique. Authorizing themselves as the owners of the theatre, they demanded that the rape scene be cut. Shortly after this intervention, [director] Itzhak left the group. The promising rhetoric of community-based theatre as 'of the people, by the people, and for the people' was betrayed in practice.

The Katamon case represents the two poles of the contested formation of community-based theatre in Israel: community development versus alternative radical theatre. The former stemmed from a liberal, patronizing position, approaching the Mizrahi minority as the 'other' in need of improvement aimed at integrating them into the hegemonic order; while the latter, based on a neo-Marxist ideology, defined theatre as a people's weapon aimed at changing the dominant social order. While the institutional sponsoring bodies did, and still do, expect a compliant performance, the local theatre group usually creates a self-representational text making publicly clear their otherwise invisible wounds and needs. Generally, the more resistant the performance, the more it exposes the ideological gap between the community-based theatre and the establishment, thus intensifying the struggle over who really owns the performance.

Lev-Aladgem, 2004: 120

---

20 Reflection exercise

There are many more areas where 'official' policy and local empowerment clash, and where a community arts worker can find her- or himself in conflict. Turn to a colleague, and discuss some of these potential problem areas. Draw up a list of five further points of potential conflict. Think about ways of moving within these constraints. What tactics can you employ?

Performance and notions of cultural specificity, expressed in dance, theatre and art, have a long history of political activism. In Nazi Germany, large-scale amateur performances were part of political spectacles, and the power of these massive displays helped to bind German people effectively to a propaganda of racial superiority (for a discussion of the relation between nascent community dance and Nazi aesthetics in Germany, see Berson in the *Reader*). In the USA, Ku Klux Klan members staged large-scale rallies with costumes, ritual circles and fire displays, often culminating in the brutal lynching of slaves.

Dance researcher Joan Huckstep spoke about community performance's potentially problematic use at the Congress for Research on Dance, Tallahasee, Florida, 2005. She described how in Zaire in the 1970s and 1980s, animators under President Mobutu worked as part of the Ministry of Information. Dances were part of official jubilation protocols, and fell under the Authenticity Code: an enforced code of cultural authenticity. People could be forced to dance in these showcases, and in daily pre-work sessions in Kinshasa. These animators' work included reporting on non-participants, who could be imprisoned.

Reenactment

Today, participation in US Civil War reenactments is high, but in *Confederates in the Attic: Dispatches from the Unfinished Civil War*, journalist Tony Horwitz (1998) describes how the majority of these events are all-white affairs, and he claims that through these ongoing battles reenactors nostalgically keep on fighting for the Confederacy.

A different kind of nostalgia and sense of agency emerge in a Philippine example of community performance reenactment: Joi Barrios writes about mass art forms, and comments that

> another popular form was the 'reenactment'. In 1985, the Artex Cultural Group reenacted the strike they staged the previous year. True to the incident, actors portrayed hired goons destroying their picket line, resulting in bloodshed. Performed by those who actually had participated in or witnessed the event and staged during the anniversary of the strike, the reenactment was like a ritual.
>
> Barrios, 1998: 259

Whether political march or festivity, political reenactment, or political ritual, the political agency of community performance is manifold, and cannot be located in any one message. In many societies, performances are used as ways to exclude, stratify and align a populace.

These examples show that animating a group of people into art practice is not necessarily inherently politically liberating, as seen from a contemporary Western democratic viewpoint. What the examples do show is that the arts can be powerful, and that political leaders can use them as forms of indoctrination. In your own practice,

Figure 2.14 Nyoongar children on a float at the Fremantle Festival Parade, Australia, 2005.
Photo: Petra Kuppers

how can you ensure that diversity has a place? How can the group ensure that dissent can be expressed both within the aesthetic production and within the larger framework of setting up your project? These are hard questions that have no easy answers. These questions make up the core of community performance work, and provide one of the differences between community performance work and single-authored art labor. In community performances, aesthetic cohesion is usually secondary to keeping diversity and communal action alive.

The arts are only one of many strands of activities that go into a contemporary animator's profile. Here is an example from Ontario, Canada, where community animators encourage:

- increased awareness and understanding of the social, environmental and economic determinants of human health and the links among them;
- adoption of a healthy communities approach, including broad inclusive community participation and multi-sectoral involvement in planning and decision-making;
- incorporation of healthy community principles within organizations and activities;
- collaboration with other groups and organizations in the community to ensure optimal use of community resources for the benefit of all;
  - involvement and support of local government in healthy community coalitions and activities;
  - networking with local, regional and provincial leaders and organizations;
  - promoting activities and accomplishments within communities;
  - implementation of evaluations to track progress over time.
  - increased awareness and understanding of Ontario Healthy Communities Coalition (OHCC) and the healthy communities movement.

Rachel Fensham, an Australian critic, sums up some of the tensions between community arts workers and institutional environments, and she points to the opportunities open to art practice:

21 Research exercise

Research the healthy communities movement. Go over the list provided above. How can community performance practitioners impact these various points? How are their activities relevant? Do you see any problems working as an artist within these kinds of frameworks?

The concept of community cultural development has been actively promoted as a policy framework by the Australian Council and so it is useful to understand some of the contradictions arising from this policy context. In her recent history of the Community Arts Board, Gay Hawkins (1993) analysed the historical and contingent forces which made 'community', a goal of government instrumentality. Initially, the 'community' consisted of those groups regarded as in a condition of 'cultural lack'; due to social disadvantage or those who needed help or support to find appropriate cultural expression. In this scenario the raising of funds for a community dance project predetermined that the themes should reflect positive outcomes for a community. . . . In practice this still meant that artists were engaged in projects that affirmed their participants in acts of communal solidarity. That these social objectives have tended to privilege an aesthetics of social realism and individual authorship has often been denied in the name of a collective truth. According to Hawkins, this blinkering of the field of community arts to debates about the nature of representation and in particular, to the dissemination of meanings through popular culture, has limited the possibilities of it developing into a radical arts practice.

My own view is that community artists employ a range of aesthetic decisions in their work and are far less compromised and naïve than Hawkins suggests [in relation to community dance]. Modern dance has only a limited history of social realism, and the corporeal and emotional contents of dance expression do not easily contribute to fixed representations. . . . If policy requires tangible outcomes then dance may not be able to offer them, because its meanings can be ambiguous and its felt experiences hard to quantify. That is not to say that dancing cannot give shape to the aspirations and fears of particular communities and in the process, give people new experiences.

Fensham, 1997: 17

2.6 Arts in service

Using the arts for non-arts purposes lies at the heart of animator and cultural worker debates, and community performance negotiates these fields. Other forms in which community performance aligns itself with other tasks include literacy development and many other agendas.

Many cultural workers believe that participation in the arts can function like a form of inoculation: it can be a safeguard, a helper, keeping young people and other social groups engaged with their communities. This way of thinking about relationships between art practice and development focuses on resilience.

> ## 22 Reflection exercise
>
> If you have acted in the past, or worked as a musician or dancer in a public performance, think back to this point. What positive experiences did you gain from the experience? What negative ones? Do you agree with James Barnes, or do you see any potential problems? Are there people for whom this kind of Readers Theatre might be particularly problematic? What issues would you need to think through in offering this method to different audiences?

Using the arts to foster other agendas: Readers Theatre

Some students find acting a very daunting experience, though most English teachers know that dramatic presentation helps students develop important literacy skills. Readers Theatre allows the student a less threatening experience with dramatic readings in a more physically static performance. The reader is challenged to use all the oral fluency skills that he or she has been developing in the language arts classroom as well as to understand new vocabulary words in context for proper interpretation. . . . In presenting a Readers Theatre script, the student can hone presentation skills, oral fluency, vocabulary, projection, selfconfidence, and literary interpretation under the evaluative eye of the instructor.

Barnes, 2004: xiii

Resilience

Resilience is about the ability to succeed in the face of obstacles, perhaps even *because* of the obstacles. . . . A popular model for creating resilience in young people shows that they [should] have available to them:

* people – who care about them and can be mentors
* places – that are safe to congregate in
* activities – that develop a sense of belonging to a group
* contributions – to their wider community to engage them

The arts are a vehicle for providing these four factors to young people. Arts activities, in particular arts centres and creative youth spaces, bring young people together in a safe environment. With the aid and guidance of tutors, young people are provided with activities that draw them out to examine their own identity and their place in society. The associated artists provide role models and mentors.

Eames, 2003: 37

This way of thinking about the arts sets art work apart from art therapy. While many community art workers have experience in and of art therapy, the goals and tools are often different. Many community performance artists see their work as specifically political, designed to change wider social structures as well as the individual. Changing communication structures, hierarchies and ways of thinking about inclusion and exclusion are some of the ways of thinking about 'making a better world', but there are others as well.

Art/art therapy

Here Kevin Finnan discusses his perspective of the difference between the work of Motionhouse, the company he is part of, and art therapists. Motionhouse spent eighteen months working at HMP Dovegate, a high-security prison in Staffordshire, UK:

> We are very clear that we are not therapists, care workers or missionaries. We are artists. We acknowledge that our own experience of our work has taught us that it can be therapeutic, liberating, empowering and affirmative. It can offer these things but because it is art it can also be disturbing, painful, challenging and a bloody grind as well. A therapist uses a set of tools to help a person to recover. We do not know how to do this – we have not trained to do this. We know how to make art and we attempt to share this experience because we believe it to be a vital and fundamental element of the life force that sustains us all and helps nourish our humanity. When we share art we are being present to the moment together. In our work there is an exchange.

Finnan, 2003

23 Research exercise

What do you think about community performance practice and art therapy? Research art therapy, itself a wide field. Where do you see differences and overlaps? Why is there a culture of 'accusations' of therapy leveled at some community performance work? Is it an insult, and if so why? Discuss with a colleague.

Use of performance in an adult literacy framework with offenders in a UK prison

PRACTICE EXAMPLE

Who ran the project?
Keith Palmer from the Comedy School, together with Juliet Lopez from BOP Collective for the two-week drama component and Shan Gayton, a comedian who works for the School, for the comedy component.

When did it take place?
From March 12th – March 30th 2001.

What was it about?
The first week was a stand-up comedy course culminating in three-minute routines to a small inmate audience. In the following two weeks, the participants explored ideas through drama and put together a show that was performed twice: to an inmate audience in the afternoon and to an invited audience in the evening. It was called 'Achievments' with the 'e' missing to communicate the barriers to achieving that they had experienced in their own lives. The show was framed as if people in the audience were at a live recording of a TV magazine show. Rudi Lickwood, a well-known comedian, warmed the audience up and

each act, sketch or interview was prefaced by Keith checking the sound, the quality of the previous 'take' and introducing the next part of the show. This provided an imaginative structure for controlling the show and validating all the material being presented. If there was a mistake, that piece could be re-run within the internal logic of the performance.

Where did it take place?

The project was based in the Education Department for the first week and then moved to the chapel where the performances took place.

Who took part?

16 people started the project; 11 completed it.

How were they recruited?

Level 1 candidates were targeted within the Education Department and there was a preliminary recruitment meeting with Keith and the Unit a week before the project began. All participants signed contracts that committed themselves to completing written tasks for key skills communication at Level 2 as well as taking part in the drama and comedy.

How supportive was the prison?

The Governor and Education staff were extremely supportive and a Key Skills tutor was attached to the project to oversee the written tasks.

What were the educational outcomes?

All eleven participants gained this qualification.

Sample 'Task' from the assessments/exercises used to put the performance experience into an assessable qualification framework

Take part in two performances. This could be the Comedy School performance and one of the March 29th performances or the two performances on March 29th. Fill in a self-assessment sheet on your experience of taking part in the show.

Also, find an image that will illustrate one of the characters or events in your piece of theatre and write a brief note about how this picture illustrates this character or event. Attach it to your self-assessment sheet.

Unit for the Arts and Offenders, Getting Our Act Together, 2002: 44–6

---

24 Reflection exercise

Go back to the previous practice example (Readers Theatre, p. 50), and compare the two kinds of literacy projects. In what way do they differ, in what way are they aligned? What are the relative merits, issues, challenges? How do issues of resilience feature in this work? Share your observations with a colleague – different life experiences might lead to different evaluations.

P
R
A
C
T
I
C
E

E
X
A
M
P
L
E

Jen Angharad, Welsh community dance practitioner, on dance and language training

I feel that the experiential integration of movement and language vocabulary is a fundamental partnership in the development of communication. I have, for many years, been exploring how the texture and quality of the Welsh language can influence movement.

[. . .]

Yr Wyddor – the alphabet

The training began by exploring the sounds of the Welsh alphabet – 'Yr Wyddor'. Time was taken to familiarise ourselves with the quality and texture of sounds, playing with where and how the body is placed and moves through space while producing the sound i.e. sitting, rolling, lying in prone and supine positions, standing, walking, rolling through the spine etc. This developed an awareness of where sound can resonate in the mouth, head and body. It is this awareness that encourages the flow of movement from one posture through to another. . . .

Angharad, 2004

Another example of the use of performance for non-arts purposes includes personal development. A case study for this is Psychodrama, and related forms, such as Playback Theatre. Psychodrama is the work of Jacob Levy Moreno, 1889–1974, originally from Vienna, who later developed his work in the USA after his move in 1925. It shares its origins with psychoanalysis, and focuses on the integration of different aspects of an individual's life and being through group drama work.

Moreno on psychodrama

Psychodrama can be defined as the science which explores the 'truth' by dramatic methods. It deals with interpersonal relations and private worlds. The psychodramatic method uses mainly five instruments – the stage, the subject or actor, the director, the staff of therapeutic aides or auxiliary egos, and the audience.

Moreno, in Fox, 1987: 13

Figure 2.15 Community dance workshop, Cultural Development Network and Ausdance Victoria at Dancehouse, Melbourne, Australia, 2006.
Photo: Petra Kuppers

By rehearsing everyday situations, differentials between 'gut reactions', thoughts, emotional reactions, levels of aggression etc. can emerge, and be analyzed and integrated into a new level of self-awareness. Participants can try out new behaviors, rehearse reactions and connections between different kinds of responses.

Playback Theatre

Playback Theatre is a form of drama use that developed out of Psychodrama, but that focuses more specifically on group processes, and on finding a form for people's memories. Its form has been shaped by Jonathon Fox and Jo Salas, who formed the Playback Theatre Group in New York in 1975. A conductor (rather than director) elicits stories from participants, and orchestrates forms for bringing these stories to life, either by working with the story owners, or with professional actors who take up the material and improvise. Today, Playback is used in many communities internationally. An example of the process in Galicia, Spain follows.

P R A C T I C E   E X A M P L E

Maria Elena Garavelli about the use of Playback Theatre in Galicia, Spain

In March 2003, in a public square in Pontevedra, a city in Galicia, Spain, I conducted an open performance of Playback Theatre, which was convened by various organisers and called 'Stories of Tar'.

The performance had been convened by the Galician movement Never Again, a non-party grouping which was formed after the sinking of the ship Prestige on the Galician coast and caused the oil slick – oil spilt by the boat – which sowed death on the beaches where the people used to fish and have the benefit of the clean waters of the sea. In the Plaza de Verdura men, women and children told their 'stories of tar', their particular stories about what happened on the Galician coast and how the residue of the oil – the 'tar' – affected their lives. Their stories told of the beaches where they had grown up; of the oil slick devouring the blue waters of the sea; of solidarity, with world-wide sympathisers working with the Galician people to clean up the beaches; of the oil slick threatening the future of children, who were thinking of emigrating to other countries; of their anger with politicians and those in power who had not kept their promises. The stories were played back with the participation of groups trained in Playback Theatre, and spontaneous actors who emerged from the audience. The music was performed by a Uruguayan violinist who had been asked for the first time to improvise with us. This was a team made up of Galician actors and actresses, a Uruguayan musician, and an Argentine director, among all of whom there flowed support for the task of giving voice and representation to the community through its narrators.

Garavelli, 2004

Playback Theatre is often used in workplaces, and in large corporations, where it becomes a tool for the creation of empathy between workers, in order to create a more humane (and ultimately, more productive) work environment. Indeed, offering performance workshops to corporations has become a lucrative form of employment to many workers in community performance. As a form of 'workplace therapy', this use of Playback Theatre and other forms brings up yet again the sets of questions articulated at the end of the previous section: how does the person/entity/ institution paying for community performance impact the content and development of that work?

The more arts are perceived to be in 'service' (that is, in services other than those traditionally associated with the arts), the harder it can become to argue for funding for community performance projects. Within the New Zealand context, cultural critics Dianne and Peter Beatson sum up this problem, as they write about the Arts Council of New Zealand's attitude to community art:

Figure 2.16 Two actors of the Nairobi-based Free Travelling Theatre perform a play about alcohol abuse in rural Meru Province, Kenya, September 1997.
Photo: Eugene van Erven

> While some Council members have been sympathetic to the cause of community art, others regard it as irrelevant to the central mission of the Arts Council which, they argue, is the fostering of art, not redeeming the world, overthrowing capitalism, empowering ethnic minorities or saving dolphins.
>
> Beatson and Beatson, 1994: 121

What is 'the fostering of art'? What is not? What do *you* think?

Theatre for Development

Theatre for Development (TFD), a form of theatre for adult education, has had a significant impact on African, Caribbean, Latin American and some Asian countries. Since the 1980s, development workers have used theatre as a tool to teach, help and foster self-expression. Boal and Freire are significant touchstones for this work, but many TFD projects have a more specific pedagogical function, teaching about issues such as health, water management, early marriages, ecology etc.

Issues of sustainability, expertize, grass-roots involvement, buy-in by local leaders and governments, and the flow of funding are important considerations for TFD work (see also Ubong Ndah in the *Reader*). Many practitioners of TFD are very aware of these thorny issues, and find ways of addressing power inequality and the political agendas of their funding sources in their work.

Tessa Mendel on theatre and social change in African nations

Theatre which has social change as its explicit objective goes by various names including popular theatre, theatre for development, community theatre or théâtre utile (useful theatre) in francophone Africa. While these terms are often used interchangeably, in general, popular theatre is the more inclusive term, with its widest definition encompassing any theatre which stands in opposition to classical, bourgeois or established forms of theatre. Popular theatre is also used to describe theatre that uses traditional media or is based in an indigenous culture.

Theatre for development, a form of popular theatre, is often used by non-governmental organisations (NGOs) or community based organisations (CBOs) to promote social goals. They may, for example, sponsor, either alone or in partnership, theatre within a community as an educational tool or to facilitate the participation of that community in a development process. Community theatre also falls within the general category of popular theatre and normally indicates that there has been a significant measure of community involvement in the theatre process, as opposed, for example, to the entire process having been undertaken by outside theatre professionals.

There is a continuum in popular theatre that runs from largely didactic, educational or propagandist forms to those that are more participatory and which promote dialogue rather than top-down communication. At the didactic end of the continuum we have, for example, theatre used by governments to promote health education messages. A range of civil society organisations also use theatre in this way to disseminate information and as an educational tool. Used in this way, theatre does promote freedom of expression, but of relatively powerful actors – in the examples above, of governments and organisations not of the dis-empowered or those with limited access to the means of communication.

At the participatory end of the continuum, the theatre process is often based on an analysis of Paulo Freire's pedagogical process of conscientisation where the community is involved in voicing its concerns and discovering solutions to problems.

Mendel, 2003: 3

25 Research exercise

a   What kind of issues do you see with terms such as 'Theatre for Development'? How do issues of naming 'developed/undeveloped' nations impact on the concerns of this form of performance practice?

b   Brainstorm with a colleague: what kind of problems arise when theatre becomes a form of teaching? Who teaches whom? What power relations pertain to particular situations? Is there a problem with predominantly urban-based 'experts'? What kind of knowledge might be favored by a technique that relies on expressive methods presented in a public arena?

c   Research a particular TFD project on-line or in a library. Chart the way that theatre workers respond to challenges and problems. Is the position of the worker her- or himself problematized?

TFD faces significant problems in many countries, and one quote shows the depth, urgency and impact of community performance. Sulaiman Abdu speaks about TFD in Eritrea, and about the violent suppression of its workers by the state:

> The government clearly wants to exert its influence on its citizens' thinking. Such behaviour impedes Theatre for Development which needs independence of government influence if it is to be an effective tool for the community, where they could discuss and analyse issues that affect them. Such independence is difficulty to attain in today's Eritrea. How would a Theatre for Development project operate in a community affected or displaced by the Badime war? Will the government look away when theatre practitioners and the community decide on a theatre play which demonstrates that without such a war this community might not have suffered, might not have had to leave its home, might not have had to be hungry and go from being a completely independent community to one that relies on foreign agencies for the provision of basic necessities of life? Clearly not, because this kind of theatre will lead to a critically aware community, one that may criticise the government and one that may eventually go into action against it.
>
> In the post-independence period of most African countries, the governments have disallowed a free theatre to develop which is bound, at certain times and in certain ways, to question governments' lines on various issues. In fact, they went further and started to squash empowering theatres, through censorship, imprisonment (the case Kamiriithu theatre project workers in Kenya) or murder of theatre workers (e.g. Byron Kawadwa, killed by Idi Amin in Uganda).
>
> Abdu, 2003

Outlook

In this chapter, I traced outlines of different historical and conceptual narratives that impact contemporary community performance practices. These accounts are open, deliberately multi-vocal and attempt to resist validating any one storyline. Community performers cite many of the figures or movements I discussed as part of their influence, but they also point to the fact that they hybridize, mix and match, and improvise their way to their own ever-changing practice. In the chapters that follow, many more practitioners, historians and critics speak, and this chapter's concepts – politics, community, folk, history, empowerment, reflexivity, interculturalism, nation, access or identity – emerge again and again as core concepts in community performance work.

Figure 2.17 Traditional Luo performance group entertaining before the performance of the Kawuonda Women's Theatre Group, Sigoti, Kenya, September 1997.
Photo: Eugene van Erven

CHAPTER 3

Setting up and running a group

You are ready to begin a project. Ideally, a project emerges from a community need and communal decision, and you and others might lead sessions because of a mandate given to you by the group. This kind of close-knit relationship is not always already established, and you might need to find other ways of building your community. For this chapter, I assume a different scenario: you are in search of a group to work with. You might have a first idea, a theme, or else a festival that's coming up, a local celebration, or the charge to work with a particular group of people. Where do you go from there?

3.1 Set up

3.1.1 Making contact

With whom do you wish to work? Why? Do you see yourself as part of the group? Are you a member of a neighborhood, an 'identity group', a community of interest, a person associated with a school, a retirement home? Think about the network you yourself are part of: which people does your life touch?

---

26 Reflection exercise

Create a network map. Take a large sheet of paper and put a circle with your name in it in the middle. Now create a spider's web or a wheel, placing around you all the people or groups you are part of. Keep at it – think about second-degree associations and potential contacts – you'll be astonished at the wealth of connections that open up! Think about the kind of journeys and contacts you make in a given month – places of work, education, medical attention, shopping or recreation. Now look back at your chart: can you see potential connections between this map and community arts projects?

'Ready-made' groups

- Community arts centers
- Hospitals with community arts programs
- After-school clubs
- Political party offices – in a place like this, you might get good leads to people who wish to work actively in community settings, addressing a particular issue
- Retirement homes with meeting places, and regular organized events who might look for a community artist/animator
- Hospices who might work with volunteer personnel
- LGBT (lesbian/gay/bisexual/transgender) groups, or other groups organized around a specific pride issue
- Diasporic groups
- Drop-in centers (whether focused on drug issues, mental health, women's centers, youth centers)
- Miners' welfare halls or other organizations and spaces associated with specific community groups
- Horticultural societies (great for landscape/garden projects)
- Adult education centers
- Bartering societies (arts services and the provision of specific experiences can provide a useful barter item)
- Church groups
- Farmers' organizations
- Reading groups
- Boy Scouts/Girl Guides or other youth associations
- Student groups
- Dieting clubs
- Sports clubs
- Parent/teacher associations
- Local amateur theatre associations
- Choirs
- Charities
- Any group or organization that meets regularly or has multiple contacts, has dedicated members who are already interested in grouping together around a specific topic.

With all of these groups, make sure that your aims and politics are well aligned with the groups and their agendas. Researching a group's support system, funders, founding members, trustees etc. will give you a good sense of their potential direction, but an actual chat with current group members will also be very useful before approaching them with a specific project idea.

Figure 3.1 A map of connections. Participant in Community Performance Professional Development Workshop, DANZ New Zealand, 2006.

Photo: Petra Kuppers

3.1.2 Motives

If you do not identify as a member of the particular grouping you plan to work with, what are your motives for your wish to work with them? Remember that the notion of 'group membership' itself is fluid, and that alliances are formed strategically. Clarifying your motives is a useful step towards shaping your idea, preparing the ground for the interaction with participants, and also for creating language that can be useful for funding applications.

27 Reflection exercise

Part of a group set-up is communication and debate. What's in it for everybody? Write down what you have to offer, what the people that are to become a group have to offer to each other and to you. What does the project you are proposing offer to them as individuals, to them as a group, to the place, location or organization you wish to work with or in?

28 Reflection exercise

Find a partner. Tell them about a project you conceived of, and might wish to carry further. As the project emerges from your mind, or from the writing on a page, notice how different ideas are coming to you in the process of speaking. Encourage your partner to ask questions. Answer them. Try to find ways of asking and answering that are neither offensive nor defensive, but that help you to develop your project idea. Share your experiences: how did your partner perceive your presentation style?

'Capacity building' is a key phrase referred to by many funding organizations when they consider applications. It refers to the ability of community art work to develop other, non-art-specific skills. When describing your project idea to others, it can be useful to think about these issues. They can lead to better 'buy-in' by the local community, particularly when the art project idea itself is still open.

Many community performance projects are open to change, collaboratively conceived, fluid and responsive to multiple inputs. What that means in practice is that things will change, should change, and you won't stay in (total) control. The persuasion or wooing part of the project is a great place to rehearse some of this openness. As you enter a meeting with a user board, a school official, a social worker or a leadership committee, you can present your idea, and it will change in the telling, and in the interaction with these people, even at this first stage.

Exercise note: As this chapter proceeds, I will ask you again and again to think through your project from different perspectives. Of course, you can change your project every time, trying out many different ones, or you can see one project all the way through.

3.1.3 Money

Do you need funding to run the project? Do you require funds either for yourself, as an artist fee, or for other aspects of the work? What do you need, what are the budget items for your project?

'Capacity building' issues in community performance work

Active participation
Skill building
Basing work on participants' ideas/issues
Sense of place
Building group identity
Giving the group ownership of the product
Leaving a pool of equipment for future work
Participants passing on their skills to their
  community

List taken from Arts Council of Northern Ireland

Who gets paid?

Some people like to fund all members working in a community group. This belief might be based on an analysis of cultural labor, and on the fact that work is differently valued when it is 'paid'. In this way, providing payment 'professionalizes' the contribution of community artists, even if the payment is only a token amount. Your politics, and the economical politics of your project, can guide you towards making a decision about this issue.

If you can, don't take existing models for granted because 'that's the way things are' – economical processes form one of the areas community performance can touch. Even if you can't or don't wish to pay your participants, be aware that they are investing time and effort, and probably some money, in the group. Exchange and value-generation can happen in different ways.

Sample budget items

Fees	Video-tapes
Transport	Marketing/publicity
Insurance	Postage
Space rental	Copying
Costumes	Copyright fees
Props	Food
Materials	Storage
Development fees for photos	

3.1.4 Ecology

Your project doesn't happen in a vacuum, it is embedded in its social, cultural and natural environment in many different ways. If you think seriously about this embedding, your project can grow in new and interesting ways.

An ecology of art making

Most directly, your project is part of the ecology of art provision in your target area. Even though it might feel as if you are on your own, you are most likely part of an ecosystem of artists, social workers, health workers, activists and others who share some of your concerns or beliefs. All the practical issues discussed so far, from group set-up to money issues, and many of the issues that still need exploring, have been faced by these people, and they all have found different answers to them. If you can find out some of these answers, sharing information respectfully, you and your project become part of a wider network of expertise and knowledge that isn't often shared in official and written ways.

29 Reflection exercise

Create a second network map, placing your name (or icon) in the middle. On this map (which might coincide with the first one in some ways), map out the art providers, individual artists and community artists, body work practitioners, elders, spiritual leaders, your support network of family and friends (whatever is appropriate for your project and genre of practice: think broadly). Embellish the map, make the linkages and symbols you use appropriate to the individuals or groups you are identifying: use different colors, icons, small sketches. Even in sparsely populated regions, a colorful and dense network will most likely appear. You can add to this network as you continue: when you find leaflets announcing art workshops or body work left in newsagent windows, when you see announcements of poets and their publications in the local paper, or see a display of local artists in your local library. The map might become a valuable document to you, a beautiful art piece displayed on your wall, a record of connections and potential contacts.

After you've identified the beginnings of the network of artists and community practice you inhabit, you can begin to think about ways of supporting this ecology. How can you nourish its diversity, make it strong and vibrant? How can you use your personal money, bartering products or services, skill, attention or energy to strengthen its life and become more fully part of it? I will discuss strategies for network building later on in Chapter 7, but it is useful to mention these connections at this point, to show that our communities are one of our primary ecologies.

An ecology of ideas: copyright

Sometimes you might think that your idea is so unique and special that you do not wish to share it with other art providers and community artists. You might be concerned with issues of ideas theft, copyright and ownership. These are valid concerns, but think about the aims of your project: are you working towards an economy of scarcity, where limited resources go towards competitively vetted projects, and where only some can win? Or are you working towards an economy of plenty, where ideas enrich ideas, action is collective, and resources are limitless? What economy would you like to work towards? Sometimes, a shift in perspective can help to see new opportunities.

The ecology of art making doesn't exist by itself: it is made possible by many different other worlds. These worlds include funding mechanisms and the wider national and international economies they are in turn part of, family arrangements and time management partners, the physical structures of communal meeting spaces and their maintenance, car parks, beaches, farms, parks, plazas etc. on which community arts projects take place.

In the following practice example, the artist/facilitators had to shift sites and modes of engagement in order to fit with the patterns of behavior appropriate to the people they wanted to work with.

No workshop take-up? Working with creative expression where it happens

Cultivating your palette: a recipe for arts, food, health and culture, by Australian art workers Joyce Louey and Lisa Philip-Harbutt, at Parks Community Centre, 2001

The aim of this project was to create a mixed media collaborative art work that celebrated the diverse nature of the local people who use the Parks Community Centre (PCC). PCC is located in a culturally diverse (including new arrivals and refugees) and low socioeconomic area of Adelaide. The phase 1 skills-based workshops were very successful. We had difficulty, however, in re-accessing the range of communities needed in order for the project to progress to the next phase. The reasons identified for this were a high turnover community linked to the redevelopment of the area at that time and the constraints of budget and timeframe which did not cater for the diversity and uniqueness of many of the participants. After several attempts at engaging community groups in a variety of ways, we came to the conclusion that in order to reach the goals of the project, we needed to take a vastly different approach from what was initially planned. Therefore, with the approval of the funding bodies we devised a change in strategy so that the targeted communities participated in alternative ways to the originally planned phase 2 art making workshops.

PRACTICE EXAMPLE

There was a strong response when we put a call out for the communities of the Parks to provide us with photographic evidence of their association with food. We suggested this could be a picture of their favorite food, a picture of what a meal or food meant to them, a picture of themselves, their family or friends, work colleagues etc. at meal time or some moment in time where food was an important part of an event or celebration. We asked the communities to inform us of when their family, workplace or community group were having a get together that involved food and we attended and took visual and audio documentation. We also put a call out to local artists who may have 'food' as a topic for their art making. We documented paintings, objects, photos and poems. The documentation was then used to produce a video that celebrated and acknowledged the socially and culturally diverse communities of the Parks and celebrated their relationships to food. The video is often played in the foyer of the Parks Arts and Functions Complex.

As the practice example shows, flexibility is key in community performance work: find ways to connect with the people you wish to work with. Here, hooking into existing rituals and uses of space and time allowed the artists to engage a wider group of people.

WIDER WORLDS

Cameron, 1997: 11

Different eyes in Australia

I've worked over the past few years with a group in Terrigal on large scale environmental work, *Homage to the Elements*. Working with people like Nina Angelo, Victoria Monk, Suzanne Holman and a host of environmentally aware artists we've specifically looked at environmental problems through dance and theatre and celebration. By performing this way you are then linked to the environment and you never look at it in the same way again. Your eyes for that place will always be different. Modern life tends to alienate people from nature and their natural environments so what we were saying was 'Come on, let's go back, let's dance on the rocks, let's go to these natural theatres and link ourselves, not only in a symbolic way, but in a physical way with the environment.'

Beyond these ecologies of art provision and community life is the wider ecology that encompasses human and non-human life. Clearly, not all community arts projects will deal explicitly with this kind of ecological thinking, but I found that giving (more than) a thought to it, and its energy, can be a great reminder of issues of scale and of generosity.

You've just placed yourself into a specific subset of ecology in your area. There are other ways in which you can place yourself into your environment – and in which you can see yourself as being seen from other perspectives, different from your own.

The birds have vanished into the sky,
And now the last cloud drains away.
We sit together, the mountain and me,
Until only the mountain remains.

Li Po (Chinese
Poet, 701–62)

Find out more about the place you are standing in, have grown up in, working in, or are visiting. Questions you might wish to ask include:

- What is the nature of the ecosystem(s) in my region?
- What are its dominant features in terms of landforms, soil, weather patterns, dominant flora and fauna, precipitation, etc.? When looking at the birds, fish, mammals, insects, reptiles and others, ask which inhabit the region, and which migrate? What connections exist between this place and others, through migration?
- When did large-scale changes in these patterns happen, and why?
- How has human life woven itself into the fabric of this place?
- What challenges do humans face in this region, and why?
- What challenges do other life-forms of the region face, and why?

Now you have a slightly different map of your region: one that presents the environment as one that is collaboratively inhabited and used by both humans and non-humans. How does this decentering of human society impact your thoughts on your project, or future projects? Can you see connections, opportunities, challenges? Do you feel an interest in incorporating non-human life in your project, in some way, be it directly or symbolically? What do you take, what do you leave, how can you act responsibly? How does your art project use and impact on the non-human world?

30 Reflection exercise

(Adapted from New Zealand ecology dance artist Ali East)
Find yourself some space outdoors. Anchor yourself, stand firmly, and begin to turn on the spot. As you turn, call out everything you see: sky, cloud, bird, tree, house, horse, lantern, shop etc. Keep turning and calling, and find a rhythm of step and call. Modulate your speed: what features come most often into your mouth? What happens as you speed up?

This exercise also works well when you interlink arms with a partner, back-to-back, and begin to call and step in rhythm with each other, in call and response. Find a chanting rhythm.

Figure 3.2 Dancing on the beach during an environment and dance weekend in the Catlins, New Zealand, led by Ali East, as part of a community dance course, University of Otago, New Zealand.
Photo: Petra Kuppers

Artist Robert Janz,
quoted in Gablik,
1991: 90

Footprints: self-erasure art?

Significant worthwhile art today seems to me to be that art which points to, which focuses on, the problem of restoring the balance. We don't need an art of imposition anymore. We need something else. It is the subtext of art that is the issue. The subtext of important art today, saleable art today, is power and prestige. That is the real subtext in a Richard Serra sculpture or a Frank Stella painting; it's Brand Art for a Brand Culture. A big corporation buys this important 'brand art' and it says: 'We brand the land. We are powerful and prestigious, and we impose. We make things happen.' That is the subtext of contemporary art. Whereas what we actually need, since we've become a cancerous society, destroying our planet exactly the way that cancer cells destroy us, is an art whose subtext is balance and attunement. Art also pollutes, consumes the world. What about self-erasure in art – art that cleans up after itself.

P R A C T I C E   E X A M P L E S

Eco-performance!

Welfare State International: Patch-work

Patch-work will be an original work of art, a site specific installation with fire, ceramics and Cumbrian/Cuban percussion. Directed by John Fox, Patch-work will be created by Welfare State International's Engineers of the Imagination, especially Martin Brockman (kiln builder extraordinaire) and will also feature Boneshaker, the band.

Patch-work will be a miniature outdoor extravaganza and a rite of passage (in carnival mode) conceived for this multinational gathering. At one time the Lancaster University campus was farmed. Now, again, clay will be dug from local seams to construct a kiln in mythic animal form. Participants will create small boats to be fired in a mass open air firing accompanied by stilt walkers, malt whiskey, drummers and a wild choir. As the kiln self-destructs in gusts of flame ceramic gifts will be raked from the morning embers.

So, in keeping with the spirit of the conference, in a four day process the local will be re-discovered, cherished, mutated, exchanged and transported back home.

Hence a Patch-work. An assemblage of parts. An installation to celebrate the art of many hands.

Proposal for performance at the Between Nature conference, Lancaster, UK, 2000

The Procession of the River Species

The Procession of the River Species invites the Fort Collins area community to bring the wild to town! Transform yourself into a local native wildlife species by making masks and costumes, or join us to 'drum' the flow of the river. We will form a procession, accompanied by drummers and rhythm instruments, which will dance, march, flow, fly or swim through old town and down to the Poudre River to join RiverFest on June 1st. It will start at the Museum of Contemporary Art and Oak Street Plaza at 1:15 PM and will arrive at Heritage Park at 2:00 PM. The procession will feature locals, maybe even you, dressed in masks and costumes, representing animals who need river and stream corridors to survive – including our native otter, kingfisher, osprey, trout, raccoon, fox, coyote, deer, fish, bugs, and others.

Become a river animal, samba in the streets, help preserve wildlife corridors.

The 16th Annual Poudre River Fest Rendezvous, June 1–2, 2002, Fort Collins, Colorado, USA

Simon Whitehead: somasonicspirit

soma . . . body as distinct from soul
sonic . . . of, or relating to, or using sound or sound waves
spirit . . . animated/life-giving principle in a person or place

Beginning at sunrise, a remote performer (Simon Whitehead) walks an upland moor locating springs and water sources. At each source he drinks, leaves an offering and (via mobile technology) transmits the sound of the water to a room. In this empty room, a sound artist (Barnaby Oliver) receives the transmission and releases this signal into the space. Through a constant and delicate dowsing and mixing of this material, the sonic and ambient image becomes the territory. During this translocation, the room becomes a receptacle of spirit; symbolically, nature is invited into a cultural setting.

The viewer enters the room for contemplation, to move, to dream, to remember . . . at intervals a performer (Stirling Steward) will gently intervene. An animating spirit, she interacts with or becomes witness to any viewer present.

The work ends at sunset, during a final transmission. The sonic element fades with the sun. The space at this time will be open to those who have encountered *somasonicspirit* during the day.

Publicity material, performance at the Between Nature conference, Lancaster, UK, 2000

For many traditional ritualists (such as shamans, priests, witches and others), and also for many contemporary ecological artists, art is a way of communicating between self and Other. In terms of human/non-human ecologies, practices seen as 'art' in Western societies can serve as communications and exchanges. David Abrams writes about one figure who has often served as a focal point for these debates: the shaman. He or she is often on the edge or limit of their society, often living outside the village, or in other ways 'separate', and their charge is a special attunement to the wider ecology:

> The traditional or tribal shaman . . . acts as an intermediary between the human
> community and the larger ecological field, ensuring that there is an appropriate
> flow of nourishment, not just from the landscape to the human inhabitants,
> but from the human community back to the local earth. . . .

To some extent every adult in the community is engaged in this process of listening and attuning to the other presences that surround and influence daily life. But the shaman or sorcerer is the exemplary voyager in the intermediate realm between the human and the more-than-human worlds, the primary strategist and negotiator in any dealings with the Others.

Abrams, 1996: 7

Quoted in Wendy
Pond, 1995: 61

A line from a Hiva Kakala, a light-hearted song, often a love song, which here is a love song to the landscape of Tafahi, Tonga:

> To u lata 'I ho hala kakala.
> I'm at home in your sweet-scented paths.

31 Reflection exercise

Clarify for yourself, and for this moment, how ecology and community practice relate to each other. What do *you* think? Abrams writes about traditional shamans – but does this description echo in any way your thoughts on community arts practice? Or are you uncomfortable with the juxtaposition of shamans and community artists? In what way, and why? How else can you bring ecological thought and community arts practice together? Discuss the issues with a partner. There is no right or wrong answer, of course, but calling yourself to clarity on this issue can focus your community art practice.

Figure 3.3 Jay Critchley, 'Immunity Mandala', Provincetown, USA, 1983. A beach AIDS ritual for the community.   Photo: Grace Consoli

SAMPLE RESOURCE: TEACHERS' GUIDES

Teachers' Guides can be very useful tools for community performance projects: you can learn a lot about local issues, specialist issues connected with areas of expertise (such as specific ecological sites), and the kind of issues and conflicts that pertain to them. Many eco-institutions, history sites and different kinds of museums have excellent teaching materials. Ask your local organizations if they have guides available: they will be filled with useful information, ideas, and workshop material. There follows an example that pertains to the use of performance in the investigation of eco-issues.

From Wetland Care, Australia, wetland teachers' resources drama/study of environment and society

Hypotheticals

Discuss with the students different wetland values in relation to the Wetland Complex. Assign each student the role of one of the wetland users as listed below and explore the following situations. Take each situation in turn and discuss whether this might be a 'Dream Scenario', 'Worst Nightmare' or 'Scenario of Little Consequence' for each of the users. Examine conflicting perspectives and whether these may be resolved.

- A 'Friends of Wetlands' group forms to manage a local wetland.
- A mosquito plague leads to demands to spray or drain a wetland.
- The government guarantees more environmental flows, i.e. higher than normal level river flows specifically for the environment.
- An algal bloom interferes with recreational use of the wetland.
- The wetland is opened up for grazing during a drought.
- A new weir is installed in the higher reaches of the catchment and used to stabilize wetland water levels.
- The council has fenced the vegetation to protect it and public access is now restricted.
- A bushfire burns the vegetation around the wetland and along the creek.
- Reeds are left to choke the inlet channel connecting the wetland with the main river channel.
- A local wetland is declared significant under the Ramsar Convention.
- The wetland becomes a centre for eco-tourism activity.
- Flow control structures are installed and a drying phase is introduced to the lagoon.
- The number and size of native fish being caught by recreational fishers is declining noticeably.
- Riparian (fringing the edge of the wetland) is being eaten by rabbits.
- Scientists advise that the wetland should be allowed to dry out completely from time to time to maintain biodiversity.
- The boardwalk is extended and more recreational facilities are installed.

Users of wetlands

- Birdwatchers
- Picnickers and campers
- Housing developers
- Commercial fisherman
- Tourists
- Duck hunters
- Recreational water users
- Farmers and graziers
- Scientists, teachers and students
- Local council

Based on 'Wetland Dreams and Nightmares' from WCA (2000)
Living with Wetlands – A Community Guide

32 Reflection exercise

This material presents an extensive analysis of situations and stakeholders surrounding a specific site.

a   How can you adapt this teaching material for use as impetus in eco-performance work?

If you can, visit a local site such as a nature park, city park, wildlife center, a proposed marine sanctuary, a wetland.

b   Create a similar list of situations and stakeholders for a local environment near you.
c   Find four different ideas about how you can get representatives of the different stakeholder groups to come together for a community performance project (rather than just 'role-playing' them).

3.1.5 Access

Thinking about access issues grows out of an ecological awareness: an awareness that there is more in the world than your own experience and life-circle. Most likely, you will want to work with people who are not all like yourself. At the same time, we all know most about our own comfort zones, and our own ways of communicating and inhabiting space. If you want to actively grow your community, and invite others in, you need to think about the assumptions of access that underlie your project.

33 Reflection exercise

Gather (or think back on) any community art announcements you've seen or heard recently. What are the assumptions of access both in the announcements themselves and in the activity they are advertising? Think about:

- ability to read;
- ability to use and access to a telephone;
- ability to use and access to a computer/Internet/email;
- ability and willingness to spend a certain amount of money as participation fee or for transport;
- ability to find child care;
- ability to access a certain space – space where note is displayed, and where activity takes place;
- ability to communicate in a specific language;
- ability to work in certain group sizes;
- access to a car/public transport/group van;
- availability during certain time slots – who can best use time slots such as 8–9 a.m., 12–1, 1–2, 3–4, 6–7, or 8–9 p.m.? What assumptions to these slots make? What tacit assumptions about religious practices and familial availability does the day of the week choice make?

Continue with building the list.

Most community activities have unspoken or implied access requirements, and these access issues pre-select potential participants and target groups. When the access criteria and target group match, this might not be a problem, but when they do not, it is hard to get participants and project together. These mismatched access issues are not by any means mainly physical. To use a hypothetical example: a city council decides to run a community arts session as a way to build more community spirit, active citizenship and involvement in the local area. They advertise a weekly group session with an enticing name and an interesting description – but they are advertising it in a newsletter that lists all their other community outreach sessions, including tax clinics, adult literacy courses and workshops on setting up your own business. What could potential effects be on the group of people who self-select to become a member of this new community arts activity?

To some people, council activities are potentially problematic, too closely associated with state institutions and other agencies experienced as negative, punitive or restrictive. People who have experienced state and local government interventions in this way might not read the leaflet with the council information.

While a community arts group could be great way to address some of these stereotypes, and create other narratives about citizenship involvement, those people furthest from council activities might not find out about it, or else read the announcement with already closed minds. If the council really wants to open up its boundaries, the publicity worker might need to rethink his or her strategies in order to ensure wider access to the activity. This might mean creating a separate leaflet, not too closely identified with the institution, and finding creative ways of reaching out.

ACCESS AND DISABILITY

One large component of access thinking focuses on disability, impairment and access requirements. The single most useful piece of information about good ways of ensuring access is 'when in doubt, ask'.

If you want to make a community theatre session accessible to people who have mental health diagnoses, ask them. What does it take to make you comfortable with a space, an environment, a group? The answer will most likely depend on a huge number of factors, and will be specific to the group you are working with.

What we call ourselves, and what others call us, are important aspects of cultural life and social interaction. If you call people by a name they find offensive or inappropriate, you might lose potential connections, and shut down opportunities for

Figure 3.4 Disability culture pride tableau with the Disabled People's Assembly, Dunedin, New Zealand.
Photo: Petra Kuppers

engagement. In writing this book, I had to make my own choices about naming. In relation to disability, I use the terminology of 'disabled person' together with 'people with specific impairments'. This language use shows a sensibility born out of British disability culture. In this context, the term 'disabled' is embraced as a sign of a shared cultural and structural oppression (structurally similar to the term 'black' in British usage). Individual differences and medically labeled conditions, when mentioned at all, are called 'impairments'.

In contrast, in the US context for instance, other sensibilities often rule: here, a 'people first, disability second' politics leads to formulations such as 'people with disabilities', 'people with visual disabilities' etc., and the term 'impairment' is avoided.

There are three models of disability, as well as many variations. Only the third one is currently endorsed by many disability organizations.

Medical model of disability

Disability is part of a person, and needs to be fixed, and medical interventions try to address the difference.

In a related model, social interventions also locate the source of the problem in the disabled person, and try to normalize her or him: make her acceptable to the wider social world (for instance, by engaging in dangerous and purely cosmetic surgery on people of small stature, to lengthen their bones).

Moral model of disability

This model sees moral issues in different bodies, senses or intellectual development. These differences can be associated with sin and shame, and blame can be allocated either to individuals, their families or social groups. These cultural beliefs about disability can lead to self-hatred and social exclusion. Much rarer, these differences are culturally associated with positive values: being singled out as special by religious entities, or being cast as moral guides for a community.

Both negative and positive moral values of disability find their way into many mainstream cultural practices: Hollywood films, for instance, often use these stereotypes as a form of narrative short-hand, presenting blind people as pure, intellectually impaired people as innocent, people with mobility impairments as twisted and bitter.

Both negative and positive assumptions set up specific roles for disabled people, and restrict their life choices.

Social model of disability

The social model definition reflects the idea that disability is socially constructed. In this model, disability emerges when individual differences (such as impairments, but also purely cosmetic differences such as unusual facial bone structures) clash with social conventions and notions of normality. In this model, disability is *not* part of a person, but of the social field, and the negative attributes of disability are created by the attitudinal, architectural and environmental features of our world.

Examples:
- The stairs disable while the wheelchair itself does not. Think about how often stairs and steps are used in museums, churches or buildings associated with public functions as architectural features to display 'loftiness' or 'power', without necessarily enhancing or providing functionality.
- The social reliance on predominantly visual information disable people with visual impairments. Think about Internet communication, and about the use of visual icons rather than text descriptors as navigation tools!
- The social reliance on petrol-driven vehicles as the main form of transportation disables people with asthma.
- The social reliance on eight-hour, relatively undisrupted office work while sitting in standardized chairs disables people with fatigue-related impairments, who might be able to do the required tasks, but in different time-slots, with larger breaks, and different postures.

Social change, and in particular civil rights can ensure that as many people as possible can participate in the public sphere. Of course, problems can arise from this as well: visual icons are often a useful form of communication for people with intellectual impairments. Cars in cities are often indispensable for people with mobility impairments. Imagination and socially responsible planning can minimize hindrances to social participation in most circumstances. In the social model of disability, normalization (making people as close to the norm as possible) isn't seen as a positive value.

The two ways of speaking about disability are incompatible, so I made the decision to employ British usage, born out of my own membership in the disability culture community, and my own political perspective. For your own purposes, whether you identify as disabled or non-disabled, make sure you find out what the currently acceptable way of referring to the issue is (acceptable to disabled people/people with disabilities). Phoning a self-advocacy group is usually a good way to go about this. But flexibility is most important: different people have different agendas and ways of thinking.

We should celebrate that these different codes show the impact disability politics and liberation movements has had on our languages.

When I was a wheelchair user, I tended to answer questions about necessary access depending on the resources available to the person asking, and to the status of the institution represented. Thus, I would feel comfortable with a single step and no properly accessible restroom for a visit to a low-budget local performance group, but I would expect full access and code specifications when I was asked to participate in meetings with local governments.

Clearly, there is a political component to access provision, and to the struggle over right of access. Community performers do well to remember that the issue of access isn't neutral, or specific to getting one individual into a building, but that the issue speaks about exclusion and decades of discrimination.

Below is a list of access issues that might or might not apply to a given situation. In all cases, these access issues are not exclusive to people who identify or are identified as 'disabled'. Many of the mental health access issues I discuss first can be helpful to many different people, and the issues raised by them apply to most other group settings, as well (in particular in relation to stigma).

The mobility issues are useful reminders for working with people who are older, or have short-term mobility issues due to accident or ill health, or are pregnant or nursing.

Many of the sensory access issues do not pertain to the specific languages of Deaf people or Braille users, but make sense to all people who use their senses: many people who hear still prefer written information, and many who use spoken languages prefer kinesthetic information sharing.

Thinking about access is about respecting difference, and allowing diversity to thrive.

MENTAL HEALTH AND ACCESS

Mental distress is a disability that has consequences both at the social and at the personal level. Accommodations can help to make workshops accessible, but we cannot provide a final answer to mental health access issues here: what is most important is to be open and respectful, and to ask people what kind of provision they require.

> ## Stigma
>
> Stigma is an attribute that is deeply discrediting within a particular social interaction.
>
> Goffman, 1963: 3

The term mental health issues covers a wide terrain of conditions, many of which are not stable in time, and many people have different needs at different times. There follows a number of concerns that have become important in my own work, but the list is neither final nor universal. While I group these issues into specific headings, they all pertain to most workshop/performance project situations, with non-disabled and disabled people of all kinds.

Access issues when thinking about setting up a project
• When trying to set up a workshop, try to find a user-led forum in which to speak about the planned work.

- Be open about your motivation. In the case of the Olimpias workshops, I try to be clear what my political aims are, how they relate to my own experience of disability, and how and why I want to work with mental health system survivors: I am fascinated by the differences among us, and want to enrich our social world by bringing more voices into the centre of attention. What is your motivation?
- Establish as soon as possible a schedule for your workshops. Many people value a familiar scene, therefore it can be useful to start up workshops just before or just after regular meetings.
- Think about school times, childcare issues, religious services or practices, and transport issues. Not everybody drives himself or herself, and you might need to take public transport times into account, or set up a transport scheme with a service provider.
- Make sure that the room you select is appropriate to your task: many rooms echo power-relations very clearly (schools, service settings etc.). It would be good to start thinking about hierarchies early on, and to try to find environments that can help to establish that. Are comfortable chairs available, set in a round? For most short writing tasks, tables are not really necessary, and hand-held paper might well do.
- Are social facilities nearby? Can you have a tea or coffee break, become comfortable with one another away from the main workshop tasks?
- Are health and safety issues dealt with: do you know the nearest first-aid person, fire extinguisher, telephone etc.?
- Overall, be flexible in your physical set-up. In the Olimpias workshops, we have found that there are seasonal as well as individual differences: we have fewer participants in the darker winter months. Sometimes, people might like to participate, but can't leave the home for disability-related issues: in the past, when we knew about these issues, we have held meetings at each other's homes.

Access issues when thinking about sessions

- People tend to be happy that you have taken the initiative and set up the group. Don't beat yourself up or think of your group members as a resource. Have fun.
- Be aware of differences in concentration, attention span, different agendas for joining etc. Every group member is different, and the group is richer for that. Try to find ways to value everybody's contribution. Sometimes, that might mean letting someone be part of the group even if he or she is completely silent and passive: 'being in a group' in itself can be valuable to them!
- Don't pry. If people want to share, they will, eventually. But the workshops are not therapy sessions: you are probably not trained to handle what might arise, and these disclosures might not necessarily be that useful for your group's creative process. Try to keep the artistic and expressive nature of your meetings in mind.
- There are other ways of communicating than in long sentences, or even in words at all. Previous participants have just offered individual words, which were then woven into the group work. Others have brought in musical instruments, rather

than speaking or writing. There are so many possible art approaches to a theme: writing, dancing, singing, drama, still images made out of bodies, music, photography, a small, still ritual.

- When you feel frustrated, try to rethink your own agenda. There is no predetermined aim or speed. The process is as valuable as the product. And if a group, or group members, feel that they have to talk about their lives rather than sit down to the tasks you might have set them, that might be important as well.
- In my years as workshop leader, I have not yet found it necessary to ask a group member to leave. I have found other group members very tolerant of each other, and sometimes the process just has to change if certain things are not possible. Exclusion is such a fundamental experience of mental health system survivors that it is important not to duplicate this experience within the groups!
- It might be good to have someone to talk to after the sessions, to debrief, and to help you deal with your own emotions as they well up. Try to have a mentor, a friend, someone with whom you can share yourself.

Other issues to think about in relation to impairments include the following.

ACCESS ISSUES IN RELATION TO MOBILITY

- Parking.
- Length of paths inside and outside buildings.
- Stairs/elevators/escalators.
- Width of doorways – different requirements for manual and powered wheelchairs.
- Flooring – thick carpet isn't a good surface for manual wheelchair users, as it grips the wheels, and waxed parquet or linoleum can be hazardous to people using sticks, crutches and walkers.
- Restrooms – low or high toilets, handrails, placement of mirrors, accessibility of faucets. Also if you are running a dance class where you are expecting a good number of wheelchair users, is there more than one accessible restroom within easy distance?
- Stamina – many pain- or energy-related conditions mean that people find it hard to stay in one position for a long time, or to work continuously for certain periods. Breaks, and comfortable resting places, can help with this.

Access issues in relation to sensory impairment/difference

If a sign language is the first language of many people in your projected project but your own first language is spoken English, how can you achieve both adequate communication flow *and* show respect for the existence of more than the spoken language in the room?

Since not all people with hearing impairments are Deaf (with 'capital D deaf' signifying members of the cultural group of sign language speakers), just as not all people with visual impairments read Braille, how can you ascertain that the modes of communication you are setting up are appropriate to the group?

Options

- British Sign Language/American Sign Language (BSL/ASL) interpreters (assumes BSL/ASL/etc. ability);
- transcription of dialogue onto a screen for people to read (assumes reading skills);
- induction loops that allow people with hearing aids to participate fully (assumes hearing aids/residual hearing);
- screen readers (assumes reading skills);
- skilled audio transcription to translate visual information into spoken word (which not all people with visual impairments like).

Asking not only shows respect for personal communication needs, but also for the existence of different cultural groups. Generally, useful tools for many people are:

- Print-out of papers or notes, some in large print.
- Keep lighting levels adequate, and encourage the person speaking to have her or his mouth visible – both of these issues make communication easier for lip-readers, but also enhance clarity overall.
- Think about appropriate use of microphones.
- Think about appropriate use of talking sticks. (A talking stick is a stick or other object that gets handed around. Only the person who holds it is able to speak at that time. It is a great device to ensure that all people get to speak, and that they do not get drowned out by others.)

ACCESS ISSUES IN RELATION TO DEVELOPMENTAL IMPAIRMENT/ INTELLECTUAL DIFFERENCE

- Self-advocacy groups such as 'People First' campaign for the use of clear language, icons and images to ensure respectful communication practices.
- Clarity in decision-making: who is making decisions? How can decision-making be delegated so that all participants feel ownership of the work?
- When recruiting for your workshop, how do you negotiate issues of advocacy?
- How can you speak to the people you want to work with directly?
- If you fill in a slot in a day-center, and there are no alternative rooms in this center, are you happy with this, or would you prefer your participants to have a voice in deciding if they want to participate?

Alice is creating beautiful arcing movements with her arms above and around Kelly, who watches them with delight. She begins moving her body to match and gradually her arms, usually held tight to her chest in a flexion pattern, begin extending out. They are reaching and arcing, diving and swooping, dancing with Alice's arms and with patterns in the sky. Alice and Kelly continue dancing in this manner long after the exercise is finished.

Workshop notes from Community Dance course, visited by members of a local 'special needs' group, written by Caroline Plummer and Ralph Buck

Elias Katz on art centers and adults with developmental disabilities

Since the 1970s, I have visited many art centers for adults with developmental disabilities in the United States and other countries, and observed many benefits to the artists with disabilities attending these programs:

- Over time, there usually are changes in the art work created. In some artists there may be rapid change in color, shape, detail, and subject matter. In others there may be a very slow growth in their expression of these elements.
- Since creativity is emphasized, each person is encouraged to seek more personal choices, to select themes and resources.
- Many artists with disabilities have never (or rarely) expressed their feelings or moods, especially those which are related to fears, anxiety, depression. In the art studio, they are able to express their feelings through a variety of media, thereby allowing for release of pent-up feelings.
- Many people with disabilities have been neglected, denigrated, and made to feel inferior. In the studio, each artist with disabilities is treated with respect as a productive, expressive person. The self-image as a creative artist is emphasized, and frequently incorporated into their art by the artist.
- We have frequently seen instances where the artists with disabilities become more expressive in spoken language, as they discuss their art with their artist-teachers and with their colleagues and visitors to the studio and gallery.
- When artists with disabilities use paints, clay, linoleum blocks and cutting tools, they develop greater skills in using these materials and equipment.
- Basic activities of daily living and elementary demands, such as being on time, paying attention to instructions, as well as skills like manipulating clay and operating a printing press can be practiced in the studio setting, and may lead to full-time or part-time jobs.

Katz (2002) president and co-founder (with Florence Ludins-Katz)
of the National Institute of Art and Disabilities in Richmond, CA

Overall, there are numerous ways of ensuring successful and respectful communication. Many are obvious, and make the workshop environment more welcoming to many different people. Others are much more specialized, but people requiring these kinds of access needs are usually able to provide information about them and their set up (an example of these specialized equipments is the bliss board, a tool for some people who have cerebral palsy, which allows people to communicate with eye movements rather than speech).

As artists, you already have a wide variety of communication paths in your arsenal, and you can use these to make access possible. How do touch, sound, spatial awareness and visuals interact and play with each other? How can you design workshops that pay attention to all these different ways of sensing and being in the world?

34 Research exercise

Research access tools for disabled people (a sign language, Simpson boards, breath-controlled power wheelchairs, white sticks, screen readers). What do they do, how do they work? Investigate at least five different tools. Knowing what they do can help you to become aware of different communication strategies.

35 Research exercise

How does the disability origin myth on p. 80 compare to other cultures' notions about disability difference?

Figure 3.5 Coastal mappings workshop, Dunedin, New Zealand.   Photo: Petra Kuppers

Adam Benjamin

In 1997 I was teaching at a school for deaf students in Tokyo. My words were being translated into Japanese and then into Japanese sign; the students' sign language was translated into spoken Japanese and then into English. This in itself demanded an economy of words and a reassessment of teaching methods. Try stopping a studio full of deaf students, who don't speak your language, half of whom have their eyes closed, and all of whom are concentrating intensely on dancing with their partners; it is quite obvious, in the way it can only be on the metro on the way home, that this was a problem I should have considered before starting.

In response to this problem I introduced the idea of flock [where an open attention means that participants respond with imitation to cues given out by others, without words, and through a form of 'group osmosis']. A single leading student was able to take a signal from me and bring her partner to stillness. The other leaders gradually became aware of this couple who were no longer moving and stillness spread effortlessly through the studio. This method encouraged us all to be aware not only of the bodies moving in space but also of the space itself.

Benjamin, 2001: 119

PRACTICE EXAMPLE

Disability and origin myth

A Chinese origin myth about the making of humans presents an interesting view of disability:

> The Creator Pan Gu separated Heaven and Earth, and then brought plants and animals into being. But he felt unhappy with his handiwork, because none of the birds and beasts had the power of reason; he decided there ought to be one creature with the ability to care for and make use of other living beings. With his strong, skilful hands he began to mould the first people from mud, and as he finished each figure he set it to dry in the sunshine. Some of the creatures he filled with the female qualities of yin and fashioned into women, others he endowed with the male qualities of yang, turning them into men. He worked all day beneath the hot sun, piling up his people against a rock outcrop.
>
> As the sun went down he straightened his aching back and looked up at the sky, where he saw a bank of dark stormclouds. Some of the clay people had not yet dried and he realized that his handiwork would be obliterated if the storm broke over the figures. He hurried to move them into the shelter of a nearby cave, but as he worked a great wind arose, whipping up the clouds until they filled the sky. Pan Gu cried aloud with anguish as the thunder cracked and the rains poured down while he was still moving the figures. Those damaged were the ancestors of people with unusually shaped bodies of disabilities.
>
> Phillips, 1999: 39

36 Reflection exercise

With a partner, brainstorm and research access issues for one cultural group pertinent to your own environment: Scots, Thai, Bengali, New Englanders, German, Black British, African American etc. In order to even begin to focus on access, you also need to have some idea of the project you wish to lead: oral history workshops and drama groups might have to think about different access issues than dance sessions or action painting.

Access strategies are not necessarily only for disability access – they are very useful tools in managing many different communication situations, since they emerge from a sensitive assessment of specific situation. The 'flock' practice example (on p. 79) is very useful in many situations.

ACCESS ISSUES IN RELATION TO CULTURAL DIFFERENCE

Disability and its cultures provide access issues, but other cultures and identities have access issues as well. Different cultures have different ways of dealing with:

- group situations;
- social hierarchies;
- ways of communicating;
- body language;
- gender issues;
- intergenerational attitudes;
- religion and its practices;
- personal space;
- mobility within urban or rural environments;
- stereotypes;
- discrimination;
- cultural and personal history;
- issues of authority.

Opposition, racism and sharings: the uses of anger

Any discussion among women about racism must include the recognition and the use of anger. This discussion must be direct and creative because it is crucial. We cannot allow our fear of anger to deflect us nor seduce us into settling for anything else than the hard work of excavating honesty; we must be quite serious about the choice of this topic and the angers entwined within it, because rest assured, our opponents are quite serious about their hatred of us and what we are trying to do here. . . .

For it is not the anger of Black women . . . that launches rockets, spends over sixty thousand dollars a second on missiles and other agents of war and death, slaughters children in cities, stockpiles nerve gas and chemical bombs, sodomizes our daughters and the earth. It is not the anger of Black women which corrodes into blind dehumanizing power bent upon the annihilation of us all unless we meet it with what we have; our power to envision and to redefine the terms upon which we live and work; our power to envision and to reconstruct, anger by painful anger, stone upon heavy stone, a future of pollinating difference and the earth to support our choices.

We welcome all women who can meet us, face to face, beyond objectification and guilt.

Lorde, 1984: 28, 32

A complex ritual guides visits to Maori marae, maori meeting houses, sacred sites, and community gathering places. The visitors to a marae enter the site after the kai karanga, a woman caller, offers a welcome such as this:

Haere mai ra	Come forward
Nga manuhiri tuaarangi e	Visitors from afar
Haeremai, haeremai.	Welcome, welcome.
Mauria mai o koutou tini mate	Bring with you the spirits of your dead
Kia mihia	That they may be greeted
Kia tangihi e.	That they may be mourned.
Piki mai, kake mai,	Ascend onto our marae,
Whakaekea mai te marae tapu	Ascend the sacred marae
O te iwi e.	Of our people.
Haeremai, haeremai, haeremai.	Welcome, welcome, welcome.

After this call has been received, visitors enter the marae.

'Karangi', quoted in Tauroa and Tauroa, 1986: 34

CULTURAL USE AND PERMISSION

Permission is one issue you might have to consider when working with local myths, stories, legends, with traditional dance movements, or with poetry used in traditional ritual.

37 Reflection exercise

Think about places with sacred, historical or otherwise special meaning in your environment. If you wanted to work in or near these sites, who would you have to contact?

Is the use you are planning respectful (even if you disagree with the tradition involved)? Will your participants feel uncomfortable or disempowered if you use traditional elements with them?

For members of some cultural groups, including some students in classrooms in American universities, engaging in yoga can trigger discomfort. Using a ritual structure such as the Christian Stations of the Cross in a secular context can be painful and upsetting to some people. Some Australian Aborigine myths are only told under secrecy, without permission to retell them. Sacred sites, whether South Pacific marae, Celtic stone circles, or pilgrimage routes, mean something to someone, even if not necessarily to yourself, and if you are planning on using these sites, you might find it useful and sensitive to ask for permission before you do so.

If you feel that the content of the rites, sites or myths you are engaging with are themselves repressive or in need of change, you can of course create work about that – but you might find it easier to gain acceptance and a response from your community if you do not desecrate places and disrespect people who disagree with you.

Personal reflection and residual racism

In an interview with Ron Scapp, bell hooks writes about problems in addressing residual or systemic racism or sexism in teaching situations:

> This fear of being found personally wanting in some way is often one of the greatest barriers to promoting critical consciousness, especially about racist and sexist domination. Since the practice of critical thinking requires that we all engage in some degree of critical evaluation of self and other, it helps if we can engage individuals in ways that promote self-motivated interrogation rather [that] reactive response to outer challenge.

hooks, 2003: 107

In all cases, as workshop facilitator you should be aware of what you are doing, open about your motivations, and able to shift and change your ideas in discussion with your participants. This does not mean that you can't address culturally sensitive material, or should avoid points of pressure: it merely means that you should do so mindful of people's feelings and in awareness of what you are doing.

ACCESS ISSUES IN RELATION TO AGE DIFFERENCE

The final group of access issues I wish to discuss here relate to age issues, and to working with elders, children and intergenerational groups.

Access issues in elder work

- Stereotypes: do you have set ideas of what to expect of elders? When you think about these issues rationally, do they make sense? How do you wish to be treated when you get older?
- Age-related disability access is similar to the issues mentioned in the various lists above. But some issues might be more prevalent:

  - conditions associated with memory loss;
  - depression;
  - loneliness;
  - institutionalization.

> ## 38 Reflection exercise
>
> With a colleague, come up with five examples of the kinds of jargon, attitudes and practices Francis discusses, which might impact community performances, in these different institutional settings:
>
> - elder home;
> - hospital;
> - hospice;
> - prison;
> - kindergarten.

In some elder work situations, you might also encounter end-of-life issues.

An important aspect of working in institutions of any kind is finding ways of maneuvering successfully within the culture of the place.

> ## Fi Francis, a British practitioner and writer, on training issues for dance artists who want to work with older people
>
> These places are also other people's work settings. Training would need to deal with how people in these different institutions work – with their employment and care practices, management structures, staff attitudes and philosophies, institutional routines, traditions and jargons. Time and again artists have told me it would have been handy to have known how a residential home worked before they were, in their words, 'thrown in at the deep end'. As a dancer you may understand the workings of a dance centre but be flummoxed by the workings of a hospital ward. Training could help you make use of opportunities a particular work setting offers, avoid its pitfalls, liaise well with the staff and their expectations. You would become a dance ambassador, trained to communicate the best of the dance world, to show what older people can do in dance in that setting – to smooth away anxieties about working with a dance artist because you have been trained to know how to enable this meeting of work cultures.
>
> Francis, 1999

Need ammunition to argue for work in an elder home?

One significant stride toward [a] transformation [on work on aging and creativity] came in 2000 with the publication of *The Creative Age: Awakening Human Potential in the Second Half of Life* by Gene Cohen. Cohen's book was the first to articulate a new paradigm and an emerging field: creative aging. His book documents recent discoveries in neuroscience that radically challenge conventional assumptions about the aged brain. For example, studies have shown that it is not the number of neurons that dictates brain function, but the number and strength of the connections *between* neurons. While the human brain does in fact lose neurons throughout life, it does not lose its capacity for forming and deepening connections between the neurons that remain. In fact, studies have found that between one's early 50s and late 70s there is actually an increase in both the number and length of branches from individual neurons in different parts of the brain that are involved with higher intellectual functioning. However, neuroscientists believe that in order for the brain to maintain connections between its neurons, and especially to forge new connections, it needs to be challenged. In other words, it is not old age *per se* that reduces the brain's functioning. It's stagnation that threatens the brain, like the stagnation that occurs when elders are cut off from meaningful opportunities for stimulation and growth. This is why quality arts programming is so essential in the late years of life: It is deeply challenging because it calls on the elder to tap the most essential parts of their personal and their cultural identity. Through the creative process, elders learn new skills, discover new aspects of their selves, and find new ways to express and perceive the world.

Perlstein, 2002

ACCESS ISSUES IN WORK WITH CHILDREN

Structures: think about the way that many children's lives are deeply structured and timetabled. How can your project or workshop avoid being just another task? How can you create a space apart?

Figure 3.6 A starkly drawn conflict: mother and grandmother disagree over the effects of mother's smoking on her daughter's asthma. Theatre Lucha/de Madras a Madras at Holy Name parish, Houston, TX, 2004.   Photo: Rene Magdeleno

The law and working with children

Make sure to familiarize yourself with any legislation and policy issues regarding contact with children. Depending on where you work, you might need to agree to background checks, on specific gender ratios and leader/children ratios, and guidelines for interaction with children. In some countries, cuddling a crying child is not permissible. Make sure you know all rules, and decide if and how you can work under these circumstances.

Mini Movers – how parents and toddlers dance sessions re-invigorated my dance practice

I would like to share with you my work with Mini Movers – a parent (or carer) and toddler dance session that runs at Ludus Dance Company in Lancaster. I had never worked with parents (or carers) and toddlers together and never worked with such small people with dance.

I love working with this age group because they challenge most of the guidelines I ask other participants to adhere to, from concentrating, to listening and staying on task to attending group activities!

Mini Movers do what they like, when they want to do it.

My skills of observation were put to the test as I tried to take in that 'Johnny' is choosing to do his moves in the corner facing the mirror, 'Henry' is discovering that he likes to be upside down, 'Emily' is practising the moves from 10 mins ago and 'Sarah' sitting very still watching everything.

Let alone that, the parents are equally varied, as one seeks to help her child do the rolling 'correctly' as she pushes her down to the floor, child resisting, another is oblivious to their child licking the floor as she discusses the price of fish at the supermarket and another is caught between wanting to help his child enjoy sliding on the floor but being far too self conscious to actually do it himself.

The very nature of the group has challenged me to notice what they like to do and why, in order for the session to appeal to them. Witnessing this unforgiving 'audience' in how they interact with dance caused me to reflect on whether my work to date had been as 'CHILD CENTRED' as I had thought, with its STRUCTURED tasks/improvisations with pre-determined OUTCOMES.

Working with these groups has reminded me that the name of our company, Ludus, is from the Latin meaning 'to play, (sport) and learn' and that the element of play can be diminished when working towards stated outcomes and/or performance.

I have witnessed parents and children discovering a new dimension to themselves and their relationship – each parent and child can inspire each other to dance, and to develop. What I found through those Mini Movers classes I can relate to all groups of any age and I have relearned the value of promoting play.

Anna Daly, Ludus Dance Company, UK

39 Research exercise

Research dance activities for children in your local area. What is on offer? How do these offers relate to Anna's experiences of the different pressures on dance classes?

Figure 3.7 Ludus Dance 'Mini Movers' with Sure Start, North Lancaster, UK.

Photo: Alan Dowthwaite, Ludus Dance

ACCESS ISSUES IN INTERGENERATIONAL GROUPS

In many modern environments, spaces for children, adults and elders are apart and separate: schools, work environments, nuclear family homes, sheltered living accommodation, elder care institutions. How can your community project bring them together? How can knowledges, wisdoms and information flow between them?

P
R
A
C
T
I
C
E

E
X
A
M
P
L
E

Creating Postcards from the Past, Sending Postcards into the Future

The Pawtuxet Village Freedom Project

Creating Postcards from the Past, Sending Postcards into the Future involved Pawtuxet Village residents in Rhode Island in a yearlong exploration of local history. In 2003, a community activist, Marianne Cocchini, invited fellow residents of Pawtuxet Village, including myself and other artists, historians, educators and neighbors, to gather at a local coffee shop. We planned a series of workshops which introduced children and adults to the variety of concepts of freedom that village 'ancestors', from same and other cultures, might have held.

We invited children and their parents to participate through presentations given to 9- to 12-year-old pupils at area schools. We began with a walking tour of Pawtuxet Village from a Native American perspective with Narragansett Indian Preservation Officer Nancy Brown-Garcia. We learned of significant sites, Native customs of sharing and living with 'mother earth', and how Narrangansett Native people used the surrounding land, river, cove and bay. In the next workshop, educator Tricia Wolf and I (in my role as visual artist) led the group back to pre-colonial contact times through an imaginary journey based on what we had learned from Nancy. The children photographed important places in the village from the point of view of a Native person.

The third session opened with historian Al Klyberg presenting information about the growth of the village from colonial times to the 1800s. Native people were mostly sold into slavery as a result of King Philip's War in 1675, and white settlers increased in number and power. The presence of African Americans increased with villager's participation in the Triangle slave trade.

Familiar with this historical context, children participated in the play *Negro 'Lection Day: A Day We Felt Free*, created by storyteller Melodie Thompson-Thomas from research gathered by folklorist Michael Bell. Melodie introduced the children to history through theater by interacting with them as Sarah Jones, an imagined domestic for a white family in Pawtuxet Village in 1836. In kind, the children were invited to become fellow Negroes in a recreation of a Negro Election, an annual holiday for freed and enslaved Negroes that had taken place in Pawtuxet Village for almost 75 years.

Building on the previous workshops the children created a collage image of themselves as a Narragansett from the 1600s or a Negro from the 1800s. They had a list of Narragansett words and typical African-American names from the period, historical images of Native

Americans and African-Americans, related architecture, landscapes, plants, texts, colored paper, glue, scissors and cardboard to collage an imagined self-portrait.

After workshops that introduced immigrant stories of freedom, including work with Trinidadian drummer Jason Roseman, and workshops with elder residents of the village about what life was like 40–60 years ago, the children wrote a message to go along with the collage. To prepare them I led them on an imaginary journey filled with descriptions of the village as it changed and stayed the same in the 1600s, the 1800s and today. Along the way questions were posed for each child to add to the imagined picture: 'What do you hear, smell, touch and see?' Working with an adult in a small group each child filled out a character worksheet then shared his/her chosen name, a description of his/her life and what freedoms and dreams he/she had and wished for. Finally the message was written on the back of the each collage. The postcards from the past were complete.

Netop,
I am a hunter. My name is Wild Fox. I use bows and arrows to hunt. I am free to stay outside for a long time. I really like being outside. I hunt deer in the summer for my family. My dream is to fly like a bird. I also want to be a sleek fox to sneak around. I want my tribe to have peace.
    Wild Fox
       (Reuben Graff, age 8)

                                       April 12, 1836

Salutations,
My name is truth. I am 7. I like to cook and at free time I pick flowers. I play with my kitten liberly with my extra yarn. I smell blosms, erbs, spises, crisp air and bread bakeing. I hear baby animals, rushing water and my mother calling me. My dreams are my dad not to be a slave, and to git a better educton becus I want to read better. My idea of freedom is mom not to be a slav or I.
    Yours truly,
      Truth
        (Lyza Baum, age 10) [misspellings intended]

The postcards were then mailed to interested adult residents who had been informed about the project through an annual Pawtuxet Artist's gathering and other public community events as well as during the course of the workshops. Each person received a letter of instructions and blank card on which to reply. The adults responded to the children's cards in kind with images and text describing present day life in relation to the life presented from the past and expressing concepts of freedom in their lives today.

My name is Strong Heart,

I am 21 years old. I have a dog named Zeke. My idea of freedom is being able to get back to school even though I finished and for being able to be free. My dream would be to get married and get paid more. I smell wood I cut, I hear children playing, I see miles and miles of trees and I feel wind blowing against my skin.

Sincerely, Strong Heart

(Ian La Plume, age 11)

Response:

Dear Strong Heart,

My idea of freedom is all the people who came before me, dreamed of making life better, and worked hard to make their dreams come true – like you. Perhaps you even lived in the house I live in now. Though I live in 2004, perhaps we walked the same path next to the Pawtuxet River and felt the wind blowing against our skin as we dreamed our dreams.

Sherry Brown

Netop,

I am fishing in the Pawtuxet river. My name is Wompsacuck, it means eagle. My life is very adventurous. I like to paddle out to the ocean. I hear the water gently lapping against our canoe. My life is great because I can travel freely. I am very content with my life in nature.

Wompsacuck Quauog

(Isaac Dressel, age 9)

Response:

March 12, 2004

Greetings:

My husband and I live in Pawtuxet, on the Pawtuxet Neck as it was once called. The photo on the left is us going to a party. Left, top is a photo of Pawtuxet Cove with our house on the left. From our house we can see the waterfalls by the Bridge. Did you know that water power once ran a textile business where the bridge divides?

We also like to go out on the ocean; we go on the Block Island Ferry, top center. Bottom right is a view of New Harbor, the Coast Guard Station and a visiting Tall Ship.

There is also a small picture of some of the shops by the Bridge, and top right is Diido, the wonder dog (who is NOT allowed on the couch!)

Maryann Dember

In early 2004, participants gathered at the local library with the sets of postcards to meet their correspondent and discuss the issues of freedom raised. The individual nature of the postcard exchange enabled heartfelt exchanges between correspondents, which grounded the discussions of war, sovereignty, equal rights, land use, and civic responsibilities in a personal perspective between child and adult.

The postcards were finally presented as inlays on a six-panel Pawtuxet landscape housed in a locally made wood accordion frame behind Plexiglas. The screen toured to libraries and schools in the area and is permanently housed at the William Hall Public Library where most of our workshops met.

In some cases before the adult met the child correspondent he/she felt the child's postcard exhibited some confusion about the life of the imagined person but when the correspondents met the adult was surprised to find out that the child's understanding was more complex than the adult anticipated. In a couple cases in which this occurred the person imaged by the child was a Native American who was a slave in the 1800s.

At the end of the project the children shared that they most enjoyed the hands on arts activities, especially the play and making the postcards. The adults were fascinated by the information presented by the scholars which then led to a series of lectures for adults in the broader community at a neighboring library. From this project Voices and Visions of Village Life was formed (www.voicesandvisions.org).

As an visual artist who has worked with various communities in the Midwest and New York City area I was surprised, when I moved here eight years ago, by these New England village residents' strong interest in local history. I've realized the wealth that local history as subject matter provides me as an artist who works with and for others. I was moved by the genuine care the adults took in responding to their child correspondent. Hopefully we have all been a pulled a little closer together with a more humbled sense of 'ownership' of the place where we live.

Written by Holly Ewald

40 Reflection exercise

What kind of differences came together in this project? What competencies, collaborations, ways of knowing, ways of communicating?

Do you feel that any of the modes of engagement used here are age-specific?

In what way are they designed to be accessible to different people, children and elders?

Figure 3.8 Melodie Thompson-Thomas with children performing *Negro 'Lection Day: A Day We Felt Free*.
Photo: Marta Martinez

Figure 3.9 Reuben Graff and Ed Greer discussing their postcards.   Photo: Marta Martinez

3.1.6 Publicity and marketing

The community performance idea has taken shape, you have thought about many of the practicalities of making it happen, you've got an appropriate location, warm and safe, and you have made it accessible to many different people, or targeted it at the group you want to work with. How do you let people know about it? A different way of thinking about this issue starts from a different place: what are the relative benefits of local, regional, national and international publicity to the people involved in the project, and to the community or communities they represent? What might be useful to you as a working artist might be relatively useless to the community group you are working in. Try to find a balance that both sustains your career and is sensitive to local needs.

In this section, I cover a wide range of communication tools that can help you to get the word out. Of course, community performance projects do not necessarily depend on large numbers, or on the kind of publicity and outreach at which these communication media aim. A project is just as valid if it is impromptu, with an audience of traffic lights, waves or seagulls, or if it is taking place in the main national art gallery. When you are engaging in your project, your energies might well be limited, and you might not wish to write press releases or phone editors. Delegation might be useful – you might have a project participant whose skill-set or inclination makes her or him a useful publicity person, and who would be happy to contribute to the project in this way.

Most people, of most cultural groups, go out of their home at some time or other. Where they go and what they might see depends very much on their individual and cultural circumstances. Your personal maps created earlier in this chapter can give you clues to places to put advertisements, leaflets, and how to tell people by word of mouth. The list on page 59 can also help you to find people and groups that might be useful to you.

Multiplicator thinking

Multiplicators are people who might not be in your potential target group themselves, but who are valuable resources to you: they might be gatekeepers (such as school secretaries, social workers, medical staff) or hubs of information (storekeepers, publicans, neighborhood organizers). Make sure you find ways of distributing information via these people!

LEAFLETS AND POSTERS

These are the most common ways of getting the word out about your project. When you design your leaflet or poster, do not forget to include:

- What?
- Where?
- When? (Time and exact date, length etc.)
- For whom? (If you want to stress that the performance workshop is open to all levels of expertise, or only to people with certain experiences, make this clear.)
- By whom? (Depending on the workshop, a sentence about your experiences might be appropriate.)
- How much? (Will you charge people? Will you pay them?)
- Contact details. (If you can, give more than one way to contact: telephone landline and cell, email, postal address etc.)

If you can, and if it is appropriate, a design element or photo will help to attract people to the leaflet or poster.

Being clear about the 'what' might be hardest of all: community performance workshops are often open-ended, or process-based, and you might not know yet what will emerge. You can mention the dominant art forms you plan on using, or some content that might bring people together.

> ### 41 Reflection exercise
>
> Design two different posters for two different workshops/ performance projects, aimed at different populations or target groups. Compare your work with a colleague, and critique each other's work: what works, what doesn't, how do you know the difference, what could be clearer?

Examples of community performance participant calls, announcements and 'write ups'

For a call for participants, aimed at advocates and groups (for Magpie Dance, a UK company working with people with learning disabilities):

Magpie's Youth Group is for young people aged between 16 to 25 with learning disabilities.

Magpie Youth Group aims to enable young people both with and without learning disabilities to explore creative movement and related arts in a supportive, safe and stimulating atmosphere. All Magpie Youth Group activities will be carried out in a clear, understandable, open and fair way, with the young people fully involved in the planning, execution and evaluation.

Sessions take place during term-time at:

United Reformed Church,
20 Widmore Road,
Bromley, Kent

Autumn term Wednesday 14th September to Wednesday 7th December 2005

For further information about the Youth Group or to book for any workshops listed above please contact David Nurse – Youth Group Director on 07813 855036

'I liked watching the show. I wasn't nervous'
Chris Skelly

'Superb!! . . . we all felt proud that Christopher was able to take part'
Mrs Kim Skelly

If you would be interested in a session for young people at your venue, please contact **David Nurse, Youth Group Director, on 07813 855036 or 01245 475770**.

For a final performance (from veteran community theatre company Cornerstone, US):

You Can't Take It With You by Moss Hart & George S. Kaufman
October 9–26, 2003
An American Muslim Remix Adaptation by Peter Howard
Directed by Mark Valdez

A contemporary adaptation (the first ever in this classic American comedy's 67-year history) that revolves around the lives of a high-spirited Muslim family in Los Angeles, exploring themes of faith, family, individualism, politics and love.

Cornerstone has spent more than a year collaborating with local individuals and organizations in preparation for this project; including Kamal Al-Marayati, who served as a Cultural Consultant. Community Partners include *The Muslim Public Affairs Council,* a public services agency working for the civil rights and integration of American Muslims; *The Council on American-Islamic Relations*, a resource organization for the promotion of a positive image of Islam and Muslims; and *The Council on Islamic Education*, a national resource providing education materials and scholarly resources.

This show is part of Cornerstone's Faith-Based Theater Cycle, a 4½ year series of projects exploring the question: How does faith unite and divide us? Since the fall of 2001, Cornerstone has been collaborating with communities of faith throughout Los Angeles.

Los Angeles Theatre Center
514 South Spring Street, Los Angeles 90013
(wheelchair accessible) LATC is a facility of the Los Angeles Cultural Arts Department

Quoted from publicity materials

EMAIL LISTS

Another good and useful place to advertise for participants is the Internet and the multiple email listservs that facilitate communication between people with similar interest. Classified Internet sites such as Craig's List or local 'What's On' are available in many communities – a quick survey of friends, family and co-workers might help you broaden your own existing list of sites. The same applies to email lists. A multitude of lists serve many communities: try to find some that relate to your project in location or theme.

When you work with email communication, you need to be even more aware of the brevity of communication: many people receive hundreds of emails a day, and if your call is to be useful, it needs to be clear and upfront: find a punchy and highly descriptive title line.

Figure 3.10 A scene from Cornerstone Theater Company's production of *An Antigone Story*, performed in the cavernous Subway Terminal Building in downtown Los Angeles (2000).   Photo: Arturo Castillo

Internet and collaboration

Many years ago, I initiated a project called Landscaping Women. This project took place predominantly in Wales, but it touched upon issues of rural isolation, female roles, landscape art and myth work that apply to many different areas. I sent out a call for collaborators and dramaturgical support people on international listservs, and got fascinating responses. At that point, I had never visited the United States, but I made one of my first friends there through the project call – she set up a response project with migrant women in her own location in Michigan. When I managed to find funding for holding a workshopping week in London, she flew over and joined us, and visited Wales and the original project site. I am still collaborating with my US partner now, after many years, and my contact with her is just one of many examples where the Internet has enriched my own local practice.

NEWSPAPERS AND MAGAZINES

Local newspapers are a wonderful way of getting the word about a local project out. They are often interested in copy, and will most likely be glad to work with you. Phone the head office or regional office, and try to find out who is the local feature editor or arts editor. You can follow up a well-presented press release with a personal phone call. If you manage to capture their attention, you might find that you get more coverage than just a listing.

WRITING A PRESS RELEASE

Your local arts council will most likely have important information about this skill, appropriate to your own location. There is an art to press release writing, since you have to both get an editor's attention, and convey all the important information in a succinct manner. In the end, though, I have often found that the personal phone call is the most useful way of making contact, so do not think that the press release means that you can skip this step!

Above all, keep it short: usually, local and regional newspaper or radio editors don't seem to want to see more than a one-page press release.

OTHER STRATEGIES

Word of mouth

Word of mouth is the most useful way of getting people through the door (or into the forest, the beach, the car park or wherever your project performance or sharing takes place). Discuss with all project participants what the best strategies might be to get the information out to people known to them.

Visits

If you are creating a project on policies surrounding the local garbage dump, for instance, think about who might be interested/should be interested in this. You might be able to arrange visits to local schools, local government offices, a brief coffee break presentation to garbage truck drivers, political party offices etc. Even if they do not agree to a visit, they get to know your project, and might take an interest.

Street theatre

How about a street theatre scene as an advertisement for your performance? If participants are happy with the idea, you can access new audiences by presenting a scene in the local shopping center, a city square or a park. Depending on your location, you might need to get permission to present material and hand out flyers etc. in these venues – it might be useful to check with authorities (unless you are happy and willing to deal with the potential consequences if your project content might make it undesirable to ask for permission to work in public spaces).

Exhibit

Instead of presenting a live scene, you can also show material from your performance in order to attract curiosity, or show other local residents that your material is of interest to them.

3.2 Running a group: agency, control, openness

Your project is running. As you move along, you will find that patience will be the core virtue that will enable the work: community performance work needs time to develop.

Everything depends upon trust and credibility. I discovered that, with the exception of a few upon whom initially everything depends, people are very cautious to commit themselves until they are certain they won't be made to look foolish; that people will begin tentatively to give – in whatever ways is in their nature; that once people are secure they will give and share unstintingly their time, energy, talents, skills and enthusiasm and as they do so they will become more warm and friendly towards each other; that you must perhaps accept that some people are unable ever to commit themselves; that theatre can use and involve people of virtually every age, background and intelligence – everyone can be involved; that it needs time for this process to grow – you can't suddenly bounce in and expect it to work – the town has to get used to the idea, take it on board, make it their own.

Jellicoe, 1987: 9

There are many ways that you can think about communication techniques inside the group in order to develop trust and credibility.

3.2.1 Leadership styles

Community performance practices can have many aims and objectives. These aims shape the sessions and projects, and the style of leadership that is appropriate to them. These styles are most usually unconsciously adopted, and reflect patterns of behavior and experience. There are many different styles, and their mixtures, and multiple ways of leading, facilitating and decision-making might be employed within one workshop session. In the following, I am discussing three different kinds of styles – in practice, most sessions will have shades of all of these ways of leading. My aim here is to help you to reflect on your practice: there is no one way to work with and within a group.

Figure 3.11 The Olimpias Tracks workshop, Rhode Island, USA, 2004. 'Celebrating our Circle'.
Photo: Jeannine Chartier

- *Tending towards autocratic*: in this style of leadership, decisions are made by one person, by the project leader. Material might be generated in improvisation and through input from different people, but the ultimate decisions about inclusion and exclusion, and the shape and direction of following sessions rest with this one person, who might or might not consult with others in the group about these issues.

- *Tending towards group-led styles*: in this style of leadership, decisions are made by a group of people who emerged (or presented themselves) as more experienced, talented, eager or loudest.
- *Tending towards democratic*: in this style of leadership, decisions about the project and its shape are taken by all members of the group. Individual choreographies, theatre sequences and produced materials are judged together, and choices are made by majority vote, or by a sustained discussion that ends in consensus.

---

42 Reflection exercise

Think back to arts sessions you've participated in (whether community arts sessions or others). What leadership styles have you experienced? What were the positive and negative effects of these forms of leadership on you, your sense of ownership of the materials generated in the class/session, and your development? Create a diagram that charts the negatives and positives of each style you can identify (and there might be more than the three I have outlined above).

Maybe you think it is easy to see which leadership style would be 'best': the democratic one. But there are many issues to think about when deciding on appropriate decision-making protocols, and in my experience all of these models, in one form or another, can be appropriate for different kinds of groups.

TOWARDS THE AUTOCRATIC MODEL

This style of leadership aligns very well with both traditional and modern ways of thinking about art: someone is a specialist, trained and knowledgeable, and hands on her or his knowledge to people who are learning, or who are 'material' for her or his vision. The traditional performance artist might feel a responsibility to tradition and the underlying reasons that established that tradition, which might have spiritual, cultural or familial origins, and a desire to do justice to standards of excellence and execution. The modern artist might feel the need to express a unique and individual stand-point, honed and crystallized by training, thought and self-development. In both cases, the work resulting from the sessions will be shaped according to notions of quality and attention.

Many workshop or session participants recognize these qualities in the artist leading them: these values infuse contemporary cultural life, and 'come naturally' to many people who think about joining a drama club, dance session, video class or sculpture meeting. There is a specialist, who knows what she or he is doing, and she or he will tell you what to do. If a leader fulfills this role, participants can feel reassured and safe, and can begin to open up and explore their own potential within this safety.

A facilitator might choose this leadership style in order to give a group a sense of purpose, to get a project off the ground quickly and effectively, and to set up a comfortable framework. But he or she might also need to negotiate issues of ownership, expectations about the creation of 'product', and try to find ways to foster all participants in their project.

TOWARDS A GROUP-LED MODEL

In this model, group participants can find a recognizable structure, and can fit themselves into it. People can find a voice in keeping with their sense of their own ability and comfort level. Oftentimes, groups organized in this way can have relatively flexible and permeable notions of 'the leading group', and participants might be able to slip in and out of decision-making situations depending on what they feel like at a meeting. If they don't feel like engaging with the pressures of leadership, but are happy to be part of a group, this model can allow them safe spaces. Leading a group like this might require some sensitivity to the specific group dynamics of relative introvert and extrovert orientation: can a person with great ideas, but a quiet voice, be brought forward, her or his work recognized, and his or her voice listened to? How can a group facilitator ensure that the leadership layer remains dynamic, and that people can cycle in and out of decision-making moments?

TOWARDS A DEMOCRATIC MODEL

This model allows for the highest transparency and can ensure that all participants have a voice. But decision-making might be hard in such an environment, and patience and a recognition of the value of process are indispensable for this model to work. In many cases, the democratic process itself might become the heart of the project – the processes of decision-making, listening and finding appropriate access for everybody might be the essence of the content. Facilitators need to think about issues such as: What is their own role? To what extent does the fact of setting up a space and time for people to work together constitute leadership? How will the issue of recognition and leadership be negotiated if the products of the group travel outside the

Figure 3.12 Urban Bush Women lead Summer Institute performance, *Are We Democracy?* (July 2004).
Photo: James Burwell

group environment (performances, exhibitions etc.). Who signs the work and owns it? What happens to the facilitator role in the action session – does he or she have a special voice, or can he or she let go of steering completely? How can democratic values work in other than verbal ways – in particular if facilitator and group decide that 'rational' discourse and well-argued speech might not be the most appropriate way to negotiate art making?

---

43 Reflection exercise

a   Think about specific art forms, and their relation to specialist knowledge, learning, practice and innovation. What connections can you see between these different leadership modes and art forms such as:
   • ballet;
   • contact improvisation;
   • devising;
   • community playwriting;
   • oral history projects;
   • the creation of a community mural;
   • a community music band;
   • a video production.
   What opportunities and challenges can you see?

b   Here are a range of skills and abilities that can be enhanced and fostered by different leadership and group communication styles. Which can be best enhanced through which kind of strategies?
   • recall and memory;
   • precision;
   • ability to follow instructions;
   • observation;
   • critical attention;
   • respect for others;
   • respect for self;
   • assessment of own skill;
   • development of creativity.

An example of a different openness to power

1   Have respect for the mask. The mask is an affective artifact – a power-filled image. It will affect the wearer according to the respect given to it. A workshop participant should not carry it around by sticking her fingers through its eye or nostril holes. Handle it properly – masks can be fragile. When putting the mask down, place it face up, with the back of the mask on the surface.

Eldredge, 1996: 42

Most facilitators will work in an environment that has aspects of all of these leadership/ group dynamic models. Reflecting on them makes it easier to spot problems: avoidable silencing of others, recognition of communication patterns that endanger participants' ownership of the process, 'tyranny of the majority', and problems that might arise from participants' and the facilitator's need for structure.

Urban Bush Women

Jawole Willa Jo Zollar founded the Urban Bush Women (UBW) in 1984, a dance ensemble that creates life-affirming work based on women's experiences, African American history and the cultural influence of the African Diaspora (see more on UBW by Anita Gonzalez, in the *Reader*). Community engagement occurs in a variety of ways: UBW set up workshops surrounding their own performance, they create performance projects in different public settings, and they train their artists in dance and community engagement.

The following statements are UBW on **dialogue** and its importance in their Community Engagement Projects (all cited from handouts provided as part of a UBW workshop):

Dialogue is a learning *process*, not simply a communication tool.

The dialogic process gives *equal value* to the insights drawn from personal experience and the knowledge gained from intellectual study. Book knowledge is not more important than experiential knowledge.

Taken together, intellect and experience help people *construct a larger truth* or a broader, deeper understanding of reality.

Dialogue is a learning process that invites people to *surface the assumptions* that inform their beliefs and actions.

People who participate in dialogue are willing to engage in *exploration, inquiry and discovery* about themselves and others for the purposes of learning.

People who participate in dialogue acknowledge that their own ways of thinking, believing and acting may be *influenced* by the experiences, ideas and beliefs of another person or persons in the dialogue process.

The process of dialogue assumes that it is possible for two different perspectives to be *right at the same time*.

The process of dialogue requires participants to establish, protect and maintain a *culture of mutual trust*.

There will be many issues of progression and development, frustration and stagnation in any community performance project. Handling these different emotions and situations will be an important part of your work as a practitioner. In the following material, Canadian practitioner Johanne Chagnon gives an insight into the diversities, perspectives and emotions that impact on a day's community performance workshop.

EXAMPLE OF A DAY

With mixed voices

I have initiated a community art project with members of the organization Le CARRÉ (Centre Aide Ressources Référence Entraide) in the Hochelaga-Maisonneuve neighborhood of Montreal (Quebec) – this organization is working with people living in poverty situation. Each Thursday from January 2003 to July 2005, we met and worked together creatively. We have produced together exhibitions, posters and public interventions but mainly three theater/video creations. Now the project is in a new phase – towards more autonomy – with me withdrawing progressively and the participants having chosen among themselves someone to take over the coordination.

Here is summary of what one of those Thursdays looked like. . .

ME: I arrive with some good ideas of activity – a schedule for the day. . .

HE: I have to leave earlier because if I don't take care of some urgent bills, I will be in big trouble!

ME: I love so much the feeling of our space – that we call the 'attic' – completely dedicated to our own creativity.

SHE: Each Thursday brings me something positive. Thanks for giving me confidence.

ME: It irritates me that the projects don't go as fast as I would like, it makes me breathless.

SHE: What I hold of this project is that, no matter what we do, nothing is lost and useless. Each time, something inspires me.

ME: I love the gang, the team spirit that wraps me, the cheerful complicity.

SHE: It's the first time, at 49 years old, that somebody tells me that what I create is nice.

ME: I feel not respected by the fact that the participants don't arrive on time.

SHE: *The pills that I take prevent me from concentrating well.*

ME: I am discouraged by the smallness of changes.

SHE: I cannot come this morning because I have to put my hands urgently on my boyfriend's welfare check before he spends it all in dope and leave me alone to pay the rent.

ME: I am now able to delegate more responsibilities.

HE: *At the group meeting, I felt the need and was able to talk with the others about what blocks my creativity.*

ME: What an improvement if she now considers that artists are not superficial people, and that art isn't made by pretentious people!

SHE: I find that my creativity work hasn't move these last weeks, I don't know how to manage it.

SHE: Today, I laughed and I cried, and both did me good.

ME: I feel a lot of interest and a great determination, each one dedicated to her project and its realization.

SHE: I wish the days would be more structured, and the schedule more clear. More firmness!

ME: I am able to develop more my own creativity, and to do this together with the others. And I go farther than foreseen because of the initiative of some other participants.

SHE: *I feel myself living, despite my dysfunctions. The art space is where I can breathe the best.*

ME: That some people now are able to act more freely and are not afraid of being 'ridiculous' makes me happy.

SHE: I can now live fully and with satisfaction, instead of anticipating and, because of that, trying to escape the situation. That's a giant step for me.

ME: I finish the day, my head quartered, like if it is splitted at many places. I must accept that the days aren't always as expected.

But what a formidable human experience!

Written for this book by Johanne Chagnon

COLLABORATION IN COMMUNITY GROUPS

Democratic styles of art making can be threatening to some people in community groups, and they might feel uncomfortable and reluctant to accept the responsibility and voice that comes with this style of working. I have found that modeling dialogic, open-ended and respectful communication by working closely with another facilitator

44 Reflection exercise

In a group of three people, collect two objects each – objects that interest you, because of their shape or function, either material found in the street or the outdoors, or else architectural details of the room you are working in. In a short improvisation, individually create movement responses to your chosen objects. Now come together, and work on creating a short choreography out of the two movements each participant brings to the group – how can you translate another person's movement into your movement? How can you modify it, bring dynamics, different shapes, energies and levels into a group choreography?

The challenge in this session is to work without words – try not to speak while working out the group choreography. Pay attention to the ways that you and the others 'speak', 'take the floor' and demand others' attention. How are decisions made, how does the choreography grow?

Now try the same exercise, but with a selected leader (each group member in turn) who puts together a choreography out of the different movements the group members present to him or her.

Pay attention to the differences that emerge, and discuss the merits and differences between the different results in a supportive and respectful way.

can be a useful way of opening up the group to ways of being with one another which might very well differ significantly from their everyday experiences.

Collaboration is also a great way to enhance art practice, it can help you as a facilitator to step out of a rut, and challenge you to develop further as an artist.

RESPONSE AND CRITIQUE

One important aspect of community performance sessions is critique. How can we speak respectfully with one another? How can we help each other towards fulfilling our goals?

In order to address this issue, you need to first clarify a related issue: what is the point of critique after an improvisation or group performance?

What is meant by critique?

* acknowledgement of an event;
* praise for effort;
* stating of powerful moments for observer;
* interpretation by observer;
* responding to a performing group as a group;
* responding to a performing group by singling out individuals;
* constructive criticism: offering ways of improving;
* taking things further: offering ideas for development;
* negative criticism: without offering avenues for improvement.

In a music session in which participants improvise and play with the sounds of a found or conventional instrument, and are asked to respond to each other's sound making, how can you critique short performances by small groups?

The answer depends to a large extent on the aims and desires of group members. If you are all at a stage where you wish to use sound making as a means of allowing expression, to bring your individual voice or sound out, any critique of these sounds, or of the ways these sounds interact with others, might be inappropriate, and might run counter to the group's aims.

If the aim is to enhance the way we listen to each other, call and respond, some suggestions and interventions might be very useful: the addition or subtraction of visual cues, for instance, or some commentary on moments of (dis)harmony that stood out to the spectators.

3.2.2 To perform or not?

Do you wish to perform publicly as part of your community performance project? The answer to this question depends on the definition of performance and audience that your group has settled on. For instance, who is your audience? Think about these different groups:

* the actual group;
* a small, pre-selected audience where everybody knows everybody else;

- an audience that might include people that hold power over participants, for instance social workers, doctors and other medical personnel;
- a general audience in a live setting;
- a general audience, in contact with the group through media such as videos and photographs;
- a wider specialized audience, reached through material generated as part of the workshops (such as politicians to whom postcards are sent).

A conventional stage performance in a theatre is not the only way that you can share performances created within a project. There are many reasons why stage performances can be problematic for participants. The theatre as an institution has a history of exclusion (socially, culturally, age-related), and many people do not feel at home in its spaces. Many proscenium theatres create a large distance between performers and audiences, and this kind of distance might not be of interest to the group. The kind of behavior scripts usually employed in theatre spaces might not be desirable (keeping quiet, sitting still, sitting in the darkness). But there are many other ways in which you can think about performance.

Skits

Many community performances develop as cabarets, or skits: short scenes montaged together. There are many advantages here for community performers:

- a single scene can be put together quickly;
- not all participants need to be at all workshops;
- energy can be sustained more easily with smaller numbers of participants;
- it is easier to identify dramatic line, a moment of held tension or of silence, and core image in a skit;
- different viewpoints and perspective can find expression in adjacent scenes.

Challenges of the form:

- sustaining dramatic arch/tension/suspense over the whole show;
- getting bogged down in scene changes;
- reliance on pace and variety.

Figure 3.13 Scene from *Confrontar el Dragon!* Breast Cancer Health Project, Fortuna, California, 2006, a play performed after Mass for a predominantly Spanish-speaking audience.
Photo: Petra Kuppers

45 Reflection exercise

Alternative sharings

Think about different ways of sharing work. Look at the following examples. What are the advantages and challenges?

- parade through a town;
- bonfire performance;
- masquerade;
- picnic;
- video;
- website;
- site-specific performance (such as the performers moving with their audience through spaces in a housing estate).

Think about further examples of alternative sharings!

WORKING WITH THE AUDIENCE

If you do perform, think about who your audience is, and what they need in order to 'get into' your performance. Are they used to performance presentation? Is there a fit between the mode of performance you have chosen, and the aesthetics or life experiences of members of your audience (for instance, think about the costumes your group uses for its dance performance).

SKILL DEVELOPMENT

In most community performance sessions, skill development is not the primary objective. You probably do not wish to emulate the kinds of skills, methods and aesthetics of mainstream performance work: it might not be appropriate to your group's aims.

P R A C T I C E   E X A M P L E

Confrontrar el Dragon!

In a community performance show in Eureka, California, a group of performers sharing a show about breast cancer used a variety of techniques to engage with their chosen audience. The group emerged from the Humboldt Community Breast Health Project. MFA students from Dell'Arte International School of Physical Theatre who facilitated the project found out that their collaborating organization would welcome a performance as a way to present messages about breast cancer to Spanish-speaking populations. So the students, volunteering breast cancer survivors and other local community members put together *Facing the Dragon*, a skit-based performance that brought their experience as cancer survivors to the stage to communicate about the importance of screening and early detection. The play celebrated and supported the central role of women's health to their families and their communities. The show was performed in Spanish, although not all members of the group are first-language Spanish-speaking. The audiences addressed by the show were Catholic Latina/Latino Californians. The group approached local Catholic churches, and arranged performances after weekend mass. In order to bring people 'into the theatre', the group used a variety of techniques: they used fire-jugglers and clowns to lead a parade from the church entrance to the nearby community hall where the play took place. Before the hard-hitting personal stories of the cancer survivors and their families, the group presented a clown performance, preparing people for the make-believe of theatre, drawing them into the magic of the stage, and engaging the children. This pre-performance featured the Los Puentes Project, which offers free after-school theatre programs to Latina/o young people in Humboldt County. *Confrontar el Dragon!* used many magic realist techniques that flowed well with the preceding clown/magician material: 'Cancer' hovered around the stage as a dragon's skull (a piece of driftwood), held by two clowns/day of the dead characters.

Proud difference: challenging aesthetics

James Stewart, a member of the Muntu reading and performance group in North Philadelphia, writes on the black arts movement:

> In our movement toward the future, 'ineptitude' and 'unfitness' will be an aspect of what we do. These are the words of the established order – the middle-class value judgements. We must turn these values in on themselves. Turn them inside out and make ineptitude and unfitness desirable, even mandatory. We must even, ultimately, be estranged from the dominant culture. This estrangement must be nurtured in order to generate and energize our black artists. This means that he cannot be 'successful' in any sense that has meaning in white critical evaluations. Nor can his work ever be called 'good' in any context or meaning that could make sense to that traditional critique.
>
> Stewart, 1968: 6

At the same time, if you plan on performing in front of an audience, you might find it useful to employ some training exercises in order to prepare your performers. From a different perspective, many exercises that aim at developing voice, finding space in the world, and taking a firm stance are psychologically and physiologically useful even if you are not aiming at conventional stage situations.

Think about what your group needs to strengthen. Have your participants expressed preferences and wishes? You might want to sit down and discuss it with them: would they like to develop themselves in some way? You might find it useful to think about managing expectations, though: is it in the interest of your group to think about relative strength and weaknesses in relation to perceived standards? Will there be tension, and can they be handled and dealt with productively? Will members perceived as 'weak' be put under pressure, or be humiliated? How can you avoid this?

When discussing potential skill development issues with your participants, you might want to discuss this history of experiences with them, to allow everybody to see alternatives to issues of stage diction, learning words or movements by heart.

46 Reflection exercise

Think about performances that have moved you. What have you witnessed? Depending on your background, you might have witnessed performance art, experimental dance and theatre work, environmental art happenings. What skills impressed you? What abilities allowed you to have a memorable experience? Make a list of these skills, and think about how you can foster them with your group.

Singing in the river

John Martin shares this performance exercise in his handbook on intercultural performance:

> The south Indian singer and voice-guru, Sivasankaram Pannikar, recalls his own training in voice as a young man. His guru used to take the students to a fast flowing river early in the morning. The students had to stand in the river, up to their chests, facing upstream so that the current was exercising a strong pressure on their abdomens. They had to sing long steady notes, resisting the strong current with their abdominal muscles. Over months and years this produced enormous strength in the voice support.
>
> The following exercise is based on that experience.
>
> Work in pairs, facing each other, in a low centred position, knees unlocked.
>
> One partner places a hand firmly on the abdominal wall of the other and starts to apply a moderate force, which would normally push the other person backwards. The second partner resists this to stay in the same position and take a deep breath and starts to produce a neutral voice.
>
> One partner is producing the force of the river flow, the other is resisting it and using the pressure to strengthen the voice. At first each breath may be quite short, but slowly it will lengthen and you will find the voice stronger from this support. . . .
>
> Note that again we are finding maximum performance effect by utilising a tension and counter-tension, exactly as in shaping the physical body.
>
> Martin, 2004: 133

Finally, community performances can offer unique ways of engaging audiences in performances, blurring the lines between performers and spectators. Fully engaged people can engage in celebratory behavior, using energy, joy and fun as access points to communal activity. These moments can emerge spontaneously, or openings for them can be structured into the group activity. In all cases, how can you ensure that all can participate?

Figure 3.14 Performance still from *Siren*, an Olimpias community performance piece presented a part of the Sea, Sky, Wind Newport Sculpture Festival, USA, 2004. The piece ended with a large picnic for performers and audiences on the red cloths which were spread out on the sand of the beach. Local storytellers entertained us while we shared our food with each other.   Photo: Petra Kuppers

Final performance of *Meet Me at Kissing Point*, in the Townsville Community, Australia, 1994

The final evening was an electrifying ending with a huge congo line of all 400 participants, as the musicians played reprise after reprise after reprise of the finale. Leading the line, I had nearly completed the length of the circular pathway and was heading onto the sandy foreshore, when I looked back and saw that performers were still entering the pathway! The audience was going wild and we all finished dancing on the beach and in the water.

Stock, 1997: 127

This chapter provided an overview of many issues that you might encounter in the set-up of community performance groups. I have tried to present these issues as opportunities: as ways of thinking about the aesthetics and politics of the project, not just as 'problems'. As you work, you will encounter many such issues, and by turning them into places of development, your practice can strengthen. In the next two chapters, I provide numerous session ideas and practice examples to help you develop creative practice within the community project.

P R A C T I C E   E X A M P L E

CHAPTER 4

Finding motivations

Images, sounds, tastes, touches

In this and the next chapter, I offer ideas for sessions and performance projects. Some are taken from my own practice, often themselves inspired by workshops and projects I have witnessed or participated in; some are from other practitioners, and from experiences told to me. All of them are offered here as points of inspiration, not as prescription.

The main theme or impetus for a session or project is often excitingly present: you might know exactly what you would like to offer to a group. It might be harder to find exercises to flesh out the core idea, to think of stimulating and new warm-ups or to keep a workshop going over weeks of engagement. These chapters offer ideas and thoughts on practice by giving community performance examples for a range of core themes.

In addition, this chapter offers itself as a meditation on the specifics of community performance. Many of the examples offered here focus on bodily experiences and on our senses. These experiences are usually private, experienced as something specific to an individual. Many of the exercises will be familiar to you from theatre, dance or visual art practice. Here, they are openings to ways of thinking about communities, group building, forms of human and more-than-human communication. In their form here, they challenge you to think about how to use them in community performance.

4.1 Warm-ups

Name games, getting-to-know-you exercises, clarification of goals and a preparation of space and people for collaborative work: these are all important functions of workshop warm-ups.

Introduction games

Stand in a circle

Step forward into the circle, and introduce yourself with a movement: for instance, a movement from your favorite activity, or a physical description of the landscape you grew up in. Say your name while you are executing the movement (I am Anna . . . and I like . . . or I come from . . .). Step back – and everybody else in the circle repeat the movement, greeting the person (Hello Anna).

This basic game can be adapted in many different ways: play around with it!

In a New Zealand setting, I used three different introductory rounds, using a large exercise ball as a means to enlarge movements, and create connections between participants. In the three rounds, we shared a movement representation of the landscape we grew up in, something about the waterways that surrounded our childhood, and something about our family – this pattern of introduction echoes Maori whakapapa.

Tag

This introduction is very useful for sessions that involve fiber work, craft work etc. Bring in materials: paper, twigs, colored pens, fabric. Get everybody to create a tag for themselves, sharing some aspect of themselves: again, I have found landscape of origin an interesting and diverse theme. Other themes include sounds of a name, or persons close to oneself. Names can be part of the tag, but do not have to be. As glue, scissors, fabric pieces are shared out around the table, introductions will be made informally.

Reminiscence

Share the first story, the first dance, the first song, the first theatre experience you have had, and what you loved/hated/found most interesting about it. This introduction can be particularly useful for work with older people. I have found it very interesting to ask people to share memories of their first storyteller – the question is open-ended, and requires no definition of what a 'storyteller' (or 'theatre' etc.) actually is.

Folk dance

Many cultures have repeating dance steps, often in a circle form, that are easily taught and learned. A three-minute round dance can be a very useful warm-up: everybody is working together, movement, music and spatial form all come together and create a first success event for participants, and participants can be aware that their activity is part of a larger chain of cultural activity. Although the steps are often very easy to remember, the mode of transmission is kinesthetic – these short folk dance sessions help to transmit the global heritage of movement.

P
R
A
C
T
I
C
E

E
X
A
M
P
L
E

Finding ways of sharing and preparing

Ohwęjagehká: Ha'degaénage is a non-profit organization based on Six Nations of the Grand River in Ontario, Canada. The aim is to help preserve and nurture the Iroquoian languages and songs. On their website (www.ohwejagehka.com), they share instruction for social dances where everybody who comes should be able to join in and enjoy. Their site provides not only basic step instruction but also music examples.

47 Reflection exercise

Read through the examples given on p. 109. What kind of information about potential group issues could emerge from them? Can you imagine first signs of potential friction, tensions and clashes between people? Within these warm-up ideas, how could you deal with them as facilitator or lead artist? Or, how can the group make them core themes for the body of the workshop?

My own primary practical training is in dance, so I always think of warm-ups as the beginning element of any workshop. In genres other than dance, a physical warm-up might not be quite as vital in the same way, but by dividing sessions into warm-up, main part, cool-down, a structure emerges that can be reassuring and practical for facilitators and participants. I often lead workshops of three hours and longer, and I structure an extended coffee or tea break into the workshop, followed by a new short warm-up and a different kind of engagement with art making. Also, if possible, my cool-downs flow from the room or environment we are in for the workshop to the nearest eatery or living room: the Olimpias workshops often end in shared food, a ritual ending that emphasizes communality and the fostering of friendship and respect that shapes much of our work. You will find a workshop structure that is appropriate for you.

A warm-up warms more than muscles:

Figure 4.1 African dance troupe from Perth, Australia, performing at the Fremantle Arts Centre, in the grounds of an old asylum, 2005.   Photo: Petra Kuppers

- it is a good place to warm up a sense of self and others;
- it allows people to get to know the space they will be working in;
- it allows people to get to know you;
- it helps to let go of the form of sense engagement that is appropriate to everyday living;
- it creates an openness towards different physical, sense and social experiences;
- it can help people to loosen their bodies, shift tensions;
- raised body core temperature, lubricated joints and gently stretched muscles provide benefits that many community performance participants seek.

Finding place

This warm-up is one of the most-used exercises in the performing arts, and you might be familiar with many different versions of it.

- Everybody starts walking. Move around the space you are working in – the community center, studio, outdoor space. Look at the space, take it its shape, smell, sound. [Call for varied speeds: slowed down, speeded up, on tip-toes, low to the ground. The aim is to experience the space in different ways – shaking off the everyday, opening up to different experiences.]
- Find a point in space – and move to it, touching it, or pointing to it. Find another one.
- As you continue walking, begin to see the others in space. Acknowledge each other. Smile. Nod. When the facilitator calls for it, touch hand to hand. Move on, find someone else. [If the group seems ready to touch and engage in ways different from everyday conventions, you can extend the touch: touching leg to leg, head to head, leg to head . . . you can play with different ideas, but keep an eye out for social discomfort.]
- Touch two people at a time. Touch four.
- Everybody touch.

Depending on how you facilitate this warm-up, you can focus on the physical and sensual environment you are in, or on the people, bringing them into contact. You can incorporate hints of the main session to come into this warm-up, creating echoes and connections across the different workshop elements. You can also gauge comfort levels, observing how comfortable people seem with the progression you are offering, how easily touch comes to them, and how they use space.

Games

Games are an excellent warm-up for all kinds of community groups. One of the most important practitioners in this area is Augusto Boal, and his work with games has influenced the whole field. Games can help to not only loosen the body and the mind, leaving normal life and its certainties and hierarchies behind, but they are also very useful in setting up new community relations. In games, new social dynamics emerge, and people can rehearse new forms of communication and interaction.

Figure 4.2 Lucas explains why diabetes management is so important to Tia Jo-Ann before Mass at Iglesia de San Felipe. Teatre Lucha/de Madres a Madres & Colonial Cameron Park, Brownville, TX, 2005. Photo: John Sullivan

BOAL'S GAMES

Games for Actors and Non-Actors (1992) by Augusto Boal is a book full with extremely useful and evocative exercises and games. Here is just one of them.

The glass cobra (from blind series)

Everyone stands in a circle (of in two or more lines if the group is very large), with their hands on the shoulders of the person in front of them. With their eyes closed, they use their hands to investigate the back of the head, the neck and the shoulders of the person in front. This is the glass cobra in one piece.

Then, on an instruction from the joker, the cobra is broken into pieces and each person sets off around the room, still with their eyes closed. In Brazilian legend, this type of cobra, 'the glass cobra' shatters into thousand pieces; but one day the pieces find each other again, these small fragments that are harmless on their own, but become dangerous the moment they get back together, because when they do they turn into the dangerous steel cobra.

The cobra in the legend is the people, obviously! In the game it is simply the participants who, after having moved around the space for a few minutes, on a signal from the joker must find their way back to the person who was in front of them before the cobra broke up. They must reconstitute the cobra(s). As in the legend, this can take time . . .

Variation

The same thing except that the whole exercise is done with the participants lying on the ground and dragging themselves around like snakes.

Boal, 1992: 108

Below (p. 113) is a version of a Boal game that I have encountered in many different settings. This basic exercise can open out in multiple ways. All participants can rearrange themselves to express a specific moment in time before the conflict (a minute before, an hour, a year . . .), and each participant can speak a line that would help to avoid the conflict, or reshape it differently.

Another development could center on fleshing out the conflict in more detail: given names, dates, specific place names to the people involved, creating biographies and contexts.

In smaller sub-groups, participants can create smaller tableaux, with some of these persons, to move up to and around the central conflict.

This exercise can lead to the creation of a whole developed and multi-layered community performance.

As part of this performance (to the group or beyond), any tableau can open itself up to change: inviting audience members to intervene, to come into the circle, tap someone on the shoulder, and step in.

Tableau

The group stands in a circle. Two volunteers step into the circle, and create a frozen picture. The other members of the group are then asked to find a content to the picture presented: what is the narrative they see? This exercise is particularly useful for investigating conflicts or relationships that are important to members of the group at this point in time. Once a theme becomes apparent, the group can move on.

Again, the group sits or stands in a circle. Two volunteers step into the circle, and create a frozen picture about a topic given by the facilitator or 'difficultator'. Themes can vary widely: landowner/farmer, scientist/mother of child affected by asthma, survivor of domestic violence/perpetrator of domestic violence. Once the image is established, other members of the circle come forward and add additional figures to the image – with other stakeholders in the conflict presented in the middle. Once the full tableau is in place, the session facilitator moves between the people, and lays a hand on their shoulders. If tapped, a participant vocalizes a thought of his or her character.

Disability Culture community performance tableau, Leicester, UK

In this tableau, we used Boal's techniques to collect images, phrases and gestures that deal with social attitudes to disability. As the final moment in our improvisation, we re-created the material on the public car park outside the centre in which we were working. We used chalk to write the phrases on the asphalt, and took up our positions, highly visible in an urban environment. The highlight of the workshop was the rain that fell later that day: it erased the insulting phrases on the car park, wiping the slate clean.

48 Reflection exercise

In what way can games challenge existing self-images, open up new ways of seeing oneself? Articulate for yourself the effects these exercises can have. Think about how the facilitator should/could behave. How can a facilitator avoid 'leading' the group?

Figure 4.3 Chalk performance piece/Disability Culture Pride, as part of Workshop Skills for Disabled Artists, two-week full-time professional development course, Richard Attenborough Centre, Leicester, 2000.
Photo: Petra Kuppers

The warm-ups I have presented here provide a few starting points for community performances. There are many other approaches: joint meditations, a shared walk in a neighborhood, a doodling exercise.

49 Reflection exercise

Think back to warm-ups that
have worked for you. Try to
remember three of them, and
write some of their instructions
and ideas down, so that you
can recreate a similar warm-up.
This can be the beginning of a
resource box or journal that
can help to inspire you.

4.2 Session ideas

Our sense experiences provide one of the richest reservoirs of
session ideas – what we see, hear, touch, smell, taste, intuit, or
feel kinesthetically. There are many exercises that take their cue
from our embedment in our world. In the following examples,
one of the challenges is to work from the personal to the group:
how can you develop these ideas, many of which come from
traditional theatre, dance or visual art backgrounds, and make
them resonant for community performance work?

4.2.1 Session idea: the moment

50 Reflection exercise

Lie down (or sit or stand quietly). Breathe
in deeply, breath out. Pay attention to your
breath moving in and out of your body.
After your breath is deep and slow, turn
your attention outwards. What do you hear?
What do you feel? Does air flow over your
body? Do you sense any masses or other
bodies elsewhere?

Now think about using the experiences
you've gained in a community setting: how
can these enhanced sense experiences inspire
a session segment? How can you make the
link from personal body to group experience?
Come up with at least three different session
ideas. Share them with a colleague.

Examples:

- Small incidental sounds move a
  paintbrush held by many hands.

- The sound of individual breaths shapes a
  communal breath choir: sounding as
  breath flows out.

- Kinesthetic sensing of others leads to a
  group dance with closed eyes.

51 Reflection exercise

Refer to the practice example on
p. 115. What are the challenges to this
work as community performance? How
do you see the relationships between this
work as therapy, as personal expression,
as group expression, and as political
labor? In order to answer these complex
questions, you might want to work out for
yourselves what the object of change is:
the self (as a form of therapeutic journey),
the self and the social world, the social
and physical environment we inhabit,
the future?

Practically, what challenges do you
see? What kind of facilitation is needed to
give people the freedom and the safety to
explore themselves in this way? What
kind of time do you think you would need
to work up to this level of trust?

There follows a description of a project in Berlin,
Germany, which uses sense impressions and an
attention to the moment to move a group, and
develop different patterns of interaction.

Group visioning in Berlin, Germany: Dream Score, by iLabs facilitators, Tiffany von Emmel and Dietmar Brinkmann

With a desire to generate life-affirming ways of developing communities, we started a project called 'Improvisation as Inquiry', which experimented with using body-based site-specific performance. A group of 12 people came together in K77 dance studio in East Berlin. Members were diverse in age, abilities, gender, sexual orientation and class. We were from Spain, Austria, US, Israel, Italy and Germany. As facilitators, we designed the project to be participatory in nature and increasingly transferred facilitation skills to other members as the group developed. Experiencing the group as transformative, members have continued on for years to improvise as a community of practice as well as in public places, in the workplace and with family at home. As facilitators, we have returned each summer to work in this community.

Members met each other for the first time on our Launch Day in 2001, three weeks after 9/11 in New York. We collectively agreed upon our intentions, the kinds of activities we wanted to practice and the qualities we wanted in our group culture. Before we had conversations about these ideas, first we did the following group visioning activity, the Dream Score.

Time: 1–2 hours; Space: Start in a sheltered open place, such as under a tree or in a room. During the activity, people will gravitate to other kinds of places. A large group is split into smaller groups of 4–6 people each. All the small groups begin at the same time in the same space. In each small group, one person is designated as 'dreamer' and the other people serve collectively as 'the dream'. The group will do as many dream cycles as needed until all members of the group have performed both roles. Between and after each dream cycle comes a dream reflection time.

Each dream cycle: The facilitator guides the beginning and ending of each dream cycle. Each cycle lasts for less than 10 minutes. The small group starts by standing neutral in a circle. The dreamer softens the belly and eyes, breathing slowly. The dreamer then initiates the action by noticing what she/he is curious about in her/his perception. It could be a memory, an image, a sensation, or words. It could be something seen, such as a bird or a person's face. Whatever it is, the dreamer plays with what is emerging moment-to-moment. Meanwhile, others equally participate in shaping the dream, responding to the dreamer's initiation.

The dream can go anywhere and look like anything. For example, one dreamer began by noticing the door and then felt the texture of the door, then opened the door. One of the other members then carried another through the door. Then the dreamer crawled out the door. Then the group moved down the stairs out into a courtyard. Then they rolled in the dirt outside, then carried dirt and rocks back into the studio where they made a dirt sculpture. As other examples, we've witnessed a group singing in a toilet stall, a group massaging each other, a group which took a dream up a public elevator and into a hotel restaurant kitchen, and a group which brought an outsider in a hallway into a dream who then joined the group.

Dream reflection time: In between each dream cycle, group members together sit in a circle, make a drawing as a response to each dream and talk. After all the cycles, the large group gets in a circle. The small groups perform briefly and share drawings. Members then identify patterns and themes shared by all. They make meanings about what is enlivening for the group.

For more information, see www.improvisationlabs.org, and von Emmel (2005)

4.2.2 Session ideas: life in water

Interactions

In art, as I have tried to argue, we have an aesthetic framework for those who believe the world is composed of discrete objects, and who are fascinated with the individualized self, but we do not have a process-oriented framework for those for whom the world consists of dynamic interactions and interrelational processes.

Gablik, 1991: 162–3

Water, its properties and its inhabitants have endlessly fascinated many different cultures, and inspired many art projects. Below are a number of session ideas and project examples that bring human bodies and watery realms into contact, into dynamic interaction and flow. How does interrelation emerge in these examples?

Session idea: water flow

Team up in twos, A and B. One member in each couple gets an invisible glass of water, handed out carefully by the facilitator. Let the invisible water flow: A empties the invisible glass over some part of B's body. B lets the water course over her or his body, until A picks up the water up at some end point – the point of the shoulder, tip of a finger, foot heel. Now B empties the water glass over A, and picks it up after its journey across A's body. Once the idea is clear, A and B empty, course and pick up the water without the invisible glass: the flow is continuous between the two bodies. After a while, the glassful of water grows into a bucket of water – movement and timing change. The bucket is shared by four people at a time, thrown across distances, and soaking more than one person at a time. The bucket becomes a continuous stream from a garden hose, a city fountain, then a small rivulet, a stream, and finally a river. You can easily vary the instruction in relation to local and regional environmental features. Pay attention to how the movement qualities change, how speed, aeration, depth etc. vary with the different waterways. Finally, bring the group together: the river grows into a river delta, and the water disperses into the ocean. As the water disperses, movement comes to a slow swell, and breathes across the group.

I have found this exercise particularly useful for creating group coherence and for raising or modulating the energy levels in a group. In most projects, people will naturally gravitate into specific groupings: creating exercises that flow from couple work into group work are particularly useful as a way to help break down the barriers that keep people from working as a group. The imaginary water has also helped me often as a way of equalizing energy levels in a group: people who are exuberant and people who are very quiet on a particular day can flow back and forth towards a balance that respects their differences, but allows them to work together.

Senses and communications: dolphin dance

Popoto or Maui's Dolphins are endangered dolphins found in New Zealand waters: there are only about 110 Maui's Dolphins left. The most significant dangers are entanglement in fishing nets and by-catch (being caught in fishing gear meant for other species). But other human activities are also a target in current conservation efforts.

In 2005, a group of activists found a powerful way to bring attention to an additional danger disrupting the dolphin's life: invasive research methods. These activists co-habit the coastal area where the dolphins live, Whaingaroa Raglan on New Zealand's North Island. Most of the activists are parents, and they want their children to grow up with the dolphins in their shared future of humans, non-humans and the land. Many are involved with the Whaingaroa Environment Centre. To protest the research actions, they created a dance.

Choreographer Ardre Foote is Maori, and she finds that this background not only influences her relation to the land, but also her way of dealing with community dance: 'Finding the dancers was easy, as most of my friends and co-workers love to dance. I also wanted to do something with mothers in our community who may have danced a lot in their youth but since having children thought they didn't have the time or talent.' The dancers were Patti, who teaches dance to children in the community; Te Kahurangi, a weaver and full-time mother; Heleina, a full-time mother of four children; Amy, a US citizen who has lived in Raglan for three years; Antonio, a father and an actor who commutes to Auckland three days a week working for Maori TV; and Te Rawhitiroa, who is eighteen and who works for Te Mauri Tau, an educational, environmental, health and community trust.

In twelve performance presentations at local sites and at events such as Eco-Reggae in Raglan, WOMAD 2005 and at the marae (Maori meeting place) at Te Papa museum in Wellington, Soul Speed Activist Theatre and Dance Troupe presented 'Popoto Whakamiharo'. The performers created a web of connection, attempting to bring audiences into a shared space of ecological connection and responsibility. In the performance, the dancers, choreographed by Ardre Foote, unwind soft muslin cords from a central pole and hand these strings to audience members. Within this web, dancers weave, taking their movement vocabulary from careful observation of dolphin movement. Scientists (rather stereotyped in white jackets and laptops) interrupt the dance and attach a box to the arm of a dancer. The box disrupts the dancer's movement until she frees herself.

Ardre Foote: 'I choreographed the piece around the story of the Popoto dolphin and its life in the sea, imagining it living freely and in harmony with its surroundings, expressing love and joy and portraying the connection and love that it wants to share with us, and then our [human] hunger for more, which was portrayed by the scientists and the need for more information.'

During the performance, the dancers plead with the audience to hold on to their strings: 'Don't let go – it's in your hands.' The performance echoes beyond its own space and time: audience members are invited to send messages to the government on special postcards provided, and members of the scientific community provided supportive statements addressing the need to change research methods.

Marine-mammal biologist Liz Slooten provided the scientific impetus behind the project. In an interview, Slooten explained how, up until a few years ago, visual, photographic and acoustic research were the dominant methods of dolphin observation. Recently, some researchers have started using biopsy darts and catching dolphins to apply tags by drilling holes in the dorsal fins.

Slooten and fellow conservationist Mary Gardner discussed ways of reaching the general public with the problems generated by this invasive research. What if somebody came up with a dance?

Slooten and her research partner Steve Dawson are well known for their innovative and effective communication methods, and in 2004, they received the Charles Fleming Award for their contribution to conservation science. In a recent interview, Slooten explained how scientific information is usually distributed by reading and writing, talking and listening. She is deeply interested in finding other ways of exchanging ideas. She was impressed with 'Popoto Whakamiharo', and with the power of dance as a form of communication about ethical and ecological aspects of conservation policies and with the evocative nature and accuracy with which the performers captured the dolphins' movements in their dance.

Choreographer Ardre Foote explains some of the alternative research processes specific to her background and her understanding of dance that have made this accuracy possible. As a New Zealander, she has often swum with dolphins. About influences on the choreographic process, she explains: 'I was having a lot of dreams of swimming with dolphins, which really helped tremendously with feeling movements and dancing them out.' And the dance itself brought the experience full circle: at the end of one of the performances taking place on a beach, said Foote, the dancers ran into the sea. There the silk costumes clung to them, creating sensations and experiences of a having a different skin, an experience she describes as magical. . . .

Excerpts from Kuppers, 'Dancing Dolphins: Approaches to Eco-Arts and Community Dance'. Arts Culture Nature newsletter, 2005

4.2.3 Session ideas: human bodies

Bodies and our thoughts about them are also a good way of thinking about community performance. For centuries, the human body has served as a metaphor for the public body, the state and for the integration of diverse parts into a whole. You can make these traditional thoughts on community resonant for your own practice.

Figure 4.4 Soul Speed Activist Theatre and Dance Troupe perform *Popoto Whakamiharo*, 2005.

52 Reflection exercise

a   Design a session based on marine mammal movement. Marine mammals such as dolphins and whales capture the attention of many cultures, and evoking them in performance work activates strong emotions and responses. But when you attempt to work with others (of whatever kind), issues of respect for difference, and an awareness of projection and fantasy are important. How can you capture aspects of the experience of animals who do not communicate with words, and whose environment is so different from humans? Ardre Foote shared some of the ways she approached the issue – how else can you learn and feel your way into another creature's sense experience? Consider video footage of marine mammals, sound recordings, technical information about weight, movement range, feeding habits, social environment etc. What kind of information do you gain from these materials? How do the different avenues of information inform each other? How do you feel about the relationship between traditional, unorthodox and scientific information channels?

b   A web is one of the core images of this performance. Create a community performance session idea based on weaving and connection, using material such as strings, pieces of cloth, or plant material. Think about how material evokes responses (think about the performers' wet silk costumes, for instance).

Session idea: the dance of the body

The group divides into smaller groups, and all are set a task of fulfilling different 'functions' through movements:

- blood
- heart muscle
- skeleton

- brain
- liver
- skin (and so on, depending on size of group).

After the improvisation period, map the whole body into space. What goes where? What interactions emerge between the groups?

The pedagogic aim of the improvisation isn't necessarily focused on an approximation or mnemonic of anatomical knowledge. Instead, the emphasis is on change, collaboration, interdependence: familiar ideas and images move into difference, and reproduce themselves in unfamiliar ways. Function and movement supersede schematic shape and line.

In my experience, this exercise always brings out surprising differentiations of movement. If the 'heart' group starts with opening and closing fists, they might, as the improvisation develops, find other ways of conceptualizing a heart, pumping actions, connectivity and flow. As time goes on during the improvisation, both conventionalized and stereotypical images of bodily function and personal meanings, experiential moments and an attention to sensation emerge in the dancers' imagination.

I have also used this exercise, combined with earth sculpture ideas, to work on different cultural ways of knowing the body (for instance, chi-based diagrams of bodies and humoreal theories) to explore intercultural difference and embodiment.

There are many ways in which exercises surrounding body imaginary can work in community performance work and beyond. What are the connections between community performance and this example of work with cancer survivors?

---

53 Reflection exercise

Re-shape the movement-based session idea above by using (a) painting, (b) sound work, and (c) earth sculpture/ sculpture with found materials.

4.2.4 Session ideas: spaces

P R A C T I C E   E X A M P L E

When I see, hear, feel . . .: locating cancer contradictions

The participants divide into three groups. Each group works together on creating a collage. The content of the collage deals with treatment, prevention, and life with breast cancer. The first group gathers images that relate to the health care system, the second ones that relate to home and family, and the third to workplace and society. After 30–60 minutes, we gather and each group presents its collage. The focus of discussion is on what was felt, seen and heard in these settings. Each group is asked to identify what their members see in their collage, to explain what they think is the main message, and invite others to comment on patterns. All points are noted on a flip chart. After each group has presented, we all explore the complexity, contradictions and challenges that breast cancer presents, and identify potential areas for action. Other questions include: What was happening in your group as you tried to do this task? Was it comfortable or uncomfortable? Participants, through this process, find ways to put into words, feelings around treatment, family and social expectations and find a context for a new understandings.

Written for this book by Pam Patterson, Toronto, Canada

Bodies in space, and the relationship between embodiment and environments are another core theme of contemporary art practice that lends itself to exploration in community performance settings. In particular, community performance can highlight the differences of embodiment within our social world.

Sensing space

In the *Body Spaces* residency, a commission for Digital Summer 2000 in Manchester, UK, I was working with young adult wheelchair users, people using crutches and non-disabled people. The impetus for the residence was to create interactive environments that allow spectators to sense different ways of inhabiting space.

We worked in dance, photography and storytelling sessions to create material for three installations. These installations were site-specific, designed to reshape three different spaces: the Royal Infirmary Outpatients' Lounge, a car park and the Contact Theatre foyer. In all of them, one element of the installation presented different pathways through the space – one was a line, taped to the floor, which followed the wheel of a manual wheelchair. When the installation creators invited members of the audience to walk this path with them, it was interesting to see how people realized playfully how differently a wheelchair user navigates corners, how certain (low) spaces were not accessible to walking people etc. Another line through the space was made up of small bits of tape, measuring the stride of a bi-pedal person: and again, people tried to 'mimic' this particular physical mapping, lengthening or shortening their own stride in order to fit the map given. In strange and intimate ways, people were dancing other people's steps and scripts.

Many community performance artists working within architectural settings stress regeneration, and the distribution of different kinds of agencies in these processes. In a series of experiments in the UK, The Public, an organization located in the West Midlands, works to transform urban environments. A description of the process shows the wide variety of interests, audience groups, involvement levels and approaches incorporated into the project – note in particular the different funding bodies involved, and their agendas.

54 Reflection exercise

Design three different community arts session instructions that could work in a disused heavy machinery factory (a site visit to a comparable building in your own community might give you valuable ideas). Think about metal and its connotations, labor practices, the kind of historical communities that formed around factories. Can you create a session idea that would reshape the environment, help to reclaim it for community use? Reflect on problems you encounter in your execution of this exercise: is it harder to think of workshop sessions in specific sites? Do you feel a division between 'natural' sites and 'industrial' ones? Do you think participants might have diverse reactions to the sites? In what way? Could the group use these different reactions fruitfully?

Radioactive

Between memory and forgetting is the space of conjecture, of imaginative reconstruction, of adventure. Visiting a derelict building is such an adventure. There is adventure in exploring old structures, in recovering bits of history and observing the traces of former activities.

David Papadopoulos

The Sozo Collective worked with The Public to transform a disused factory, part of a large swathe of derelict land awaiting redevelopment by Smethwick Regeneration Partnership, into a location for a series of temporary art installations, exhibitions, events and social activities.

The first event, Radioactive, was curated by Sozo founder Dave Pollard:

To me this represents a unique experiment in combining art with urban regeneration, community building and new ways of living and working together. Quite simply, the project is based on the idea of empowering, freeing and nurturing the innate creative abilities present in all of us . . .

The project was funded through an Arts Council Grants for the Arts award and Advantage West Midlands through their Social Inclusion to the Creative Economy program. This program supports learning opportunities for artists and other creative practitioners. Learning and professional development opportunities were delivered through artist mentoring and peer critique.

A diverse group of artists (up to fifty) were encouraged to get involved from a very early stage in transforming the building, contributing DIY skills to renovate and reshape the spaces. Through this approach, every artist participant in the project had a stake in designing and improving the environment where their work was created or exhibited and an opportunity to experiment with an informal 'non-precious' space.

Over a twelve-month period, The X-Ray Factory was used to house:

- A pre-Christmas event for school groups and families, Grotto – A series of light and sound installations, a celebration of wonderment and seasonal curiosities – which included over two hundred Christmas trees, a wicked goblin and Santa's sledge crash landed into a front room, play activities and traditional mince pies.
- The NESTA (National Endowment for Science, Technology and the Arts) Creative Laboratory, working with young people to transform the factory floor into a desert island experience.
- A series of workshops with Guillermo Gomez Pena, working with local performance artists culminating in two events during the Fierce Festival.
- A pilot Live/Work space project with artists, architects and local people – sharing creative ideas and experiment with building and construction.

Quoted from publicity materials

Reclaiming sites: community labyrinth

The Lenape Turtle Peace Labyrinth, Teaneck Creek Park, New Jersey, USA

About the process:

The Lenape Turtle Peace Labyrinth is an environmental art work created through an artist facilitated, community building process using materials found on site and recycled from the waste-stream with low-impact construction methods to make a place where humans can reconnect with nature and witness its cycles.

The stepping stone path of the Lenape Turtle Peace Labyrinth is made from broken rubble that was found in large piles all over Teaneck Creek Park. Rather than importing new material, in keeping with the ecological vision of the Park we creatively re-used available materials from the site. This emerges from a long view consideration as humanity moves to the realization that our waste is piling up and future generations are going to have to deal with the pollution of their ancestors. The path winds its way around land that was once a garbage dump. In the Fall of 2003 and Spring of 2004 volunteer groups prepared the site for the laying of the labyrinth.

About different agencies at work in regeneration:

The creation of the labyrinth is an on-going process that requires the development of a relationship between humans and the land through the maintenance of the pathway and the plants. Over time the areas between the stepping stone path will be planted with native plants while allowing space for rare native plants that show up. These unplanned visitors are known as volunteer plants and in the spring this was seen through the appearance of Skunk Cabbage. We observed that in some areas of the labyrinth plants flourish while in other areas the ground is barren – these are the areas where most of the garbage was found and removed by the volunteer groups. Many of us have been conditioned to enjoy highly manicured parks, where the grass, an unnaturally human landscaping choice is regularly mowed and controlled, however in these settings we lose the opportunity to witness nature's process. By allowing the plants to do their own thing in the labyrinth environment, as the path is walked we move through a variety of states of nature and perhaps learn more about the impact humans have on nature and its ability to recover.

How to use the labyrinth:

The labyrinth has one path that leads from the perimeter to the center. Typically the full labyrinth experience is to walk the path winding inward, enjoy some moments in the center and then to retrace the path outward. A regular practice of walking the labyrinth, once a week, once a month or each season offers a wonderful way to witness how the surrounding environment transforms through the cycle of the year.

About labyrinth building as a community process:

In the process of creating a Labyrinth people learn how to collaborate with others and Nature. From experience we see how people are enlivened when they participate in building a Labyrinth and bring it into their daily lives through walking it and caring for it. They come to know old friends and neighbors in new ways and make new friends. The Labyrinth can be a powerful tool for creating community and peace as the building process cultivates friendship, trust, inner peace, confidence and connection to an innate knowing.

Material by Camino de Paz lead artist, Ariane Burgess, US

PRACTICE EXAMPLE

Figure 4.6 Mrs Ing in her vertical garden with large bitter melon, part of 'The Growing Fence' project (artist Christina Bechstein and landscape architect Klaas Klaus Loenhert), a public art and landscape intervention on over 1 acre of community garden land in downtown Boston. The collaboration preserves both the green space and urban cultural histories that are overlooked and vanishing. Photo: Christina Bechstein

Figure 4.5 The Olimpias Scar Tissue workshops, Rhode Island, USA, 2005. Dancing the lines of our hands.   Photo: Martha Kuhlman

Global Positioning System (GPS) information, webwork, and improvisatory media mixing by disk jockeys and video jockeys: the Walking Project uses a wide range of media to connect participants with each other, and with audiences and users beyond the time-frame of the project.

Low-tech, high-tech and ways of knowing: the Walking Project

P
R
A
C
T
I
C
E

E
X
A
M
P
L
E

Erika Block on the Walking Project, a large-scale community arts project series:

> The Walking Project is an interdisciplinary performance, mapping and cultural-
> exchange project collaboratively developed by my company, Walk & Squawk, with
> U.S. and South Africa-based artists during a series of residencies in Detroit and
> KwaZulu-Natal from 2003 through 2006.
>
> The Walking Project uses the paths people make across vacant lots in Detroit and
> across fields in South Africa – desire lines – as springboard to explore the paths we
> walk and how they are formed through culture, geography, language, economics and
> love. It looks at how people make their own paths; how and why people's paths cross;
> and how changing patterns of movement can alter perceptions, attitudes and lives.
>
> In the past year I've been exploring the use of locative technologies to create
> alternative maps of desire lines by converting GIS (geographic information systems)
> data into audio and visual material for the Web, for physical installation and for live
> performance. Apart from the technology, I've been thinking about the stories maps tell,
> not only about the places they locate, but also about the people who make them.
> Denis Woods writes that maps are as important for what they don't include as for what
> they do include. As I've been learning about the process of map-making, I've thought a lot
> about information and the way it both shapes and becomes 'place,' and I've stumbled
> upon a mother lode of material about this emerging field, from tools and technologies to
> projects, policies and politics.

About the connections between different sites:

> The Walking Project has drawn connections between walking and political protest – from
> antiwar marches around the world to anti-eviction marches in South Africa and water-rate
> protests in both Detroit and KwaZulu-Natal. It has juxtaposed Gandhi's first act of civil
> disobedience in the Pietermaritzburg, South Africa, train station in the 1890s with paths to
> safe houses that were part of the underground railroad system in Detroit, as escaped
> slaves passed through the city on their way to Canada. And it has connected workers
> losing manufacturing jobs in the U.S. with workers losing jobs in South Africa.

About the new maps as part of the future plans for the project:

> These new maps will be generated by mixing and layering audio and visual material from
> the database we're building. People can make an infinite series of new 'map mixes' that
> can be stored and added to the database for someone else to sample. This 'map mixing'
> will happen in three different formats: live performances with DJs and VJs; an interactive
> montage for installation in public spaces; and an interactive web experience. New maps
> will be added to an online gallery as they're created.

Quotes from Block, 2005

4.2.5 Session ideas: new media

Synaesthetic perception is the rule, and we are unaware of it only because scientific knowledge shifts the center of gravity of experience, so that we have unlearned how to see, hear, and generally speaking, feel, in order to deduce, from our bodily organization and the world as the physicist conceives it, what we are to see, hear, and feel.

Merleau-Ponty, 1962: 229

New technologies have also long been part of stage environments: moving tapestry hangings, stage pits, candle-lit footlights or stage audio systems and microphones are all part of traditional Western stage performance. Many of these technologies have synaesthetic properties: color and light become touch and kinesthesia (such as spotlights communicating as close-ups). Community performance can challenge traditional aesthetics within its stronghold, and use stage technologies for its own aims: to widen participation, bring different kinds of bodies and sensibilities into the 'limelight', and to further dialogues about participation and inclusion.

In the following report on a multi-media stage project, I highlight the opportunities multiple overlapping access technologies and stage technologies can offer.

Figure 4.7 Performance still from *Performance in Telepresence* by Corpos Informaticos (Brazil, Germany, US). This image shows the multiple screens set up in this telematic encounter where participants at the community/performance conference could interact with dancers and performers in Germany, Brazil and the UK, where similar screens were set up. Small dances of mouth movements and hand gestures offered halting interactions.
Photo: Petra Kuppers

Performance report: senses, disability and performance technology

In May 2003 Elizabeth Goodman and Jo Gell from the SMARTlab at Central St Martins, London, UK and Clilly Castiglia and Kevin Feeley from the Center for Advanced Technology, New York University (NYU), asked me to work with different performance technologies that they were developing, and test them out in a community arts setting. We all worked together with a group of interested disabled artists associated with the Liverpool Institute for Performing Arts and North West Disability Arts Forum.

An extremely short work period meant that instead of a lengthy research of locations and their associated legends, myths and stories and personal fantasies, we had to find quick access to a unifying theme, something that would anchor our concerns with transmission, media and disability politics. We found this core in the myth of the Sirens – bird-bodied women-monsters whose beautiful voices lure sailors to their death. Much of Greek myth uses different bodies as markers of extraordinary natures, and as meaning carriers.

Our bodies on the workshop stage echoed these mythologized impairments, but as disabled people, we experience them differently. If limping is part of your way of navigating in the world, it doesn't necessarily feel subjectively negative, or 'secondary' to some idea of 'normate' walking. In the same way, the visual information perceived by someone who is visually impaired is appropriate and orienting, 'normal' to them, and not necessarily experienced as inferior. My own, pain-related experiences induce me to move in our shared world in a deliberate and attentive manner, and given my adaptive strategies, I don't experience my physical difference necessarily as a negativity – instead, it opens up new perspectives and different sensibilities for me.

For many disabled people who become interested in their particular perspective as a cultural minority, a different way of being in the world emerges as our own, familiar, central identity. The sense of disability as a form of different and therefore valuable access to the world in its own right, and as a dance language, became the core political centre of the show. In *Sirens*, we issued a call, a song, a seduction: we wanted to share some of the richness of our different access points.

In the dance choreography and the technological play with dance, connections and distances provided anchor points. Play with perspective, for instance, allowed videographer and dancers to interact in different ways, using close-ups and changing distances. One of our videographers, Max, has a mobility impairment that meant not only discomfort on the stage, but also the need to be flexible with time arrangements. Traditional performance would have problems with these access needs but our use of a more diverse theatre machine allowed for Max to be a fully integrated artistic voice – he didn't have to be physically in the theatre for his unique perspective on movement and space to be part of our show.

Two of the performers were visually impaired, and two identified as Deaf. This allowed for many interesting moments of improvisation – the vibration of the wooden floor and a reliance on kinesthesia as information source were some of the techniques we explored.

In one moment in our working process, a Deaf (i.e. someone who uses British Sign Language as her first language, and sees herself as part of Deaf culture) dance artist, Ruth Gould, gave an audio transcription of a dance between two other performers, and a camera captured in close-up her moving mouth. In a movement/live video mixing montage, these different performance moments could now interplay, and their status as 'aesthetic objects' or 'information systems' became undecidable.

Other forms of access could be provided visually at multiple points – a signer occupied a corner of the stage, and put any language used on stage or on video into an elaborate hand-dance. Using Sign Language as a fully equal partner (to spoken language) and a creatively rich source of bodily poetics on stage is by now a well established practice for many companies, including Graeae and Common Ground Sign Dance Theatre in the UK and the National Theatre of the Deaf in the US.

A transcriber provided audio transcription, and the sound engineer could feed it into the whole auditorium through the intercom system whenever she wanted to, or individual audience members could access it through an audio loop system. Many people did avail themselves of this audio-description, including those who didn't normally use it, who were neither visually nor hearing impaired: it provided another aesthetic, poetic channel of movement translation.

Captioning (spoken text running as subtitles) also functioned in a complex way. *Text Rain* was a software solution brought by the NYU team. We fed various pieces of creative writing created by workshop participants in response to the *Sirens* theme into the program, and mounted a sensor to capture movement on stage. The resulting material shows text scrolling down on the projecting screen. Where moving bodies are captured by the sensors, the text-color changes. The text seems to flow around the bodies, it moves with them.

As I am writing this, I know that this montage and mélange of sensorial access, some translated and transformed through visual or audio media, sounds like a circus, a spectacle, a mass of too much information. And it was, in some ways, but the resulting show was always anchored back in the movement material – its translation into language, image, presence, sound, smell and kinesthetic nearness provided the focal point. Many of the audience members were well used to elaborate communication set-ups – they were disabled people, like ourselves, and were willing and happy to grant time and space to serious reflection about inclusion and access. At disability culture events, many of us wait while the speech paragraph we've just given is typed out and appears on a screen, we interact respectfully with the ASL transcriber, and ensure that there is good lighting on our faces and mouths for those in our audience who read our lips. We shuffle wheelchairs, seats and move guide dogs to ensure that we can all participate. This spatial and sensory awareness of difference has always been a delight (and necessity) to me, and is significantly different from the atmosphere at most non-disability-led events I participate in. Our show's multi-layered access provision and play with technologies emerges therefore seamlessly out of a disability aesthetic, or at least more seamlessly than it would emerge from (some) non-disabled dance viewers' sense of stagework as relying on an 'invisibilized' or naturalized technology. In *Sirens*, we aimed to foreground our sensorial differences, and therefore to thematize difference not just in the choreography on the stage, but also in the choreography of the stage, and the audience/dancer interaction.

The performance was the opening evening of the Effecting Change: the Future of Disability Arts conference at Liverpool Institute for Performing Arts, and thus the audience was filled with fellow disabled people, and non-disabled allies. Once the performance ended, the audience wouldn't let us get off stage: in a world where access issues often play second fiddle to aesthetics, it was very refreshing for many to see a dance performance that deliberately plays with the call and response of video, audio and human bodies. We had a great conversation.

The show relied on collaboration: the technologist-artists went with the flow, improvised just as much as the dancers did, and the audience was happy to engage with the resulting experiment, overlooking technical difficulties, and engaging very nimbly with their audio loop gear. Access technologies, often seen as supplementary to the 'actual' performance event, became here exciting dance partners, full participants in the multi-nodal collaboration. I learned that new dance technologies and access technologies TOGETHER can play important and creative roles in the future of community dance performances.

56 Research exercise

a   What are the access technologies that enable you to witness and participate in public performances?

   Think about your different senses, and come up with performance ideas that translate experiences between senses. Are there any features to transmission of data to senses that overlap across different sense areas? Think about vibration and wave transmission, for instance.

b   Research: Do you see connections between synaesthesia and performance practice? How does synaesthesia relate to the *Sirens* project? Make connections to other projects discussed in this chapter.

c   Think about new (or old) media technologies available to you: how can video, film, PowerPoint projection or an interactive DVD kiosk enhance sensory access? How can they create different kinds of community?

   Think about your access to these resources: how accessible are they to you, how can you build teams that would allow you to enlarge the technological grasp of a community performance project?

4.3 Cool-/warm-downs

Even if your workshop is not movement-based (where a cool-down can be a physiological necessity), it is a good idea to provide an exit or closure for it. During an arts workshop, people usually experience a different attention to the world, a different pace, a different way of being with others. Find a way to release participants back into the 'normal' world.

You will find a gesture or sequence you personally are comfortable with, and you most likely will use that gesture often. I find that that repetition of a similar event at the end of all workshops reassures all of us, and I often use a circle exercise, both for greetings, and for short cool-downs.

Circle ending

We all stand together in a circle, and either hold hands or not, depending on the 'emotional temperature' of the preceding workshop, or the dominant cultural or social scripts and their suggestions. From there, we reach up, stretching our bodies up towards the sky, past any ceilings that might loom above us, and into the sunlight. We then slowly roll down, enjoying the sensation of stretching our spines, and let our hands dangle downwards, through any floor we are standing on, down towards the rich earth beneath us. Coming back into middle space, we twist towards each other, and smile: acknowledging each other. Finally, we turn back towards the middle, and bring our hands into the center, raise them up, come back, and say goodbye.

P R A C T I C E   E X A M P L E

Meditation

Many practices end with meditation – many people associate a short quiet meditation sequence with yoga sessions, for instance. A meditation can be a wonderful way of bringing a workshop to a close, as it allows participants to collect their bodies, and find their balance. Depending on the practice chosen, meditations can offer gentle ways out of communal experiences, and a space for reflection on what happened within a workshop.
   Meditation can take many forms:

- quiet sitting or lying, using breath counts as a steady guide into concentration;
- candle meditation;
- dance meditation, i.e. an abandonment in movement often using spiral movements or percussive sounds as its pathway into trance-like states;
- automatic writing, where words and phrases flow from the hand onto paper without (too much) intervention through form;
- visual meditations, circle-drawings and mandalas.

57 Reflection exercise

What kind of contemplative practices or meditation techniques are part of your experience? If they are not now, were they ever? How does cultural difference impact people's familiarity or comfort level with this kind of work? In these practices, how do concepts of individual and community intersect and interact?

Mandalas

'Mandala' is a Sanskrit word for circle, and can also mean 'community' and 'connection'. It is used extensively in Buddhist meditation work, but the form, a round shape within other geometric forms, with mirrored and convoluted interior, has appeared in many cultures: think about rose windows in Gothic Europe or Diné/Navaho sand-paintings.

Psychoanalyst Carl Jung paid attention to the mandala. For him, it was a figure that transcended cultures, an archetype or symbol that had resonance for humanity:

> The 'squaring of the circle' is one of the many archetypal motifs which form the basic patterns of our dreams and fantasies. But it is distinguished by the fact that it is one of the most important of them from the functional point of view. Indeed, it could even be called the archetype of wholeness.
>
> Jung, 1973

Mandalas can be created by individuals, and then shared, but they can also be created together, on large pieces of paper (wallpaper, rolls from newspaper printers), on asphalt with chalk, or on sand with fingers.

This chapter offered various ideas for community performance workshops, ways to structure the work, and ideas for building thematic blocks. Our sensual embodiment acted as the focus for many different exercises and practice examples. Having worked through this chapter, you should be able to evaluate workshop ideas for their potential contribution to community and group practice. Given these reflections, you will be able to adapt many exercises in common use in theatre, dance and visual arts practice for community performance use.

Figure 4.8 Post-workshop glow. Participants from the Olimpias Scar Tissue workshops in a local pizzeria, before our regular communal meal.   Photo: Petra Kuppers

CHAPTER 5

Finding inspirations

Stories, legends, myths

So far, the session ideas I have discussed were based on our senses, our sense of embodiment, space and time. In this chapter, the focus is on inspiration derived from the particular place a community workshop might be located in, and from the stories and memories of project participants. Stories, legends, myths, histories: these are some of the core materials and starting points for many community performance events.

Questions emerging in various ways in this chapter include:

- Who owns stories?
- Who tells stories? What is the role of the community performance artist?
- Who is/are the audience(s)?
- What is the role (and definition) of the community in a creative process?
- How do aesthetic processes and products relate to community structures and the wider social field?

As you work through this chapter, you will be introduced to many ways in which individual stories and memories can weave together into a communal tapestry. In different ways, community emerges, and communal politics and action are the background for many projects discussed here.

In order to give a sense of a potential workshop series progression, and the development of work over months and years, I am including in this narrative five practice examples from a project I facilitated in Wales with fellow disabled people, in particular, mental health system survivors. The project, Earth Stories, saw us working together for a long period of time, exploring many different methods.

After a section that provides examples of potential formats for sharings and performances, the chapter also discusses strategies of working with existing scripts, an important part of the working methods of many community performance workers.

5.1 Memories

Places hold memories: things happened here. People have been born, lived, been in conflict and harmony with each other, with others, and the location itself, and died. Their stories penetrate the memory of sites, and these stories are one place a community performance practitioner can access to develop material with community groups.

Legends as exits

It is through the opportunity they offer to store rich silences and wordless stories, or rather through their capacity to create cellars and garrets everywhere, that local legends . . . permit exits, ways of going out and coming back in, and thus habitable spaces.

de Certeau, 1988: 106

Earth Stories session idea 1: childhood memories

PRACTICE EXAMPLE

A rich fund of ideas for my own work are childhood memories that come to carry adult meaning in a slow movement of shaping, through surprises, coherences, echoes and inspirations. The specific example I will focus on in this chapter is a workshop series that took place during 1999 and 2000, located in rural Wales, with people who all identify as mental health system survivors. In these workshops, we worked towards the creation of two videopoems – associative montages of images and poetry. The starting points for these videopoems were two mythical figures – the Lady of the Lake and the Sleeping Giant. These mythical characters have strong story presences in the location of our workshops, and are anchored by physical landmarks. In the case of the Lady of the Lake, a particular lake was associated with her, as well as a village where her sons, natural healers, are supposed to have lived. Many local landmarks refer to her story. The Sleeping Giant refers to a rock formation – a natural hill, whose resemblance to a recumbent human had been exaggerated in Victorian times with specifically placed hedges and walls.

After becoming familiar with each other, having tea together in the Ystradgynlais User Group Home, a community center for people who experience mental health distress, we began by thinking back to the moment as children or adults we first heard about the area of the Lady's Lake, or of the story associated with the hill.

We started out by talking about the nature of memory, by naming sense impressions: smells, sights, sounds, tastes, textures etc.

Then, we wrote poems. We agreed on four lines as a format, but didn't necessary feel bound by it. We gave ourselves permission to use single words, whole sentences or fragments. Everybody developed their own style.

Here are examples of the kind of lines, poems, stories and memories that we recorded in the first few sessions of working on the Sleeping Giant. The last line of one poem 'This is not a Giant of Despair, but a Giant of Hope' became a central part of our work together: changing the meaning of things, looking for something new, searching, looking for hope – these became the main ideas for the video.

I was born not far away, in Caerbont, Abercrave.
I can say these are my hills, this is my homeland,
and those are my mountains.
This is not a Giant of Despair, but a Giant of Hope.

Hill
Eyebrow
Nose
Chin

My brother first pointed him out to me.
He lay there like a monster quite and still
I thought if he yawned, his arms would reach the sky.

What if he got angry? Shook his fists at the world?
Would he carry us all away somewhere?

One of the tasks of a community performer can be to investigate with members of the community some of the images that are resonant for them – that capture something about a location, a home, a place. There are many ways to make connection with a place. Local historians might give workshops, or might even maintain a local history museum. Oral history projects, an important feature of a sociology and history 'from below' emerged in the 1970s in many countries, and many local libraries or universities might have collections of transcribed tapes that speak about everyday life, realities of living in a location, and about the kinds of stories, myths and legends that echoed for them. Investigating these materials, and reading background information about a location's economic history, its land-uses, or its growth as a city, can provide invaluable material. Different memories are stored in different ways: try to be attentive to the relative likelihood of preservation of some stories instead of others. Do women's stories have the same status as the stories of male factory owners, for instance? How can you reach children's stories? Which accounts seem absent?

Figure 5.1 Making felt amulets while storytelling. We later used the stories we shared to create a dance, and the amulets became part of a felt bag in which many people's stories about the local environment were collected. Workshop for Rural Education Activities Program (REAP), Masterton, New Zealand, 2005.   Photo: Petra Kuppers

Figure 5.2 *Vignettes du Port Nouveau*, by Art Bridgman and Myrna Packer, at Doris Duke's Rough Point in Newport, RI as part of Island Moving Co.'s Open for Dancing 2002, a biennial site-specific dance festival of works created and performed by participants of all levels of dance experience, open to everyone.   Photo: Thomas Palmer

Stories, prisons and placements

The Performance Project began as a collaboration between two artists, Annie Dowling and Julie Lichtenberg, and eight men incarcerated at the Hampshire Jail and House of Correction in September 2004. Our work is generated through improvisations that are videotaped, transcribed, and shaped into script and choreography. Ultimately, the performers each communicate their story not as singular isolated experience, but woven together with the experiences of other members, and crafted into a whole.

59 Places (2001) was inspired by Josh Washburn, a group member who lived in 59 foster placements over a nine-year period of his childhood. Using the concept of 'home' as a point of departure, Josh's story was told through movement, letters, documents from his Department of Social Services file, and through the repetition of the addresses of 59 foster placements. His story was juxtaposed with more traditional scenes, which took place within the apartment of three brothers, and address individual conflicts, family tensions, and intimacies.

Communication by artist

PRACTICE EXAMPLE

58 Reflection exercise

What are the different places that hold information about you and your life? How could you access them? Create a list of potential avenues of information. Next to each entry, write how you think you would feel if you were to see this information. And how would you feel if others saw it?

Accessing memories

There are many ways that memories can be activated. Sounds, textures, smells: they all can act as pathways into the past.

P R A C T I C E E X A M P L E

Senses, movements, archives – Liz Lerman workshop

Liz introduced us to word-movement relationships, as she taught us a phrase based on these images: 'Tree in the wind . . . Swing wide . . . Touch gently . . . Pass through . . . Paint the sky . . . Rock . . . Wrap . . . Turn away . . . Show softly . . . Show strongly.'

After learning her phrase, we each made our own, using these words and then their opposites. This segued into a writing, talking, and interviewing exercise, which lasted all week. We wrote completions of the sentence fragment 'I come from. . .,' observed and adopted each other's conversational gestures, wrote personal stories with an emphasis on sensory detail, recalled movies and fairy tales, and assembled a personal archive, which contained everything from photos, letters and trips, to sayings, songs, scenery, illnesses and crimes.

I was intrigued by the category of 'sayings.' A lot of things were said in my family, where the *bon mot* was always preferred to the stumbling, uneven expression of feeling. I suddenly remembered the letters my mother wrote to my father in the months before they were married, which I discovered and read when I was 13.

Narrative by Maggie Kast about her experiences in the Senior Camp organized by the Liz Lerman Dance Exchange (2000). For more about the Liz Lerman Dance Exchange, see Jan Cohen-Cruz in the *Reader*

Words, phrases, 'bon mot', sayings: they have a power, and hold memories beyond their obvious meaning. Maggie Kast remembers the structure of 'bon mots' as a significant aspect of family communication, and words such as place names also can encapsulate meaning and memory. Are there phrases, words, or maybe just sounds and rhythms, echoes of a voice speaking a phrase, that conjure up significant memories for you?

59 Reflection exercise

Design a community exercise based on private memories. Think about a tapestry, a tableau with core words spoken out loud, or a music collage. What issues emerge? How can you safeguard people's privacy while still keeping the force and passion of lived memory? How can you intersect the private archive with the group's memories?

The power of words

An account by Nalungiaq, an Inuit woman interviewed by ethnologist
Knud Rasmussen (1983: 3):

> In the very earliest time
> when both people and animals lived on earth
> a person could become an animal if he wanted to
> and an animal could become a human being.
> Sometimes they were people
> and sometimes animals
> and there was no difference.
> All spoke the same language.
> That was the time when words were like magic.
> The human mind had mysterious powers.
> A words spoken by chance
> might have strange consequences.
> It would suddenly come alive
> and what people wanted to happen could happen –
> all you had to do was say it.
> Nobody could explain this:
> That's the way it was.

Personal stories, cultural memories

A right to stories and words, and an ownership of stories cannot be assumed, in particular in post-colonial environments. In a community performance project at a hospice in New Zealand (discussed in more detail further on in this chapter, p. 157), we were working with different kinds of cultural contact. Many of the Maori myths and stories that intertwine so deeply with the places of New Zealand weren't told to or known by the predominantly Pakeha (white European heritage) workshop participants when they were children, at least to the older ones who didn't receive bi-cultural schooling. When we were creating sense memories of home places, and of the stories we associated with them, many stories they shared were private and personal. They spoke about growing up without a strong storytelling practice, quite alienated from Celtic and other storytelling traditions their Irish, Scottish and Welsh ancestors grew up with, and about making up their own stories about the land. And even though they didn't know the full stories and legends, the private stories they did tell and worked with often involved Maori place names, and the fantasies these Pakeha children built around the (vaguely remembered) translations of these names: a river called 'lazy lizard' in the English translation of an older Maori word, led one of the participants as a child to imagine stories about lizards living in the sea, different and yet related to the Taniwha (water demon) stories Maoris have about the same place. We explored these echoes, bringing private stories and memories in contact with the rich story and song tradition of Maori habitation of the land. In our workshops at the hospice, we used these memories to build up a map of living in the locality, honoring the networks of habitation and home.

For Maori, these place names that proved so evocative for Pakeha children also mark a publicly preserved memory as shown here by Te Maire Tau, Principal Historian, Te Runanga o Ngāi Tahu:

> For Ngāi Tahu [tribe tahu people] living today, our world is vastly different [from the markings of time and space the ancestors used]. The main motorway defines our knowledge of the South Island [of New Zealand] and the waterways and hillocks that tell their histories are retained by few in their villages. Nevertheless, it does not take much to recall the past because the placenames still exist and we have maintained our whakapapa [genealogy] despite the corrosion of our traditions that is a result of colonialisation.
>
> Te Maire Tau, 2003: 14

Place names thus recall past(s) both cultural and personal. They are reservoirs of resonance, their sounds often as important and emotionally rich to local people as their descriptive content. Activating them through community performance work can help to create a focal point for a local community.

60 Reflection exercise

Collecting stories is an activity that is part of many community performance workshops.
Think about the activity as an exchange: stories are valuable, and in many cultures, stories are precious and their exchange regulated by ritual and prohibition. How can you show respect to the value of the story? Collect ideas of what you can give back in exchange for the story you received – a story in return, a poem, a movement, an image? The acts of gifting and exchange can become the basis for a session idea.

Ethnomethodology

Ethnomethodology is the study of the ways in which people make sense of their social world. The American sociologist **Harold Garfinkel** in the early 1960s set out its main ideas in his book *Studies in Ethnomethodology* (1967). How do humans create order out of the mass of sensations and experiences that surrounds them? How do they create narratives, shape a life story? Ethnomethodologists interested in these issues worked on many oral history projects, collecting 'history from below': the voices of 'ordinary people', charting their ways of making sense of time passing.

Historical investigations in archives and museums can make for rich and layered excavations, but the most important resource for community performance practitioners are, as always, the people and participants of the project.

Verbatim Theatre

Verbatim Theatre is the term used to describe performances which create scripts that are not theatrical in origin, and utilize 'real life' interviews, court transcripts, government session reports. Examples: *The Colour of Justice*, Tricycle Theatre, UK, 1999, on the Stephen Lawrence Inquiry and its exposure of British racism; Srebrenica, 1996, on the Hague 1996 War Crimes Tribunal, also Tricycle: Talking to Terrorists, writer Robin Soans, dir. Max Stafford-Clark, with interview material from people involved in different terrorist networks, 2005.

Figure 5.3 The Olimpias: participants in Earth Stories workshops, break-time at the old ironworks in Ynyscedwyn Ironworks Park, Ystradgynlais, Wales, UK.   Photo: Petra Kuppers

There are numerous ways you can go about collecting and gathering material. Formal **interviews** are one way of doing this. Setting up informal memory talking shop sessions are another way, initiating (or joining) creative writing groups or adult literacy groups yet another. Looking for historical photographs of sites or old family photos can also be a very useful way of gaining different kinds of memories, sense impressions, and a feel for a place's history. Before you set up a project, though, think about how you are doing it, with what aim, how you are recording it, and with whom you are sharing it. What are the **ethics** of your work? What kind of **permissions** do you have to ask for? What material is sensitive? In previous sections, I have written about issues of **confidentiality** and **ownership** – take these issues into account as you think about recording conversations.

61 Reflection exercise

Find out more about *The Laramie Project* (p. 140). Read some of its scenes, and try to watch the HBO film made from it. The original staging of the play was minimal, using a black box and almost no props. Why do you think that decision was made? What is the effect on the way you hear the words? What changes when you watch the HBO film? How does its use of well-known actors and naturalist settings impact on your reception?

The Laramie Project, by Moisés Kaufman and the members of Tectonic Theatre Project

The town of Laramie, Texas, was the venue and context for a horrific hate-crime: the killing of Matthew Shepard, a 21-year-old gay man and student at the University of Wyoming. He was beaten sadistically, tied to a fence and left to die. The play *The Laramie Project* presents glimpses into the town of Laramie, assembled by citizen's voices, and it is a hugely successful example of theatre work that uses interviews.

Kaufman *et al.* 2001, pp. vi–vii

From Kaufman's Introduction to *The Laramie Project*

The idea for The Laramie Project originated in my desire to learn more about why Matthew Shepard was murdered; about what happened that night; about the town of Laramie. The idea of listening to the citizens talk really interested me. How is Laramie different from the rest of the country and how is it similar?

Shortly after the murder, I posed the question to my company, Tectonic Theater Project: What can we as theatre artists do as a response to this incident? And, more concretely: Is theatre a medium that can contribute to the national dialogue on current events? . . .

At the time [of writing] I also happened to run across a Brecht essay I had not read in a long time, 'The Street Scene.' In it Brecht uses as a model the following situation: 'an eyewitness demonstrating to a collection of people how a traffic accident took place.' He goes on to build a theory about his 'epic theatre' based on this model. The essay gave me an idea about how to deal with this project, both in terms of its creation and its aesthetic vocabulary.

So in November 1998, four weeks after the murder of Matthew Shepard, nine members of Tectonic Theater Project and I traveled to Laramie, Wyoming, to collect interviews that might become material for a play. Little did we know that we would devote two years of our lives to this project. We returned to Laramie six times over the course of the next year and a half and conducted over two hundred interviews. . . .

The experience of working on The Laramie Project has been one of great sadness, great beauty and, perhaps most importantly great revelations – about our nation, about our ideas, about ourselves.

Theresa May, author of a play dealing with community voices, on *The Laramie Project*

As playwright and director I struggled with the moral issue of whether or not I could take our gathered interview material and write a play. Certainly there are examples to emulate: Moisés Kaufman's *Laramie Project*, in which a company of actors took interviews and developed a docudrama about the beating death of Matthew Shepard. Kaufman and the actors had to craft that script; edit those interviews; develop scenes and dramatic structure. But the uncertain distaste I had for precisely that kind of work held me paralyzed. The truth is, I have strong ethical concerns about a New York-based director who flew to a Wyoming town, mined its tragedy, and now has struck professional pay-dirt through the staging, publication and filming of that community's pain. And yet isn't that what we as dramatists do? Tell the stories that need to be told? Isn't American society more sensitive to hate crimes because Kaufman went to Wyoming?

. . . Ethics is always personal and local. I don't have answers; but I can tell you what we did.

Each person interviewed received a statement describing the project, the purpose of the interview, and a promise that they would be not only receive a transcript of their interview, but also that their words would not be used for any other purpose except this particular community-based play; that the University would not 'own' the script, nor their stories; that each person interviewed or working on the project would 'own' their own stories. But this initial clarity about our intent and methods was soon muddied in the waters of playmaking. In a clumsy attempt to track authorship, early drafts of the script, initials of the original writer and interviewee appear after each sizeable piece of text. Would everyone who either worked on the project or given an interview need to review and approve the final script? Some 100+ people, many of whom do not have email, some of whom do not have telephones. As we worked the script through improvisation, and then transcribed an improvisation, whose writing is it?

(See also the *Reader*)

Carolyn Lambert and fereshteh toosi: searching for the fourth river

Creative tactics for gathering stories and starting processes

The city of Pittsburgh developed where the Monongahela and the Allegheny Rivers meet and form the Ohio River in southwestern Pennsylvania.

Because of the rivers, Pittsburgh became a significant site for US steel production. Pittsburgh's steel industry has since declined, but the three rivers remain an important geographical feature for the region. Numerous local festivals and place names have adopted this label, including the Three Rivers Arts Festival, the Three Rivers Regatta, and the former Three Rivers Stadium. In a city that places great emphasis on its identification as the three rivers region, stories prevail about an underground fourth river.

As newcomers to Pittsburgh, we were curious: Did people know about the underground river, and if so, what could they tell us? We wanted to collect various versions of this urban legend. Could we draw attention to the significance of urban myth and provoke discussion amongst strangers?

In the summer of 2003, we developed a performance as an opportunity for dialogue about Pittsburgh's geography and the city's collective identity.

This performance was constructed around the fictional premise of two private investigators and the public interest group that hired them, the Fourth River Lobbying

Organization Working Group, FLOW. FLOW maintained a downtown window-front office that served as the headquarters for their campaign to lobby the City of Pittsburgh for a re-branding of Pittsburgh as the Four Rivers region of southwestern Pennsylvania.

As geological private investigators, Cat Furman and Macauley Brooks conducted man-on-the-street interviews. They attracted attention in colorful uniforms and life preservers. Among the leads the private investigators received from Pittsburgh citizens were a sighting of the river in the basement of a prominent downtown hotel and tips on how to find the underground water using a dowsing rod. Others told stories of river rats coming up from the river to threaten summer picnics.

Meanwhile, FLOW maintained a downtown storefront office that served as their headquarters.

The window display detailed the clues that had been relayed to the investigators and tracked their progress.

By soliciting these stories from the citizens of Pittsburgh, Furman and Brooks became stewards of the legend and also part of that legend.

Most people were receptive when this absurdity was inserted into the routine of Pittsburgh's business district. Passers-by were willing to engage with the geological investigators and conversations were sparked amongst strangers through the use of the spectacle.

Artist's communication

62 Reflection exercise

a   Close your eyes, and remember a story, legend, myth that was told to you as a child. How was it told? Can you remember where you were? Was there a smell? What was the sound of the voice like? What were you wearing? Write down as much as you can remember.

b   Work with somebody. Interview each other about the first exercise. What did you remember? Use questions to help your partner remember more. What kind of questions help in what situations? Open ones, or those that ask for a yes or no? When you are the one questioned, take note of how you feel being asked about your memories – are you uncomfortable anywhere? Do you not wish to disclose certain things? Do you feel awkward? Or do you feel happy, elated, joyful? Interviewer, likewise, record your feelings – do you feel prying, helpful? Who is in charge? Why? Can you change this dynamic? Change where the interview takes place. Sit on the floor. Share a cup of tea while you are working. What happens to your memory, to your interaction, to your physical pose? Choose a theme, or find a photograph that seems evocative – do other memories appear when you have a different focus?

c   Share your insights about how it feels to be the interviewer and the interviewee, and design a non-threatening, respectful and comfortable interview sequence for a specific project, paying attention to space, time and questions asked.

d   Extrapolate – what cultural conventions come to bear on this exercise? Does every child hear stories? Are stories transmitted in different ways? Books, TV, cinema, religious ceremonies, kindergarten, school, or one-to-one storytelling? Given these specificities, how can you be open about how to garner childhood stories and memories?

Space

What we are concerned with, then, is the long *history of space*, even through space is neither a 'subject' nor an 'object' but rather a social reality – that is to say, a set of relations and forms.

Lefebvre, 1991: 116

Figure 5.4 The Olimpias community video still: *Dancing in the Lake*.
Photo: Petra Kuppers

Bodies and books

Nina Montenegro, student, writing as part of a class exercise: dancing in the library, University of Michigan, Ann Arbor

We attempt to record our histories with our writings, desperate to convey the knowledge that is ours because if we do not it will disappear with us. But will not the books and archives disappear too? Susceptible to the destruction of natural forces; fire or water could do away with us all. Then our own bodies are not so different from a book's body, though we seem animate and they not. These books in their sturdy shelves in rows and rows and tagged by little orange stickers. How lifeless and boring. But their millions of leaves contain bodies and bodies: writers and characters and historical figures and fictional people and all the things we consider beautiful and horrible in this world. Their innards investigate the minutest detail of our bodies and then examine the most infinite space within the space of a few inches. They confront the constitutions and compile histories of their predators, fire and water. And then, they too, of course grow old, like us, losing the privilege to speak and reach the future. But there will always be more. More pages and books and articles and volumes and stacks and libraries. And voices.

Finding inspiration: 'The Lady of the Lake', written on the wall of a fish-and-chip shop in Wales

Mural at the Bwyty West End Café, Llandovery

In the midst of beautiful mountain scenery, about 16 miles from here, is the lovely lake of Llyn y fan fach. Here, legend has it that a beautiful woman appeared to a poor shepherd boy who was so taken by her that he asked for her hand in marriage. She agreed, but only on condition that he wouldn't strike her 3 times. However, he found cause to and she returned to the lake with her dowry of animals. Behind her were left 3 sons who became the famous doctors of Wales.

Earth Stories session idea 2: group visit

For our work, the groups visited places: for the Lady of the Lake videopoem, which we called Earth Stories, we spent afternoons by a lakeside in the Brecon Beacons National Park, and we went on a trip to a nearby castle.

For the videopoem Sleeping Giants, we drove around our village, Ystradgynlais, and its environs in order to find good places from which one could see the giant, which is mainly seen when one travels – from the road. This 'road-trip' imagery became the frame for the videopoem.

All of these trips allowed us to come together as a group, and to become more consciously aware of the landscape that surrounds us. By tying our stories to trips and visits, we enriched our sense memory of the places we live in. For many of us, these trips to castles and lakes brought back childhood memories: as adults, many have few means of access to these spaces, particularly if they don't have their own car. For others, these trips echoed tourist experiences, the kind of space consumption associated with a different kind of habitation. Things we saw and felt then fed back into the videos, including the theme of search, and moving across space together.

In related workshops, focused on the creation of photography websites on the themes of dragons (a strong symbol for Wales, its nationhood and its mythical histories), we spent time in the Swansea Marina and the park of Hendrefoilan House, a part of Swansea University, exploring the water/land boundary of dragons. In other workshops, we visited the ornamental pond in the park of Craig-A-Nos Castle, looking again for water stories, and an old iron smelting factory site, to capture what one of us, a former mine worker, called the Welsh dragon time: the time Wales was strong, sweaty and fiery with molten metal.

During the visits, we searched for and photographed textures that reminded us of our dragon theme: spiky, scaly, red, white, metal and water, wood, old material, shiny material, nature and steel. Out of this story focus on dragons, a different image of our locality arose.

Most localities hold myth memories of some sort, and sometimes these myths can become official, authorized, points for tourist development or civic pride. By revisiting these myths, and the places associated with them, potential new alignments can emerge: places, stories and tourist paths can open up to show the exclusions that occur at these sites. Who is the primary audience of your local tourist attractions, nature walks, nature reserves, public monuments? How can you either supplement or disrupt these sites by diversifying their uses?

Casey, 2002: 167

Choreography

Whereas geography puts its representations of the earth within the embrace of a unitary space that reduces places to points or positions – that is, regards them as *sites* – choreography takes any such space as *already diversified into concrete places*. For the choreographer, even a region is viewed through its constituent places and not as a simple block of space . . .

Session idea

'The Boat of the Dead' (Polynesian myth)

In a cloud floating above the surface of the sea lived two evil spirits. When they arrived close to the island of Hao, they saw through the waves the face of a woman. It was Takua, swimming in the waves looking for some food.

The two spirits surrounded her with their dark arms, and for an instant they brought her to a far and lifeless land. There, they entered inside her body and stole the baby she bore in her belly. From that moment on, Takua would never get pregnant again. Later, silently, the woman came back to life through the waves and the two spirits went away in their cloud.

So the stolen child was raised by the sea itself until he could live alone. The spirits called him Tahoratakarar and with foam and darkness built a big black boat for him. It was Mahina, tied with invisible ropes to the mysteries of the Other World. It sailed by night, and the men felt the chill wind that blew through its sails. It only stopped when somebody was dying, and waited for his soul.

One night, Takua felt that she wanted to take her son back, and she thought he might be the one who was guiding the mysterious boat. She dived deep into the sea, and swimming reached the boat of the souls. There was a rope hanging from a side, and she could climb up to the deck of the boat. In it, there were big corridors in which, without knowing it, hundreds of souls were constantly mingling. There was no sign of life in it, not even a breath. Takua only could see a tall man with a beard, and her blood told her that it was her son.

In the darkness, she touched his shoulder, his face, his eyes.

You are my son, she said.

Yes, mother. But now, our duty is to walk together without recognizing each other.

But your eyes reflect my love, cried the mother.

Maybe it is because they contain everything. Now you have to go. No living being can remain on this ship.

What can I do with you, now that I know you? asked the mother.

When you will reach the island again, everything will be different – finished the son.

When Takua got back to her groom, he found her very different. She had a lost look in her eyes and was always hiding. So he tied her to the table, but the table broke; he lit a fire around her, and the fire died out.

Attracted by her magic powers, many women that had dead relatives came to her, to ask her if she had seen them on the boat, but Takua said she hadn't. They asked her if she could call one, and Takua could do it, for her son let her. From that day, she always could call the souls of the dead.

And the ghost boat continued sailing forever through the islands, to help people to accept death.

(Collected through a web-interface as part of a storytelling project, for the International Year of Freshwater, 2003, www.wateryear2003.org)

5.2 The matter of memory

Memories and stories are not just 'thoughts' – they are often anchored in specific events, materials, sensations, textures, smells and tastes. If you are working in a specific building that is well known to the people you are working with (such as a hospital, a community center or a school), you can go on a roundabout – a procession from room to room, gathering impressions as everybody tells of (or shows) something that happened to her or him (or someone else) in that specific room (or the street corner, garden path etc.). And in the roundabout, a first transformation can happen: a validation of memories, a shared acknowledgment of the riches each member of the participant community can bring to the process. There are ways in which this trans-formation can be marked. This mark creates the space between the everyday group and the momentary communal group – a place between, a new creation. The location that engendered a person's memory can be recorded: a Polaroid might do this, or a digital photo. Or else a name can be bestowed upon that location, and a map be chartered on a large sheet of paper. A movement sequence can bring back memories in different ways: a dance out of the movements of excited children, of subdued or elated patients, or of shared meals or ballroom dancing events, for instance, depending on the location and the memories. Bringing back or re-inventing these different habitations in a place *changes* the place, makes it different, enriches it.

Many of the memories emerging from roundabouts, or from interviews, might be 'banal' at first sight – but the very act of remembering, and the attention given to the specific person, can be empowering, and denies banality to the process. Banality is the stuff out of which life happens, and it is in the connection between the banal or everyday and the 'elevated' realm of art as transformation that the power of community practice can reside.

Figure 5.5a *Castanheiras of Eldorado dos Carajás* (10m × 15m × 25m, burnt Brazil nut trees, oil, stone, cement, original plaque), Pará, Brazil, 1999. The monumental sculpture which marks the location where 19 MST (Landless Movement) peasants were massacred on April 17, 1996. Organized in the shape of the map of Brazil, this national monument of 19 trees was collectively created and built by 800 survivors through storytelling, dance narrative and tribunal theatre, as an intimate world theatre of healing and justice.

Figure 5.5b Young survivors of the massacre of Eldorado dos Carajás painting brazil nut trees burnt, mutilated and felled by the landlords that made their parents landless, chosen to symbolize their personal and regional histories. Ten years after the massacre, the same young people participated in a one-week transformance and workshop within the sculpture, to learn how to transform the invisible scars into resources of community and hope.

To transform these memories into something outside oneself can also provide affirmation.

Working in and across disciplines

- A photo of a location is a location taken outside of its 'normal', everyday environment, and held up in a different light, in a different time.
- A poem about a childhood memory transforms that memory, makes a new product, engaged in creative labor.
- A map allows us to see a location with new eyes. What could be written in the legend (the reading instructions for a map)?
- A dance changes the spatial memories and kinesthetic associations we have with a place, and allows new imaginations about how a place could be used to emerge.
- A theatre piece brings voices, bodies and spaces into new constellations.

Interview with Dan Baron Cohen

This interview by Katherine Anger covers Cohen's work in Brazil with the Landless Movement, his work with a community on a monument to the massacre of April 17, 1996, when landless peasants occupying and using agricultural land were killed and persecuted by government forces.

'The culture of the barricade, of opposition needs to celebrate its own lucid rage,' [Dan] explains, 'but what about that internal world behind the barricades? What happens to the doubts, fears, questions whispered in the silences between confrontations? Those voices of intimate reflection are an enormous archive of knowledge, but remain hidden behind profound doubt and fear.'

The starting-point of all his projects is releasing that knowledge 'from all its obstacles, from fear, from lack of self-esteem, from prejudice.'

P R A C T I C E   E X A M P L E

The process begins with a question. Groups of between six and eight people are asked to bring an object – perhaps an idea, perhaps the thing itself. An intimate object, an object that reveals them to themselves, that speaks of their wider meanings.

People might bring a ring. A shoe. A medicinal plant. An heirloom. As others in the group question them about their choice, slowly people begin to tell stories, present fragments from their lives, speaking about the world and their place in it. In this way they reveal themselves to one another, grow comfortable with intimacy, build a method of active listening and exchange in which all the people engaged in the dialogue are transformed.

They then are asked to choose by consensus a collective 'intimate object' for the group. No-one can propose their own, so the process of questioning and consensus-building grows. This is then repeated in a larger group. It takes time. The questions create a network of concerns, responses, curiosities which reveal the group to itself. In this way a large number of people can come to a collective proposal and rapidly build a community of empathy and solidarity. The strength and power of this emotional candour can be extraordinary.

Dan, who has been evolving his working methods for over 15 years, describes it as a process of 'learning democracy'.

He asked the MST [Movimento Dos Sem Terra – Movement of the Landless] Settlement of the Seventeenth of April in Carajas to identify objects that would articulate personal, regional, national history – in which people could see themselves and the massacre. . . .

Anger, 2001

P
R
A
C
T
I
C
E

E
X
A
M
P
L
E

Encounters: Sharrow stories, facilitated by Ruth Ben-Tovim and Trish O'Shea, UK

Encounters take up residence in disused shops, working with local people and visitors to create art works exploring the themes of people, place and community.

So far there have been three Encounters shops. All have been based in Sharrow, Sheffield, and have become galleries and meeting places in which to collect and exchange experiences, memories, objects and thoughts about everyday life in the area. The artists, who also live in Sharrow, use performance, film, photography, visual art and text to collect material and create interactive and evolving displays within the shop.

Communication by the artists, see also Gwen Robertson in the *Reader*

Working together, no one imagination rules – but remember that power is always an issue, and there will be balances, tensions and silencings in any community situation.

The next task is now to build a new piece with the stories, legends or myths. What are the affects of the collection? How can these actions reverberate?

There are many different ways in which stories can be collected, and the act of collecting itself can change the physical structures of community environments. How do maps of places change with projects such as Encounters?

Rachel Rosenthal

I know exactly how to fix everything. You know what I'm saying? The first thing you do is provide free abortion and contraception, making it totally available globally with a huge educational blitz from every country. Then you have to completely change the whole educational structure. You start Earth Studies in kindergarten, and they get more and more sophisticated as you grow up. You make Earth Studies the major function of education. You teach people where they live. They live on the Earth. And what does that mean? What kind of responsibilities, what kind of problems? What is the profile of the planet on which we live? Unless you can begin to reach people from the earliest years with the consciousness of the planet and what it means to be a human being, one of many species, one of many species of this planet, we won't survive. . . .

Even if you are not a great artist and are not going to be able to contribute on a professional level, you are aligning your energy field with the energy field of planetary creation. You are feeding that field, instead of feeding the field that destroys and kills. On that level also, art is extremely important. Again, this is not something that you can measure. Art, because of the nature of what it is, is not something that you can approach with a study group to ask, 'Is this effective and what does it really do?' You can't do that – it's like a psychic phenomenon – when you look at it, it's gone. And yet, on a spiritual level, I think that it is doing its work and has to continue to do its work. So that's where I am optimistic . . .

Rosenthal, in Lacy, 1991: 14–16

Figure 5.6 Performance still from *Warning – This Product May Contain Nuts*. Performed by Freedom in Dance intergenerational group (10 dancers aged 13–73 years), Project Director: Diane Amans, Nuffield Theatre, Lancaster, UK.   Photo: Brian Slater

**P
R
A
C
T
I
C
E

E
X
A
M
P
L
E**

Earth Stories session idea 3: digging into an image

In all sessions leading up to the recording of the videopoem, themes developed out of previously created material: there was no prescribed path, no idea that came before the workshops started. The myths were our starting point, and our common goal was communicating something of the way our minds work, including the anxieties and elations that come with the conditions many of us are diagnosed with. We all identified as mental health system survivors, and we wanted to share something of our world, but without outing specific people among us as voice hearers, people diagnosed with schizophrenia, or with bi-polar disorder.

In all sessions, we found that something someone said allowed all of us to go on a journey, focus in on a feeling, an image, an idea. In the Sleeping Giant video, that idea became 'the cave of the heart' – an image one of us had created in the Childhood Memories workshops.

In our sessions, we never discussed or queried the poems created by individual members: no one had to be afraid to be questioned or analyzed. Sharing was often enough, and expressing delight in each other's creativity. But when an image really echoed with us, we made it the theme of the next four-line poem session.

Below are the results of two exercises that took their cue from the idea of being inside the Giant's body. The Cave of the Heart exercise then led to a movement sequence: we played with candles, mirrors, a dark room and a circle made out of our bodies to create a place of intimacy, exploration and sensual communication.

Poem exercise instruction: how it feels to be in the fist of the Giant

In the fist of the Giant reaching up to the sky
The solidness of the stone feels safe and secure
I can see light through the crevices of his fingers
At any moment I could be flung with huge force into an unknown land

He will be careful carrying me in the cave of his hand.
I am as a small as a marble in a child's fist.

Follow-on poem exercise instruction: moving in the Cave of the Heart

As deep as you can go. The Giant's heart would be a cave of stalagmites and pools, an unchartered country of minerals and precious stones.

How to move along its rocky ridges and furrows?

Muscles surround me
As I unwind my hair
Weaving a shiny band.

As we continued on our journey, we wove our poem lines into a weft: a communal fabric exploring the tapestry of our memories and our relations to our landscapes.

The format of a particular legend or myth gives a good structure for a long-term project: there are always more ways of digging into the material, and finding new angles. At the same time, the narrative structure of the myth creates a sense of familiarity and closure to the work, even if people drop in and out of the workshops over the course of the project.

63 Reflection exercise

You have now become familiar with some of the working methods in the Earth Stories workshops. Think about the following issues:

- How is progression managed?
- What possibilities and problems can you see emerging in these workshops, as they unfold over many weeks?
- What strategies can you use to keep people involved, interested, moving forward together?

Story weaving

The Spiderwomen Theatre is a Native American woman's theatre company, established in 1975, when Muriel Miguel facilitated a workshop of native and non-native women in New York City. The ensemble takes its name from the Hopi goddess who wove humans into life and taught them to weave. Weaving is at the heart of many of their performances: they bring together different storylines and movements, and weave a new web with them. Their performances use collected native quilts as backdrops: communal creation, and intersection lines and texture shape their aesthetic. The three sisters who founded this vibrant theatre group call their process 'story weaving'; the meshing of stories with words and movement to create an overlay of interlocking stories in motion.

64 Reflection exercise

a   In a group of three, write a four-line poem. Use as your inspiration the room you are working in (a color, a view, a story?). After you've read each four-liner, a different person calls the next inspiration, something spontaneously emerging from the material read out.

b   After everybody has called a theme, read the poems again: this time, not each poem separately, but by going in the round, every participant reciting one line from their poem, until all three four-liners are read.

c   Discuss how it felt, and what the result was.

d   Now take three movement ideas from the communal poem you have created: three images or actions. Each person responds physically to the ideas, and links the three poses up into a movement sequence.

e   And now try to make connections between your different movement sequences.

f   End by memorizing one line from the communal poem, and recite it as the three of you move together through your different movement sequences, making connections. Feel free to improvise.

g   Discuss: what felt good or hard to do? Why? How could it be made easier? Was there anything you felt resistant to? How did timing work? How could you move the process on at this point? Where could it go?

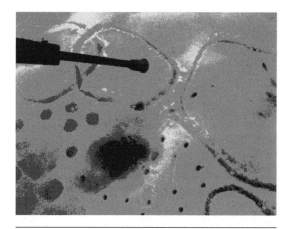

Figure 5.7 The Olimpias Tracks workshop, Rhode Island, USA, Winter 2004. Weaving addenda like wheelchairs, crutches and canes into our environment – leaving tracks in snow.   Photo: Petra Kuppers

5.3 Genre

There are many useful mechanisms of storytelling you can fall back on to create coherency without strict **narrative**. Depending on our cultural background, we tend to organize narratives and images into **genres** – romance, heroic, gothic, sci-fi, horror, news story etc. To recast stories by looking at them through the lens of a genre can be a useful way to generate new material, to find new conflicts or new angles, or to expose some of the contractions underlying everyday life. It is also a useful way to think about **belonging**, and about making connections back from individual stories to communal stories, and the larger group.

**P
R
A
C
T
I
C
E
E
X
A
M
P
L
E**

Earth Stories session idea 4: genre

In the second workshop leading up to the Lady of the Lake video, we looked in detail at the gothic genre, or the dark fairy tale.

a Brainstorming
We started out by brainstorming what 'gothic' meant to us, and we created a long list:

castles	stone statues
princesses	gargoyles
cobwebs	well
quest	owl
dragons	cave
circle of fire	poisoned apple
black cat	walled garden
witch	poison ivy.
wizard	

b Association poem
Using some elements from this list as inspiration, we all created a short, four-line poem. In order to get away from 'storytelling', we called this poem 'The Gothic Dream of the Lady of the Lake'.

Many of the lines created in this session found their way into the final video, and the gothic mood pervades much of the final product. We talked about shooting the video in black and white, to capture this 'gothic' feeling, but decided in the end against it, since we wanted to avoid falling into the 'mad woman' stereotype that some of us associated with the gothic genre, and that seemed particular problematic to us given that we wanted to show a different image of mental health difference.

One of the poetic dreams we kept in the final video is the 'marble lady sequence': the lady dreams that she is walking into a secret garden, where marble statues wait to be called to life. We liked the sense of history that statues create, and the sense of being at one with the landscape, so we shot ourselves as statues in the hills.

5.4 Ritual

Genre is one way of linking the specific to the wider, shared world. Another avenue that can be pursued is based on a physical experience, on the shared experience of time and space in (secular) ritual. The emphasis of ritual work is on the group, not on an audience. Rituals can be based on seasons, act as the root of childhood games, or are both integrated into and emerge from local spiritual and religious practices. They can also build from more abstract ideas: acts of the circulation of energy, gifting, establishing social relationships, echoing and forming patterns and geometries. Transformation and change are at the heart of many rituals; at the same time, they can work to stabilize existing social and cultural structures. This dichotomy sustains many community artists' interest in ritual work.

Figure 5.8 Community dance workshop, Cultural Development Network and Ausdance Victoria, at Dancehouse, Melbourne, Australia, 2006. Working with ideas from fibre arts, we are weaving a dance and our stories of fabric and touch memories around a piece of felt created from Tasmanian merino wool.
Photo: Petra Kuppers

A definition of ritual

Olsen, 2002: 219

A ritual is a focused container for experience. Communal or personal, the precision and repetition of ritual creates its charged effect. A simplified view of a ritual or ceremony of transformation shows three essential stages: preparation, enactment, and return, including completion and time for recovery. Thus, the end becomes the beginning, connecting to the future as well as reflecting on the past. Ritual stages also require transition from one dimension to another. This period, called a liminal state, is a betwixt-and-between time when one is neither who one was nor who one will be. It is a particular potent and dangerous period, requiring care, teaching, and support from elders and the community. These periods of vulnerability and heightened potential occur for each of us in our journey through life.

a   In a group of five or more, create a ritual sequence based on one of the following three spatial arrangements: a circle, two parallel lines, and a group and a single individual outside it. Some sample 'materials': touches, mirroring, handing something on, sounding, external objects.

b   Discuss the effects of your ritual: how does it feel to work in this arrangement? What is comfortable, what is uncomfortable? What memories came up? Who holds the power to change parts of the ritual? Is there a moment of potential, of renewal, or opening, as Andrea Olsen described? Are there any insights that you can bring into your own practice?

c   Map the shapes onto existing rituals you are familiar with: round-robins, wedding ceremonies, religious ceremonies, sports events etc.

Repetition and difference? *The Golden Bough* (1911–15)

James Gordon Frazer provided one of the most influential storylines about the echoes of myths cross-culturally, but from a deeply ethnocentric perspective located in a British Empire perspective, after collecting (often second-hand) myths from across the globe:

> Dionysius was not the only Greek deity whose tragic story and ritual appear to reflect the decay and revival of vegetation. In another form and with a different application the old tale reappears in the myth of Demeter and Persephone. Substantially their myth is identical with the Syrian one of Aphrodite (Astarte) and Adonis, the Phrygian one of Cybele and Attis, and the Egyptian one of Isis and Osiris. In the Greek fable, as in its Asiatic and Egyptian counterparts, a goddess mourns the loss of a loved one, who personifies the vegetation, more especially the corn, which dies in winter to revive in spring; only whereas the Oriental imagination figured the loved and lost one as a dead lover or a dead husband lamented by his leman or his wife, Greek fancy embodied the same idea in the tenderer and purer form of a dead daughter bewailed by her sorrowing mother.
>
> Frazer, 1922

66 Research exercise

Read the citation in the box above. Research the stories associated with the various mythological characters mentioned here, and also rituals associated with them. Then think more about the connections and associations Frazer makes. What problems emerge in intercultural ritual and myth work? Can myths (and the rituals that are often connected to them) be reduced to their structural similarities? Are there any problems in creating rituals with corn-husks, or with moon symbols, with yin/yang symbolism, or with alchemic signs? What are the relationships between cultural tourism, a sense of 'the authentic', and romanticism?

Joseph Roach, *Cities of the Dead*

The three-sided relationship of memory, performance, and substitution becomes most acutely visible in mortuary ritual. This study closely attends to those epiphanies. In any funeral, the body of the deceased performs the limits of the community called into being by the need to mark its passing. United around a corpse that is no longer inside but not yet outside of its boundaries, the members of a community may reflect on its symbolic embodiment of loss and renewal. In a jazz funeral [in New Orleans], the deceased is generally accompanied at least part of the way to the cemetery by a brass band and a crowd of mourners who follow an elegant grand marshall (or 'Nelson').

Roach, 1996: 14

Earth Stories session idea 5: ritual

In our meetings, we used movement, dance and drama as well as creative writing to bring together the images and themes of the final video. The Mental Health User Group met in a house with a garden, as well as a private home up in the Brecon Beacons, but for many sessions we left the safety of our armchairs and went out into the sun instead.

One of the movement ideas we explored was the ring, and rituals surrounding the ring. We stood or sat in a circle, and focused on the energy created by just being together, in stillness, outside, in the ancient form of the ring.

In our writing, we had heard each other's stories of going up to stone circles as children.

Small stone circles can still be found in the parks in as well as the land surrounding Ystradgynlais. We wanted to connect to some of the strength of being in a place for a long time, and taking comfort and strength from each other's presence. We found many ways of using the circle form:

- We memorized brief bits of our poems, and voiced them to another in the circle, either moving or standing still.
- We started in a circle, then left to explore a part of the garden in private, maybe taking a piece of the garden (respectfully, without disturbance), and then came back to share our traces. We created a gifting place in the middle of our circle, and, after showing everybody what we had found, placed stones there, grains of earth, a single flower, a leaf, or a line that had popped into our heads.
- We played around with ideas of rooting in the earth, standing tall, lifting our heads into the clouds: basic drama and dance exercises.
- We danced in the ring to the tune of a flute one of us brought along. Handing the flute around, we gave ourselves permission to remember long forgotten skills many of us had learned in primary school.

In the Earth Stories video, we retained the sense of belonging and strength we took from the circle as we decided to have the coming together into a circle on a hill as the final shot.

In Sleeping Giants, we used the ring and circle movement to create a sense of oneness and coherent movement in the centre of the videopoem – the cave of the heart.

PRACTICE EXAMPLE

5.5 Sharing stories

P
R
A
C
T
I
C
E

E
X
A
M
P
L
E

Near/far/in/out

This is a performance work driven and inspired by the dialogue among four generations of the LGBT communities. Personal stories of one era intersect with those of another to reflect moments of history and individual change, generating a theatrical event that incorporates text, movement, metaphor and music. A team of Dance Exchange artists led by co-artistic director Peter DiMuro will be joined by members of the local LGBT communities at sites across the country to create and perform this innovative new work.

Project description from Liz Lerman Dance Exchange, a US-based company

One of the challenges of working with personal stories and small, gesture-based movement work is sharing: how can you as facilitator bring something of the intimacy and content of your sessions into material aimed for public consumption, without endangering the privacy and integrity of your participants? How can you ensure that you do not just 'use' their material to create your own vision of the art work? In what way can you ensure that the process is community-focused?

There are no right or wrong ways of going about this, but these should be important considerations in the construction of the process.

---

67 Reflection exercise

Think about how privacy, beauty, personal voice and ownership express themselves differently when community performers share their stories in these art forms:

- stage performance – script
- stage performance – dance
- stage improvisation
- video
- film
- songs – sound improvisation
- songs – rehearsed music
- tableaux
- performances in everyday environments
- sculpture
- creative writing
- poetry improvisation.

In the following, I will discuss a range of examples of sharings, using different processes and media.

Sharing through visual arts

The exchange of personal stories was the core impetus of Coastal Mappings, a community arts project that I undertook as part of a six-month Caroline Plummer Fellowship in Community Dance at the University of Otago, New Zealand, during 2005. The Coastal Mappings project had multiple components, featuring movement choirs in public libraries, performance installations in the Dunedin Art Gallery and on a beach, and 'dance with a difference' workshops for people who experience pain or fatigue. The part of the project I wish to describe here took place at the Otago Community Hospice, where I worked in both group and one-on-one sessions with day patients and in-patients. Photography became an important component of our work, as it allowed us to share something of what we were doing with people outside the hospice. In these sessions, we began by working with regional myths, and moved towards thinking about places and spaces where we've felt comforted, that we had called home, and that acted as reservoirs of memory. Over time, we mapped parts of our life experiences onto specific landscapes, or memories of these landscapes, using movement as a way to access memory. We worked with materials I brought in response to stories told to me and places mentioned (stones, bark, wood, shells etc.), and we used small movements, gestures and caresses to respond to them and their energies. I described earlier in this chapter (p. 137) how Maori/Pakeha cultural contact expressed itself through some of the legend work, and the participants' labor with place names. Another kind of cultural contact emerged around issues of death and life: the animation of nature, including trees and stones, had a strong impact on workshop participants, as they negotiated the imminence of their own death. Many of the hospice participants worked with this beautiful and careful attention to the breath of life in nature, expressed in small tender gestures and movements.

In order to capture what we were doing, and to share it with the wider community, we took photos of our hands, with the camera circulating among us. We looked at every image together, building up further layers of impressions, stories and emotions around them. In between my weekly visits, I manipulated the colors of the images, responding to suggestions and echoing some of the content with which participants imbued the specific movement or moment captured. When I came back, we discussed these altered images, rejected some changes or enhanced others, and continued to build narrative around them, making them deep reservoirs of individuality and traces of being in the world.

The first story that began our workshops, and that we returned to again and again, was a Maori story about the creation of a lake in New Zealand's Southern Alps, not far from the Dunedin location of the hospice. The part of the story we focused on describes a giant who desired a Maori princess, abducted her, but was hunted down by the woman's lover, a warrior who slew the giant, and burned his body. Where his body burned away, water rushed in to form Lake Wakatipu. At the bottom of the lake, the giant's heart is still beating – and in response, the lake breathes, heaving slowly up and down.

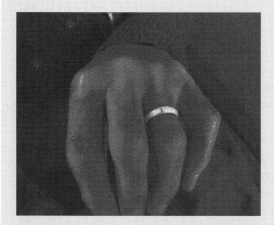

Figure 5.9 *Josephine's Unbroken Ring*.
Photo: Collaborative, The Olimpias, 2005

Figure 5.10 *Harriet's Peninsula*.   Photo: Collaborative,
The Olimpias, 2005

The story had many connotations for participants: love surviving, a heart still beating after many destructive experiences, a strange biology deep inside familiar tissue. And so the heart found its way into our photographs multiple times, as did water creatures and sea life.

The blue/purple image in Figure 5.9 is called *Josephine's Unbroken Ring*. She created the pose in response to the giant story, and also in order to show the ring that was broken during her chemotherapy, when her fingers swelled. Josephine saw no point in repairing the ring, and in all important ways, the ring she has worn for over thirty years is still unbroken. 'The other creature' – the cancer – that is how she talked about the cells talking over her life, and the final image is shaded in blues and greens to capture the Taniwha, the water creature, a figure that she remembered from legends and from the private stories she made up as a child. The ring area remains gold: through color, the break in the ring is mended.

Josephine's fingers form the shape of an anatomical heart, and she wanted to emphasize the motion of sheltering – a gesture she used to create another image, in which she holds a piece of tree bark tenderly, expressing what she felt as its loneliness, and its need for tenderness.

Another patient's image (Figure 5.10) is called *Harriet's Peninsula*, and it responds in coloring and shape to Harriet's stories about the place she has chosen for her burial: a wind-swept old graveyard far out on the Otago Peninsula with its muted greens and yellows, with a glowing sea shell. When I visited her bedside, Harriet spoke of her love for this countryside, and of her many memories of walking on its beaches as a child, listening to stories and legends about natural features and local inhabitants her storyteller uncle shared with her. She also worked with the story of the giant, picking up a Paua shell for its textures and colors, and likening it to the heart.

Harriet not only gave me permission to talk and write about some of the things she shared with me, she also felt strongly about the digital photo's status as witness and memorial to her. Most people who worked with me participated actively in shaping their images, filling them with meanings (and all images were only released once participants found them finished and gave permission). In constructing the images and stories, the outdoors and the many natural beauties of specific locations in and around Dunedin came to life in the landscapes of our bodies, filled with energy and emotion.

The photographs share a new and unfamiliar image of the hospice, of people on the edge of life, and specifically of people with terminal cancer diagnoses, with the wider Dunedin and Otago communities. In these images, end-of-life periods and the hospice emerge as times and spaces of beauty and dignity, deeply connected with their environment.

68 Hand exercise

a   Take a digital camera, and shoot images of your hands, as well as the hands of a partner. Look at your images: note the individuality of hands, their extensive movement range, their color, shape, their ability to hold tension or relax. Find ways of modulating the images of your hands – create different moods, emotions, associations.

b   At various points in this chapter, you've been asked to find a story. Use one of these, or any story/personal memory that is significant to you. Using the expressiveness of your hands, create an image that holds associations of your story.

Figure 5.11 HIV/AIDS mural project in a women's prison in Connecticut, USA.
Photo: Ana Flores

Tableaux and AIDS mural

Ana Flores shares the process she engaged in when she was asked to create a collaborative HIV/AIDS mural project in a women's prison in Connecticut. She used performance and personal writing as well as visual approaches to share the prison stories:

> During our brainstorming session, a number of writing prompts were developed to encourage the AIDS narratives from the students:
>
> - Imagine you are the HIV/AIDS virus, what would you want to say?
> - Explain to a family member or loved one that you have HIV/AIDS.
> - Write a letter to a friend who has passed away as a result of AIDS.
> - Share a memory or story with someone who has HIV/AIDS.
>
> Excited by the compassionate and creative educators I had met, I began the project with a core group of women, members of a AIDS/HIV support group and other students interested in participating. There were 12 in this small group. I showed slides of Greek vases and discussed some of the myths and battles illustrated on them. We also spoke about the often invisible battle being waged against HIV/AIDS by themselves and loved ones. They began to see the parallels between themselves, and the stylized warriors, the gods and goddesses depicted on these ancient clay surfaces. My studio was the back half of a large classroom used to teach a Health aide certificate program; during 'open studio' sessions other inmates could come in and help or just observe. I also did short workshops around this theme with other groups of women.
>
> The AIDS narrative writing theme inspired many personal essays and poems, and from these we chose compelling anecdotes to act out. Using the hallway as a small theater area, a small group was asked to act out scenes of professional and emotional support, living with the disease and mourning the loss of loved ones. The actors would freeze in different positions which captured the essence of these situations, students who were not acting would draw them full scale by tracing their bodies and shadows directly onto large brown paper. These life size figures on brown paper were then composed into monumental vase shapes outlined on wooden panels. I had chosen to work with two traditional shapes found in Greek vases: the 'Kraters', expansive, bold shaped urns with florid handles used to commemorate victories in battle and 'Lekythos', tall slim vessels with minimal handles that held oil for libations to the dead.

Ana's full project description is in the *Reader*.

Sharing through movement

Rudolph von Laban, an Austrian-Hungarian dance artist working in Germany and the UK was one of the most influential thinkers and movers in the push to bring dance away from the stage and ownership of trained dancers and into the wider community. In particular, Laban worked with movement choirs – a form of dance that combined expressionist ideas about bodies and movement and a commitment to dance by lay people, using 'natural' movement. Movement choirs rely on group work, but without a sense of 'unison' patterns (see also Benson, in the *Reader*). Oftentimes, storytelling is an element in movement choirs.

In movement choirs, the group agrees on core moments that encapsulate a significant aspect of a story told. In a group improvisation, the group expresses these moments with the participants' whole bodies. Unison and copying others is not important. Find connections, work collaboratively to bring multiple bodies together into an energy sequence. Focus on energies and tensions rather than 'mimicry'.

Now link these moments together.

In Zurich, Switzerland, Claude Perrottet taught Laban movement until his death in 2001. During his summer schools, he led movement choirs based on myths. He broke the myths down himself, and challenged the participants to find movements for them. In one choir movement, a ship is embodied by a number of participants arranging themselves into ribs of the ship, while others stepped between those as rowers, and a group of three participants created a mermaid as the galleon figure.

P
R
A
C
T
I
C
E

E
X
A
M
P
L
E

Figure 5.12 Community dance students bringing performance into the community as part of a movement choir outside the Dunedin public library, New Zealand, 2005.   Photo: Petra Kuppers

At the Dunedin Public Library, New Zealand, students in a community dance course engaged with me in a Story/Movement exchange. We stayed in the large, sprawling library that gives out into a shopping center, and spoke to patrons. After asking if they'd care to participate, we offered them a movement for a story. Many people were happy to engage with us, and the students and I received rich life-stories and confidences from children, elders, tourists and many others. After they shared their story with their listener, the listener offered a movement that honored or remembered an aspect of the story just shared.

Each hour we came together in the library foyer, and shared the stories (those where permission was given to share) and the movements. Members of the public who had spent time with us individually also joined us in these sharings. Everybody picked up the movement offered to the tellers by each participant, and translated it into their own bodies, making connections in keeping with the story that gave rise to the movement. We then linked those movements into a choir – a sequence of shared movements, with stations where sequences began and ended, and used them to move through the different levels of the library and out into the shopping center. Movement ideas we used included 'passing a rugby ball with our whole body' (one of the people who exchanged a story for a movement was the son of a New Zealand All Black rugby player), 'hiding' (from a sad childhood story one person heard), and 'the lifting of a cloud' (from an immigrant who told of his traumatic fight with the New Zealand immigration authorities).

As part of a residency at the University of New Mexico, Albuquerque, US, I led a different movement choir event around the campus's center pond, inspired by various Albuquerque locations. From the leaflet we handed out as part of the public performance:

- The chorus moments you witness grow out of the interplay of repetition and difference, as it presented itself to us seeing the public art columns at Washington Middle School Park, the lithographs in the gallery at the North Forth Arts Center, the ancient art works at the Petroglyph Momument, and in the rows of grass and stone along the Sandia Mountains.
- Working together, our differences allow beauty to emerge.
- Inspirations for the separate movements:
  - Bird curiosity
  - Tumbleweed
  - Rain on the desert
  - The shuffle of a man with feet wrapped in plastic, met along Central
  - Snow slowly falling
  - Dream movement
  - Storytellers, and the strength of finding new forms and new myths
  - Sculpture Tree: we invite you to respond to our performance by leaving something behind. Please feel free to take a clay plate, and work on it while you watch us – let your hands respond to what you see, hear or feel. We are collecting these witnessing sculptures on the site.

During the performance, which flowed from site to site three times over the span of three hours, we moved from bridges over the pond to a tree grove, from a flowering cherry tree to an artificial waterfall overlooking the site. The sculpture tree, full of small natural clay sculptures, remained on site long after the performance was over. A poet, Hana Li, and an opera student, Heather Alvarez, also joined the choir, and guided us with improvised poetry and sound-work from one of the performance stations to another.

Sharing through theatre

In *Community Theatre*, Eugene Van Erven writes about a number of international community theatre projects (see also the *Reader*). In one production, by Strut Theatre in the Netherlands, community actors work with professional playwrights to sculpt a performance from improvisational scenes. *Tears in the Rain* was an intercultural show about parenting issues. After the performance, the actors shared their evaluative comments.

69 Reflection exercise

Go outside, and spend five minutes recording mentally what you see. Now go for a short walk, and continue recording. Find a different place, and spend a last five minutes recording what you see there. Come back, and share experiences with your colleagues. Pick a small number of core images from each participant, and find ways of creating a movement choir out of them.

Strut Theatre

Tears in the Rain has made Hans [a participant] realize that there are many cross-cultural similarities in the way parents suffer for their children: 'I believe the power of this kind of theatre is that it makes people think that they can do something about their problems themselves, not by providing easy answers but by giving them a few other perspectives on the matter.' Talât, who cheerfully participated in the process from beginning to end, eloquently sums up the benefits of multicultural community theatre:

> It gets people talking; it touches them because it comes straight out of our lives, straight out of the neighbourhoods where we live, where all the parents want the best for their children, regardless of whether they are Dutch, Moroccan, Turkish, or something else. You know, when you look around you see a wealthy country; that is why our parents came in the first place. There are some things that Dutch people do well, so we tried taking Dutch parents as our example. But the thing is, you never know what really goes on behind those doors in all those Dutch households. And when you start putting some of that stuff on stage as well, then you no longer have to see them as ideal parents. You realize that you yourself do a lot of things right and that perhaps the best thing to do is to be open to other cultures and pick the good things out of each one and apply them the best you can in your own family.
>
> Van Erven, 2001: 88

PRACTICE EXAMPLE

Figure 5.13 Witnessing sculptures. Passers-by were given pieces of clay to mould while they watched a movement choir process around campus. The pieces were lodged in this tree. University of New Mexico, Albuquerque, 2005.   Photo: Petra Kuppers

70 Reflection exercise

What are issues of concern in your community or environment? Do you believe that sharing personal practices through theatre can help towards finding new perspectives on these problems? Make a list of five issues, and discuss how improvisational scenes can show different habits or actions by different people.

71 Reflection exercise

If you have access to a video camera, use it, and gather personal stories about a specific theme of your choice. Think about how you frame people, whether or not you are in the frame, what effects backgrounds have, movement and soundscape. Pay attention to how people interact with the camera, how their demeanor changes between addressing you as an individual, and addressing the camera. How can you make aesthetic use of this difference?

Figure 5.14 Community Performance/Disability Culture workshop at the first Summer University in Disability Studies, Bremen, Germany, 2003.
Photo: Petra Kuppers

Sharing through multi-media

Irish immigrant playwright Kaite O'Reilly has adapted the Foursight Theatre's *Reans Girls* for BBC Radio 4. This excerpt here from the opening of the play juxtaposes these immigrant women's lives with the racist 'Rivers of Blood' speech by Enoch Powell (Member of Parliament for Wolverhampton in the 1960s). It is provided with permission from Kaite O'Reilly, Foursight Theatre and BBC Radio Drama for the West Midlands. Shared and separate spaces, family relationships, and language (as well as accents) become important dramatic markers of transportation and co-habitation.

Reans Girls – a celebration of the women of the area of Whitmore Reans in Wolverhampton, UK, by Foursight Theatre

All the source material for this project came from twenty-four women who moved to Whitmore Reans, Wolverhampton from all over the world. These women were interviewed and each one of them was asked the same series of questions. We listened to all of the interviews, most of which were two hours each, and noted all the things they said that were of particular relevance to the making of theatre – images, smells, music references, and clear stories about the reasons why they left their homeland, their journeys to the UK, and their impressions and experiences on arrival.

The setting for the piece was derived from the many references made to the old slipper baths in Wolverhampton – where the women took a weekly bath. We decided to recreate the baths within the theatre space, with a central pool area and surrounding cubicles. We were then able to think about how and where we might place the different stories and references using the varied spaces created.

Most of what was created was either taken directly from the interviews with the women and then literally rehearsed and put into a space – or the idea was almost totally fully formed and then just put on its feet. There was very little devising in the process (unlike most of our work) – as we literally had three days on the set before we opened to the public. So for example, we would lift a story from the interview, an actor learned it and then it was directed in situ and that was it.

Our audiences were enthralled. Only twenty-five could experience the show at a time, and following a section at the beginning where they sat together by the side of the pool, they were then split into groups of five and guided on their journey around the spaces. They encountered a room of masks in which there were three real faces that whispered to them about the loss of friends, family, lifestyle. They sat in a multi-ethnic café and tasted food from around the world. They listened to a woman from Barbados tell her story to them as she bathed. They went on a bus ride around the local area, all within the confines of a cubicle on industrial springs. And they found themselves interacting with suitcase installations and sound-pads in the Lost and Found cubicle. They listened to world music, watched an Indian Kathak dancer and witnessed women working cloth together in a large pool of water. As they left, they themselves were washed in a shower of water. The nature of the piece provided the possibility of intimate exchanges – both between audience members themselves (for example, eating a meal with complete strangers) and with the performers.

The interactive, tactile nature of the piece ensured that the audience became intrinsically involved – I like to think they were *transported* for a while to a place that gave voice to their neighbors, with whom they were able to eat, laugh, cry and bathe with.

Personal communication and interview with Foursight Theatre

LOU:	(INTERNAL) You know what they say, just bang two tins together and you're home! Home. Nothing is sweeter than Badian laughter, women laughing together. You plait one another's hair and polish each other's nails and it's more than a sisterhood, it's a –
F/X:	THERE IS A CRASH FROM THE ROOM ABOVE.
	(CALLS) Winston! You're like an elephant! The neighbour's on nights – I hope you haven't woken him, boy!
F/X/GRAMS	WE PASS THROUGH THE CEILING TO WINSTON'S ROOM, ABOVE, HE IS DANCING TO REGGAE, HE RAISES THE VOLUME.
LOU:	(OFF) Winston!
F/X:	**THE NEIGHBOUR BANGS AGAINST THE WALL.**
	WE PASS THROUGH TO PADDY MURPHY'S BEDROOM NEXT DOOR, THE REGGAE IS DISTORTED. SINEAD TRIES TO APPEASE HER FATHER AS HE BANGS THE WALL.
SINEAD:	Don't, Da! I have to face him at school! Please . . . don't be mean to Winston.
F/X:	**FROM BELOW, BRIDIE (SINEAD'S MOTHER) CALLS UP THE STAIRS.**
BRIDIE:	(OFF) Sinead, Bryan, Michaela, Patrick! Get your backsides out of bed and down these stairs, or I'll tan them for you!
SINEAD:	Coming!!
F/X:	WE FOLLOW SINEAD DOWN THE STAIRS.
GRAMS:	AN IRISH BALLAD PLAYS ON THE RADIO.
BRIDIE:	(CLOSER) And where are you going in such a rush, young lady?
F/X:	SINEAD PULLS ON HER COAT, PICKS UP BAG.
SINEAD:	School!
BRIDIE:	And since when have you been so keen (on school)?
SINEAD:	(OVERLAPPING) I'm gone!
BRIDIE:	But I've got rashers cooked. . . .
F/X:	**SINEAD FLIES OUT OF THE DOOR, IT SLAMS.**
	Sinead!
GRAMS/F/X:	THE IRISH BALLAD MOMENTARILY GROWS LOUDER AS WE 'PASS' IT, MOVING THROUGH TO MINAXI'S HOUSE.
MINAXI:	(GUJARATI) You do well at school, today. (ENGLISH) Be good, beti, study hard and do what the teacher tells you.
F/X:	**THE OTHER MOTHERS AND CHILDREN ARE HEARD, SIMULTANEOUS WITH MINAXI'S LINES:**
	(GUJARATI) Kavita! Your sister is going. Kavita! Hurry, now, you'll be late for school!
LOU:	(OFF) Winston!
BRIDIE:	(OFF) Bryan, Josephine, Patrick Murphy – get down these stairs . . . !
MARGOT:	(OFF, IN HUNGARIAN) I'm off to work! Be good!
F/X/GRAMS:	THE SOUNDSCAPE OF DIFFERENT VOICES, MUSIC AND LANGUAGES, COMBINED WITH FEET RUSHING DOWN STAIRS, SLAMMING DOORS, ETC, BUILDS TO A CACOPHONY, A TOWER OF BABEL, OUT OF WHICH COMES:
	TITLES: REANS GIRLS

SCENE THREE. RIVERS OF BLOOD

F/X: ENOCH POWELL'S VOICE, BACKED BY A DISTANT AEROPLANE COMING CLOSER

ENOCH POWELL: It almost passes belief that at this moment 20 or 30 additional immigrant children are arriving from overseas in Wolverhampton alone every week – and that means 15 or 20 families a decade or two hence. Those whom the gods wish to destroy, they first make mad. We must be mad, literally mad as a nation to be permitting the annual inflow of some 50,000 dependants, who are for the most part the material of the future growth of the immigrant-descended population. It is like watching a nation busily engaged in heaping up its own funeral pyre.

F/x: THE ROAR OF THE AEROPLANE COMING INTO LAND SLICES THROUGH POWELL'S SPEECH, SILENCING HIM. CUT TO:

FOUR. IMMIGRATION – ANSWERS AS VOX-POP, DOCUMENTARY-STYLE

IMMIGRATION: How did you get here?

MINAXI: Nairobi, Delhi, London. My father a lieutenant in British Army, Kenya. I have boarding house in Wolverhampton.

© Kaite O'Reilly (script) and © Foursight Theatre (live performance)

5.6 Working with existing scripts

Many community performances work with existing scripts, often with theatre scripts, but also with other material found in many different ways. This section focuses on dramatic scripts and the development of performance work out of them. It does not address theatre productions that use relatively conventional staging methods that align themselves with mainstream theatre. Instead, I discuss methods that allow forms of engagements between community performers and scripts.

> Among the most common traits [of community-based performance], community-based performance often redefines *text*, initiates unique script development strategies that challenge time-tested techniques for playwriting, and introduces participatory performance techniques that blur the boundaries between actor and spectator in order to maximize the participants' agency.

Haedicke and Nellhaus, 2001: 3

Figure 5.15 Streets Alive Theatre Company, London, UK works to empower young people aged 16 to 25 who have experienced homelessness. The Theatre for Life course offers young people the opportunity to learn basic drama skills, and improve their self-esteem and communication skills as well as learn about study and employment opportunities.

Study questions

In what ways are letter
exchanges scripts for dramatic
action? In which ways are they
not? What is involved in staging
them?

   Imagine creating a similar
project. Write a letter soliciting
a response that might become
part of a dramatic performance.
What do you offer, disclose,
discuss?

The boundary between community performance and professional theatre practice becomes much more malleable in
relation to avant-garde performance methods, and post-modern
staging techniques. There is no hard and fast way to delineate
the borderline between theatre work staged by lay people
and community performance work: in this book, I focus on the
exciting experiments that emerge in the realms where aesthetics,
community-building and epistemologies meet. There are many
excellent community theatre groups staging shows all over the
world, and no matter where they see themselves on the spectrum between mainstream stage practice and community performances, many of the group-building, improvisation methods and
approaches to text discussed in these pages might be of use
to them.

PRACTICE EXAMPLE

What is a script? Letters and community: The Correspondence Project

Christina Tsoules Soriano, dance and video artist, and Paige McGinley, performance artist,
collaborated to explore this performance project:

> The Correspondence Project seeks to interrogate the relationship between global
> and local communities in its on-going series of postal performances. The Project
> began with a call to our friends, families, and colleagues. We asked them to send
> one or both of us a letter. We then began to create performances and installations
> based on the letters we received. Drawing from mail art, the task-based aesthetic of
> Fluxus, the everyday-ness of the domestic space, and participatory art practices,
> the Correspondence Project creates its pieces directly from the found text, inspired
> movement, and arresting images provided by our pen pals. It is our hope that over
> the course of the year, the scope and reach of the Correspondence Project will
> expand beyond our circle of acquaintances, creating a performance community as
> we go.
>   Some of the questions The Correspondence Project addresses are: How do
> letters function as a network of connection across time and space? What happens
> to letters that are written and never sent? What is a messenger? What kinds of
> relationships do people have with their mail/mail carriers? Why is it difficult to write
> a letter? Why is it a small miracle when a piece of mail arrives? Is there a dead letter
> office? What are the physical and emotional geographies of our letters' journeys?

Material written by Tsoules Soriano and McGinley for this book

What are the advantages of working with a well-known existing script?

Recognition – many people in Western societies have heard of Shakespeare plays, and have a vague notion of content and style when they see a drama named.

Instant audience – it is relatively easy to market performances based on famous scripts to local schools and education providers, or to find subscribers that recognize the cultural cachet of the show.

A starting point – performers will have a reference point, a way into the workshopping process, and a sense of what might be happening.

Embedment – you can have access to previous productions of the play, and develop strategies of difference from there. You can also address issues from within existing plays: a *Swan Lake* danced by men can subvert the messages of the play (of young women dying), or a *Julius Caesar* performed by women retools messages about power and gender. The impact can be more significant if a recognizable and acknowledged part of one's culture is changed.

Dialogue – when the original play is well established, it is possible to insert individual new voices without necessarily disrespecting the integrity of the well-known text.

What are the disadvantages?

Recognition – just as a name like 'Shakespeare' brings recognition, it also brings with it categorizing: many people might be alienated by a dead white male author, representative of a colonial nation, often given in a language experienced by some as archaic and out of date.

Instant audience – it can be harder to reach out to new audiences with existing plays and their associations. You might find that the audience you attract is not the one you would like to address. Depending on the group's aims, 'preaching to the converted' is a significant danger for many community performance productions.

A starting point – if you are still at the stage of gathering performers and community workshop members, could the name of the play/playwright hinder rather than help people to connect with the event? Might they be too firmly fixed in their expectations of a given script?

Embedment – the weight of history can be hard to shift. A difference of staging or textual manipulation (cutting, rephrasing, montage) can be lost if your audiences find themselves more stimulated by the historical inaccuracies or issues of 'disrespect' than by the nature of the changes.

Dialogue – issues of style, time distance and cultural cachet might stand in the way of community participants working freely with the ideas offered by the original script. How can their voices by heard, seen, presented?

Macbeth

An integrated performance by non-disabled and disabled secondary school children (examples are from a New Zealand school that brought me in to consult on accessible theatre practice).

Session 1: In the first fifty-minute session, after some warm-up games, we discussed what *Macbeth*, the drama, was about. Who was Macbeth? The pupils named a number of different aspects – swordsman, murderer, king. We also identified two other iconic scenes: the witches' circle, and the forest advancing to take Macbeth down. In small group improvisations, the pupils created a tableau for four elements: the witches, the swordsman/killer, the king, the forest. After sharing each tableau, one group's physical scene was taken up by everybody else. For the first image, the witches' circle, we chose a group who created a human brewing cauldron. All fifty pupils involved in this initial session grouped together in a circle, linked hands across their shoulders, and became a cauldron, swaying gently from side to side, until, on a count, everybody exploded outwards as the ingredients incinerated.

When the teachers and I discussed these initial tableaux, and their potential use for a stage performance, we came up with various ideas: various of the witches' lines could be introduced by members of the ensemble, emerging in the middle of the cauldron, and the explosion could signify the start of the play: all elements brought together in the pressure cooker of Shakespeare's writing.

Session 2: A teacher had asked me to work with a specific scene, and to model how lines could be used differently – how script material could become resonant in ways not part of traditional theatre. She chose the scene in which Lady Macbeth is trying to wash the stain of murder from her hands, and prepares herself for her suicide, commented on by her doctors.

Again, we had a fifty-minute session with the thirty-plus pupils who would be stage performers for this show, with some pupils familiar with the play and its lines and others not. I introduced only six lines from the scene, from two characters: Lady Macbeth and the doctor. After an initial short discussion of Lady Macbeth and her role in the play, and of the core issues that the scene conveys to the audience, we divided up into two groups: doctors and 'Lady Macbeths'. The doctors took on the characteristics of a Greek chorus, commenting to the audience on Lady Macbeth's behavior. They opened the scene by pointing behind them to the Lady Macbeths: each member of the doctor cast said the line, either individually or with somebody else, and then sat down, looking back behind them. The Lady Macbeths took up space in the stage back, and moved through the space, everybody by themselves, without contact with others. After the last doctor had sat down, the Ladies, in three groups, pointed to areas in the room and shouted 'out damn spot', one group after the other, three times. They then faced stage front and displayed the palm of their hands, fingers outstretched to the audience, and asked 'will these hands ever be clean'? This was the cue for the doctors to face the audience and call, lifting their shoulders and hands and letting them sink into the floor, 'what sigh is here'. Behind them, the standing Ladies began whispering 'to bed, to bed' until the whispering died away to leave silence for the haunting tones of a harmonica played by a wheelchair-using pupil in the middle of the Lady Macbeth group. As she guided the sound deeper and deeper, the Ladies sank into the earth. To make this image more compelling, and to allow more room for individual difference, we had separated the Ladies into straight and spiral sinkers: one sank down with her or his body fronting the audience, the next one in a spiraling movement. When all Ladies were on the ground, and the music had ended in a long dark note, the doctors got up and each walked to a fallen Lady Macbeth, laying their hands on the person, and saying goodbye with their touch. They then moved to stage-right, and, as they were filing off the stage, one by one asked the audience 'Will God ever forgive us?'.

In the fifty-minute session, we had time to set this scene, using ideas generated by the students, and to run it once.

In both of these sessions, the play material is generated out of the students' understanding of the play, and performance elements emerge from the students' bodies rather than from set images of Shakespearian performance. In this way, no differences between disabled and non-disabled students intrude on the creative process: all are merely material for the play.

Using this kind of approach to theatre in school settings has advantages, but also offers challenges: teachers need to find ways of adapting assessments to the differences offered by script approaches that do not identify individual actors. As part of the consulting work, we discussed some of these issues, and tried to find alternative ways of thinking about what it means to have and offer a 'sustained role', or to 'create a significant scene' – students who were required by their assessment strategy to write about researching a role could do this just as well when they were an individual Lady Macbeth as a communal one, and responsibility for improvised design could be shared out among pupils, and therefore count as 'scene development'. Other challenges offered by this method include the challenge to the facilitator: how can physical and vocal creativity emerge in a school setting? What are the ways pupils usually interact with teachers, how can that engagement be shaped differently so that new forms of creative potential can emerge?

72 Reflection exercise

Take a favorite text you have – it doesn't have to be a playtext. What kind of methods could you use to approach this text with a group of people? Think of paraphrasing the material, of setting up improvisation sessions based on the basic conflicts presented in scenes or in a text. Make a list of five different group instructions you could use to find connections between participants' lives and the material you wish to work with.

What problems arise from any tension between your wish, from the text you've chosen, and the group's (and that includes you) life world?

Figure 5.16 Moana House performers singing Maori songs for the residents at the Dunedin Community Hospice, New Zealand. Photo: Petra Kuppers

This chapter introduced you to different ways of working with one of the most significant sources of material in community performance: memories, individual stories, local histories. It offered ways of thinking about sharing material in ways that feed from individual stories, but engage thoughts about community, collaboration and communal action.

CHAPTER 6

Documentation,
evaluation, reporting

What happened? What did it mean to the people involved? How did your project do? What did others think about it? What could you or other stakeholders in the process do better? What aspects of your work or your group experience should be shared with others? Does documentation validate your processes?

Documentation and evaluations allow community performance practitioners to find answers to some of these questions. This chapter discusses final project reports (also called acquittal reports), quantitative and qualitative data gathering, and alternative modes of sharing project outcomes.

To begin with, you will probably reflect on your project within your group, finding ways of holding on to the experiences and insights that you have all found.

Tree of life evaluation

Arguilles *et al.*,
1998: 14

Create a large tree out of construction paper. On the trunk, have the participants identify all of the elements of the project – places visited, issues discussed, key resource people involved. On the roots list the names of the project members. On paper cut outs of buds, leaves, flowers and axes have individuals evaluate the project with one idea per cut out as follows:

Leaves – sources of information

Flowers – memories, feelings, and reflections about the process

Buds – hopes for the future, new ideas

Axes – things that didn't work, hopes and expectations not met, problems, conflicts and impediments to the project.

All participants place their buds, leaves, flowers and axes on the tree. Encourage participants to be creative by introducing birds, bugs, sun, soil etc. to the exercise. Once all of the elements have been placed on the tree allow time for everyone to view it. The tree acts as a focus point and catalyst for further discussion.

Documentation can be any and all forms of data that emerge from a project. How else can you hold on to the thoughts, sensations, feelings, images and stories of your project?

Forms of documentation can included:

- personal narratives
- videos of workshops/performances/discussions
- images of workshops/performances/participants
- a final one-off performance captured on tape and presented on a DVD
- questionnaires
- audio interviews
- project notes
- journals
- press clippings
- leaflets, announcements, posters.

Evaluation and reporting sift this wealth of potential information, and assemble a coherent narrative out of it.

There are many ways that you can report on a project, and many voices that can be drawn in. The most easily accessible site of documentation, attention and reflection, rests in you: the artist facilitator's narrative. And beyond the issue of reporting needs, fostering a strong reflective practice will help you to develop yourself, to become clearer about your goals and practices.

Lazarus, 2004:
11–12

Joan Lazarus on reflective practice

Reflective practice – the habit of considering and reconsidering what transpires in your interactions with students and others – is an important element of best practice. As busy professionals, we often don't take time for reflection or dismiss it as reminiscent of homework assignments. But there are all kinds of wondering and worries swirling about us each day that beg reflection. As you consider the ideas in this chapter in relation to your practice, what anecdotes or incidents come to mind? Begin a journal in which you freewrite about what you are thinking related to events that happen or have happened in your work. End each entry with 'It Made Me Think. . . .' Don't include what it made you think *about*; just describe the incident and that you are thinking about it. Like Professor Dumbledore's pensive in *Harry Potter and the Goblet of Fire* (Rowling 2000), this metacognition allows you to take your thoughts out and look at them over time. You might find patterns or recurring themes to help you in your journey toward best practice.

Questions about the boundaries between art work and documentation can give rise to interesting forms of creative expression, as the workshop example of the tree exercise showed.

Can the writing about an art work *be* the art work?

Lacy, 1994a: 176

When an artist adopts the position of analyst, the visual appeal of imagery is often superseded by the textual properties of the work, thus challenging conventions of beauty. Their analysis may assume its aesthetic character from the coherence of the ideas or from their *relationship* to visual imagery rather than through the images themselves. In this way, art of analysis draws on the history of conceptual art during the sixties, when artists explored the dematerialization of art as object and its rematerialization in the world of ideas.

In many countries, art practices and their beneficial effect on community-building, cohesion, integration, regeneration, public health and wellbeing are well recognized, and funding has been forthcoming to study the nature of art's contribution.

---

73 Research exercise

Research your local, regional and national networking environment to find out what current issues impact good practice in evaluation, in particular if you rely on public funding for your work. What are the trends, requirements, expectations? Look out for descriptions for conferences like this one: 'How Was it for You? Assessing Impact of Artists' Practice in the Public Realm', a conference organized by IXIA, Excellence in Public Art, in Manchester, UK (October 2005).

74 Reflection exercise

How can reports and evaluations be part of the aesthetic outcome, rather than a completely different genre?

A range of organizations are involved in developing evaluation tools to measure social change and regeneration agendas and the impact of the arts. In contemporary large-scale multi-nodal community performance projects, specialist assessors and evaluation specialists from sociological frameworks sometimes come on board to fulfill these necessary functions. These forms of job-sharing can be beneficial, but can also open up differences in agendas and aims. Communication is the key to good working relations: social scientists and artists need to respect their respective criteria for excellence and fulfillment, if the evaluation is supposed to be meaningful to all concerned.

If you are working within an institutional framework (social work, health provider, adult education) you are most likely required to evaluate your work. If you are working outside these structures, it might still be useful to have a record, in particular if you want to go on, apply for grants or develop yourself. The Arts Council of England lists a number of benefits to good evaluation practice:

There are clear benefits to you if you evaluate your work.

- Evaluation helps with planning, as it makes you think about what you're aiming to do, how you will do it and how you will know if you've succeeded
- Ongoing feedback keeps you on track and helps to avoid disasters
- Evaluation helps you to adapt and change as your project continues
- Evaluation is a good way of dealing with 'quality assurance' – you keep an eye on things to make sure quality is maintained
- Evaluation helps prove the value of what you are doing
- Evaluation records your contribution to the field you are working in
- Your evaluation can help others working in the same field
- Information you collect can also be used for reporting back to those with an interest in the project (eg participants, funders) and telling others about what you've done
- The evidence you collect can support future funding applications

Information Sheet: Self-Evaluation, Arts Council of England Publication, May 2005: 2

The Arts Council of England also provides a useful overview of some of the things you need to start thinking about in relation to evaluation:

You can organise an evaluation yourself or you can ask someone else to do it for you. Either way you need to include it in your budget, as whoever does the evaluation will need to be paid for their time. The things you need to sort out when planning an evaluation include the following points.

1   What kinds of information or evidence you are going to include in your evaluation – eg what people say, what they have done (process and finished work), what you have done, how an audience has responded.
2   What questions you are going to ask.
3   How you plan to answer those questions – this is really about what sort of information you need to answer the questions and how you will collect it. Do you need numbers (eg 50 people attended 20 workshops) or information with more depth? Useful evaluation usually combines both types of information.
4   When you should collect the information. As a minimum you need to collect information at the end of your project but if you can ask questions at the beginning of the project, you will have a 'before' picture against which you can look at the 'after' picture to assess change.
5   How you will collect the information. You may already have some of the information you need, perhaps from previous evaluations or findings from market research. There are many different ways of collecting information, eg keeping a register, using a questionnaire, taking photographs, videotaping people's thoughts about a project, asking them to keep a diary, etc.
6   How you are going to make sense of the information you have collected.
7   How you are going to present the results of the evaluation.
8   Who you are going to share it with and how.

Information Sheet: Self-Evaluation, Arts Council of England Publication, May 2005: 4

6.1 Sharing evaluations, outcomes and achievements: final reports

Most funders require you to submit a final report on a project you've undertaken. And even if you do not have to provide a report, writing up what you did can be an important reflection exercise. It will attune you to the specific quality of your own voice and vision – as you reflect, you will most likely encounter moments where someone might have seen the events taking place in a different light. A 'report-to-self' is also a useful archival document: you might want to hold to what actually happened in the project, which exercises were used, how people developed ideas, how groups responded. After a few years of practice, it is easy to forget particulars, and to fall into specific routines. Carefully reflected write-ups of your own projects will provide a memory space for yourself.

Here is an excerpted example of a standardized report form:

Alaska State Council on the Arts: evaluation report form

Community arts development grants

- Actual individuals benefiting: (i.e. the actual total audience, participants, students, etc., excluding employees and/or paid performers), that benefited directly form your activities. Estimate for broadcasts or large public events (i.e. Performances in the park).
- Actual number of participating artists: the total number of artists directly involved in providing artistic services specifically identified with your project. Include living artists whose work is represented in an exhibition, regardless of whether the work was provided by the artist or by an institution.
- Description of your activity. (Please be concise – what did you do?)
- Was there any change in your activity from what was stated in your application? If so please explain.
- List the communities served by your activity.
- Did you have any problems? If so, how were they overcome?

In this final report, you are also asked to compare projected and actual budget. This report needs to be completed and handed in to the State Council 60 days after the end of the funded activity.

Different funders require different kind of reports. Below is a final report on a project I was involved in, for a different institution (provided for a 2004/2005 project funded by a Rhode Island Foundation grant, here reproduced without the budget section). This report, prepared by Jeannine Chartier from VSA Arts of Rhode Island, an organization that fosters art practice in the field of disability, was accepted by the Foundation, and the Foundation has since funded other, related projects. Clearly, this format worked for them. I am providing it below as an example of a narrative account for a large-scale project – not all projects will require such long documents.

Figure 6.1 Olimpias Tracks workshop on the beach in Newport, Rhode Island, 2004.   Photo: Mary Ann O'Toole

RI FOUNDATION NEW WORKS FINAL REPORT

GRANT # 20031370

ARTIST: **PETRA KUPPERS**

PROJECT TITLE: **THE TRACKS PROJECT**

ORGANIZATION: **VSA ARTS OF RHODE ISLAND**

Grant activities/accomplishments

The grant Petra Kuppers, Artistic Director of The Olimpias Performance Research Projects, and VSA arts of RI received from RI Foundation was used to support the development of new 'Disability Culture' art works created in collaboration with affiliated video artist Agnieszka Woznicka and adult RI community members that have disabilities at a series of workshops held in rural locations of RI during 2004–5.

Our strategy was to use arts elements in close dialogue with community people unfamiliar with arts discourses and arts environments, to connect with people underserved by traditional approaches, and to utilize non-traditional spaces and public sites to be a model of inclusion in both process and product in order to create art works focusing on disability issues.

Participants were recruited through direct marketing and 'call for participation' solicitation using a variety of techniques including networking, leafleting and notices placed in RI's disability related newsletters inviting people to come and explore the meaning of disability culture and disability arts through practical art making. Overall, fifteen people participated with three artists in the various workshops and in the creation of the final Tracks art works. While this amount is slightly lower than our original strategy of 20 individuals, the smaller size/number of individuals able to attend more workshops proved to be more critical to produce the high-quality, intimate experience necessary for participants to be able to share their personal stories essential to creating our outcome works to fruition. Workshops sites included: Burrillville Recreation Center, Burrillville; Louttit Library, West Greenwich; Bryant College, Smithfield; Goddard Park, Warwick; Misquamicut Beach, Westerly; Norman Bird Sanctuary, Middletown; and Canonicus Park, Exeter.

People welcomed to the project were not limited to just those who readily identified as having a disability, according to the guidelines put forth in the ADA, but also included those who have personal connections to people with disabilities (ie: parent, personal care attendant, etc.) as well as those who have survived disabling conditions. Additionally, some of the participants identified as 'people with disabilities' and some as 'disabled people' and we spent time talking about these different languages as well the potential meanings of 'disability culture'. The participants were a diverse group of people, included men and women and an age range between early 20s through late 60s. Professions ranged from un- and underemployed RI citizens, self-employed artists, professors of local universities, nurses and people otherwise associated with medical environments. Straight, gay, bisexual, transgendered and other people mixed, and people shared their various experiences with a variety of disability categories, including mental health, physical and/or developmental disabilities; visual, hearing and/or speech impairments; cancer and abuse survivors. Ethnic diversity was less visible, although the participants hailed from a range of different countries and environments, and had diverse religious affiliations.

In these workshop sessions, lead artist Kuppers used a variety of approaches to have everyone examine 'Tracks' – consider the traces we leave in our environments and in each other – and create art works around that theme. In workshop settings, participants explored creative movement and writing, percussion music and song, and created earth art out of found materials. Video and still photography were used both as a documentary tactic and art form.

The resulting art works – a photo exhibit of digitally manipulated images taken communally during the workshops, and an experimental documentary film created by Agnieszka Woznicka – were exhibited with great success and to a wide audience in numerous places including several web site locations. Beyond the workshop producers as participants, this project reached a greater number of individuals than first planned, including passers-by as audiences in the public venues where we held our workshops, the additional audiences attending our exhibitions/presentations, the PR we distributed and the media attention we were able to generate. In addition to local press coverage, our work was recognized by the national Community Arts Network and information about the project with photos and links to our sites was distributed through their circulation. Many more people than we originally anticipated felt the impact of the project as a result of increased dissemination opportunities as this project is of interest to the local, national and international arts and disability communities, including:

June 2004: Community/performance conference, multiple sites, RI – (photo installations)

July 2004: InterFACES Bangkok, selected 'Wood Chair' image, Raffles LaSalle International Design School, Bangkok – (juried photo exhibition)

August 2004: Committing Voice Festival, Goddard College – (exhibition)

September–October 2004: Glocester Manton Library, Chepachet (exhibition)

September–November 2004: Empire Gallery, 22 Broadway, Newport (exhibition)

November 2004–February 2005: Bryant University, Women's Center (exhibition)

March 2005: Performance Medicine conference (presentation)

March 2005: Muhlenberg College, Pennsylvania (guest lecture)

March 2005: The Atrium Gallery, 1 Capitol Hill, Providence, RI (presentation & exhibition)

April 2005: University New Mexico, Albuquerque (presentation)

May 2005: Sarah Doyle Gallery, 26 Benevolent Avenue, Providence (exhibition)

May 2005: Arts Nature Culture conference, Seattle, Washington (presentation)

June 2005: Community Performance Network event week, Roger Williams Park and Perishable Theatre (workshops and exhibition)

July 2005: Tertiary Dance Festival, Auckland, New Zealand (presentation)

Audience numbers are over a thousand, and will increase as the material we produced – we have compiled the video and photos from The Tracks Project and works from the follow-on project, Scar Tissue: A Body of Work, on a final DVD – continues to be shown. We are now finding a wider national and international audience as the DVD gets distributed through both the VSA arts and Olimpias networks and shown at international festivals.

Evaluation and impact

As designed in our grant request, The Tracks Project was evaluated in several ways in a collaborative method between Kuppers and VSA arts. In addition to the quantitative elements reported above (successful community involvement evidenced by tracking numbers of participants, exhibition sites, presentation attendance, etc.) the main tool used was qualitative research with our producer group through conducting interviews with verbal and/or written responses collected. As we had hoped, the impact on participants was significant in allowing them new spaces for thinking and knowing to emerge. In their answers to interview questions, participants expressed a deep and thoughtful engagement with the ideas of disability culture and its positive uses for self-expression and empowerment.

Statement from Kuppers on personal impact/success

'Working with VSA arts of Rhode Island was nourishing and gratifying, and the discussions about the meanings of disability culture, disability languages and concepts were challenging and exciting, and have shaped my vision of what it means to work within disability culture settings in the USA. Creatively, my work on the Tracks Project has opened up new avenues for me: the Olimpias disability culture projects have always been about how to share presence and beauty in non-traditional ways, utilizing new media, and this project was the first one that allowed me to fully explore communal photography and subsequent digital manipulation.

. . . The interplay of art forms seemed to work very well, indeed: participants responded generously and beautifully to creative writing, dance, found sculpture and earth art suggestions, and, as always in community arts, the results of the work far exceeded what I might have imagined of it.'

Impact on community participants

Workshop participants in Tracks commented frequently on the positive creative energy that emerges when people with disabilities work together, valuing one another as cultural producers, and bearing witness to the cultural specificity of their experiences. In Tracks, several ideas and images about scars and body difference emerged that became a springboard – at participants' urging – for a follow-up project to respond to those acknowledged needs and will help extend the work begun in Tracks of building an infrastructure for disability culture work throughout RI.

One of the most touching things a dedicated participant shared towards the end of the Tracks Project was that she had learned to appreciate touch and touching during our creative movement work together and how that new appreciation might find a productive outlet for her through the creative process of art making. As an abused person and a person with a disability, she had always felt excluded from and afraid of touch, and our workshop activities led her for the first time to a place where touch was associated with fullness and respect. In addition, she now has expressed a desire to create art work of her own and exhibit it independently of this community project.

Her response sums up many of the comments people have made about the project experience: art making, community making, exploring/developing a shared culture, and presenting it proudly have been the core issues people have taken away from our time together in this project. All of these issues of breaking through isolation to produce art emerge in the videos made about our workshops, are mentioned in the interviews and come to light, poetically, in the communal poetry people wrote:

Circle

Your hand touches mine	Smiling at Others
Fluking Up	Draw me into Movement
Warmth from Nearby Others	By the Wind, Sailor
Rhythm	Shining Slowly Out
Close, inside	Movement
Moving Around	Free, Alive
Meeting People in a New Way	Having Fun
It is very relaxing	Invisible yet visible
It's cold, or hot, and	Connecting with other Beings
– Green Flash –	Back, okay
A Community of Never Mets	Touching Hands
Endless Space	I follow
Sway Away	Orion

Impact on organization

VSA arts of Rhode Island is using the positive results from this Tracks Project to maintain developing relationships with our new community partners and leverage additional funds from other grant sources for follow-up projects that will enable continued exploration of 'Disability Culture' and community based art projects.

The primary partnership initiated by applying for this grant between VSA arts of RI and The Olimpias has proved particularly strong and dynamic. We have continued to work together on looking for money to support additional projects – including the RI State Council on the Arts, who funded the previously mentioned 'disability culture' follow-up project entitled Scar Tissue – and brought further resources and contacts to our collaborations. These include community artists Agnieszka Woznicka and Ana Flores; arts orgs such as Dance Alliance of RI, Carriage House and Perishable Theatre; and multiple contributions – including exhibit spaces, digital cameras and editing equipment – from RI Higher education venues including Bryant, Brown University and RI School of Design without whom we would not have been able to create our DVD.

Many participants have gone on to participate in other events this project has fed into: they collaborated again with VSA arts of Rhode Island and The Olimpias in the Scar Tissue project we created to help sustain our 'disability culture' work beyond Tracks, quite a few of the Tracks Project people are now sharing their work in the Community Performance Network events and others have reported how participating in these kind of community workshops opened their eyes to the variety of art practice that is out there, valuable, and – hopefully – accessible to them. Obviously, other RI organizations need to take issues of access, both physical and programmatic, into consideration for this inclusion to happen successfully and VSA arts of RI will make ourselves available to help facilitate this process as much as possible.

This project was highly successful, and managed to enhance and expand the visibility of disability culture in Rhode Island – this feeling of validation, of shared cultures and understanding, was an important feature of the work for the participants, the passers-by in the various nature centers where we worked, for the culture providers who gave us access to exhibit spaces in coffee shops, libraries, galleries, women's centers, and for the many people who were touched by our displays either by visiting the gallery, through the publicity materials we displayed freely, or the DVDs we are currently distributing for free.

Our goals for The Tracks Project were not only successfully met, but were exceeded. We hope that the Rhode Island Foundation is going to continue funding innovative and experimental projects like ours, will join us as strong advocates for access and we remain grateful for this opportunity RI Foundation funding provided.

---

76 Reflection exercise

In this report, what information has the largest impact on you? What different information do you get from (i) the list of workshops, (ii) the list of sharing events, (iii) the quote from the participant, (iv) the poem and its evocation of our workshops?

6.2 Quantitative approaches to evaluation

As evident from the two final report examples above, evaluation can take many shapes. One of the most often used approaches employs quantitative methods. This means that you keep records of attendance and statistical information such as gender, age, employment status, benefits status, ethnic affiliation etc.

Example of quantitative record taking

This example shows an Attendance Record, taken at the beginning of project.

SAMPLE ENROLMENT FORM

1 Your name

2 Address

3 Post code

4 Telephone number: home

5 Telephone number: mobile

6 Your age
- a 17–24
- b 25–39
- c 40–59
- d 60–79
- e 80+

7 Gender
- a Male
- b Female

8 What are your employment circumstances? (*Please tick the main one that applies*)
- a Employed full-time
- b Employed part-time
- c Self employed
- d Volunteer/unpaid worker
- e At home
- f Unemployed
- g Student
- h Retired
- i Other, please specify:

9 Are you a disabled person? Yes No

---

10   Do you use:

a   Visual aids or alternative formats to print i.e. Braille, large print or audio tape

b   Communication support or equipment i.e. sign language interpreter, speech-to-text, loop etc.

c   Equipment to aid mobility i.e. wheelchair, walking frame etc.

d   A support worker or personal assistance

e   Other support, please specify:

11   Have you been involved in one of this organisation's arts projects before?

Yes

No

For later recording: sessions attended (please tick)

1 2 3 4 5 6 7 8 9 10

Annabelle Jackson Associates, 2004: 70

---

77 Reflection exercise

Look over the attendance record above. Who would feel comfortable filling this information out, who might not? What assumptions about 'normality' seem automatically built into these kind of questions?

   Can you think of any alternative formats that would still garner this kind of information, but in a different way?

Many of the forms used to get this kind of information are not all that appropriate in some situations, for instance in mental health settings. Try to think whether the tool you are using might be intrusive or overwhelming. What is involved in giving out the information requested? What kinds of power relations are established by the question and answer system set up by these forms? Is the written format the best way to gather the information you require? Remember that many of the people you are working with might have negative experiences with systems and institutions, and that there is something threatening in giving out personal data.

At the same time, your funding institutions or partners might require this kind of statistical information in order to present their work to others, in turn. Finding balance and finding ways to satisfy divergent demands is one of the performances community performance artists need to engage in.

However you deal with this kind of personal identifying data, make sure you research and respond appropriately to data protection acts that might be in force in the country you are working in.

6.3 Qualitative approaches to evaluation

Qualitative approaches stress the multi-faceted nature of engagement: people bring to projects their own life worlds, their ways of thinking, their social and cultural frames. Interviews of various kinds and focus group work can help excavate some of the different agendas, expectations and outcomes.

Definition: focus groups

Focus group work is an evaluation activity comprising of a semi-structured discussion with a group of people. Usually, an experienced moderator leads respondents through an informal discussion, allowing group members to talk freely about their thoughts, opinions, feelings and attitudes. In community performance contexts, small group discussions like these, acting as a form of evaluation, mean that people can reinforce each other, engage in dialogue, create answers together. The onus of speaking is not on an individual, but emerges more naturally from the group. The focus group differs from the full group setting in that it can allow minority opinions to come to the fore more easily.

Questions worth thinking about include:

- Do you have a sense of the associations people might have with interview situations? Think about immigration interviews, doctor's visits, care situations, closeness to student/teacher power differentials etc.
- How can you set up interviews in such a way that you do not project your desired answers?
- What is the most comfortable way for participants to give their opinions? What are the differences in comfort level between a one-on-one interview and a focus group in which a person is interacting with his or her peers?
- How can you ensure privacy, and help people to avoid showing themselves in such a way that they might later regret?
- Who should do the interviewing? How should it be recorded?

Below is an example of an in-depth qualitative evaluation, written by Loree Lawrence about a street-involved youth project.

Figure 6.2 A group of young people impacted by methamphetamine use from The RAVEN Project created a performance on methamphetamine awareness and prevention in Humboldt County, presented in a Youth Center in California, 2006.   Photo: Petra Kuppers

Qualitative evaluation

An Example of Evaluation: Material from 'The Measure of Success: Conversations with Street-Involved Youth about an Arts-Based Intervention Program'.

KYTES (the acronym for Kensington Youth Theatre and Employment Skills) is a program for street-involved youths that was founded in 1983 as Kensingston Youth Theatre Ensemble of St. Stephens Community Centre in the Kensington Market area in downtown Toronto.

In 1988, when the program received funding through Canadian Job Strategies (a federal government agency), job skill training was added to the curriculum and the program was renamed Kensington Youth Theatre and *Employment Skills*.

KYTES combined theatre, supportive counselling and alternative education to engage the youths in a full-time program where they were immersed in artistic creation and skill-building activities that highlighted the importance of punctuality, commitment, problem-solving, conflict management, effective communication strategies and community.

In 1993, 85% of the budget was lost when the Canadian federal government cut funding to the program claiming that KYTES was not successfully training youths into job placements.

The program survived and two years later, in 1995, I was hired as the Theatre Director because of my background in popular theatre and my training with Augusto Boal in Theatre of the Oppressed methods.

In 1997, KYTES was funded through the Canadian government's Youth Employment Strategy but the next year, a scandal in the government Ministry that ran the program resulted in a funding freeze and KYTES lost a majority of its funding once again.

By this time, KYTES offered full-time (from 9–5, 5 days a week) programming for 18 youths aged 16 to 24 years over a period of 4 months two times every year.

Along with the original aims, the curriculum now included alternative schooling, life skills training, social issues discussions, employment mentoring, job shadowing, nutrition and cooking classes, counseling and theatre.

Each 4-month long 'troupe' ended with the performance of a collaboratively created original play. Over the course of its history KYTES worked with over 600 youths and produced over 34 plays. In January 2003, KYTES closed due to a lack of funding.

Data collection

I used qualitative research methods to find out more about the experiences of six former KYTES troupe members. In most cases, I met with them twice for semi-structured interviews. The first two-hour interview was exploratory and the second was co-investigative. In the second hour-long interview I talked about my analysis of our first conversation and asked for their feedback on it as well as their analysis of the research questions about program evaluation.

Participants

The six interviewees were KYTES troupe members while I was the Theatre Director, from 1995 to 2000. I was looking for a fairly representative group and from an extensive list of possibilities I found these six eager former troupe members:

Stephanie, 17 years old, heterosexual, Caribbean-Canadian
Out of school for 2 years, lived in group homes and foster care then stayed in shelters and was couch-surfing, on medication for manic depression

Anna, 19 years old, lesbian Philippina/Anglo-Canadian
Out of school for 1 year, did not identify as street-involved, middle-class background, couch-surfing and collecting welfare

Jenny, 18 years old, bi-sexual, African-Canadian
Attended all-girl Catholic school, left home to get away from physically abusive brother, moved in with her boyfriend

Justin, 17 years old, heterosexual, Spanish/Anglo-Canadian
Left school in grade 10, kicked out of home, stayed in shelters and was couch-surfing, drinking and drugging 'a lot,' cutting himself and 'not caring about the future'

Robert, 21 years old, heterosexual Anglo-Canadian, out of school
Living in semi-independent housing, recently out of jail and off the streets, on a methadone program

Adam, 17 years old, gay, Anglo-Canadian
Attended alternative school, couch-surfing, on Ritalin and sleeping pills

Impacts
So what did they have to say about the impact KYTES had on their lives?

Justin: We came out with a lot of good skills.
I think it made me more employable. It showed that I could work in a team.

Adam: I only ended up getting 2 credits.
But after getting those 2 credits, I went hard-core back into school.
I've been pretty much go, go, go since I finished KYTES and I haven't stopped really. It's amazing to come this far and look back and see where that change came from.

Jenny: I think part of me thought that KYTES was a detour and what I realized after leaving KYTES was that it wasn't a detour, it was a total re-routing of my life. I think I walked into KYTES in a bubble and KYTES burst that bubble. I needed that.

Robert: I am resourceful, that's how I describe myself now. KYTES had a role in my transition from being on the streets and being in that sort of world where I expected less out of life. It was easy for me to not think about tomorrow. That's quite a skill, to get up and go.

Stephanie: I know I'm able to do something, I'm able to start and finish it.
If I didn't have that boost of confidence, I might still be transient and in the shelters somewhere.
   I was being bombarded with all these negative things about myself and KYTES was able to show me that there are positive things about me. I can go out and do my own thing and fulfill my own prophesy instead of proving everybody back there that they're right.

After KYTES

Now we'll compare what they have to say about the kinds of impacts the program has had on their lives years later with what they said about their immediate experiences after leaving KYTES.

When I asked them about what they did after KYTES ended, only one of them said that they went back to school full-time. In all of the other cases, they either didn't get a job or go back to school and if they did they didn't last in either for longer than 6 months.

Justin: After KYTES I went to Oasis and I was at my ma's place. Midway through my semester I left but I was a bit more stable.

Stephanie: After the troupe ended I finally got an apartment although that didn't last for too long and I kind of bounced around shelters again.

The People Strong Theatre Company started in the middle of KYTES. We just loved doing all the skits and games and theatre that we just didn't want it to end. It didn't last for too long afterwards.

Jenny: I think that I was lucky after KYTES because it did give me the courage and the ability and the know how to go on and apply to school and I did get into school but 6 months later I wasn't in school anymore.

Robert: After KYTES I felt really good. I felt on track but then I wasn't really working. I felt like I just did something great, now what am I going to do?

For me the words of Justin, Adam, Jenny, Anna, Robert and Stephanie speak volumes about the length of time it takes for street-involved youths to find their moorings. Programs like KYTES can't offer quick fixes to entrenched behaviours but they can provide a first-step off the streets and toward building positive identities for the youths.

Measuring success

When I asked them how they would measure success when it comes to evaluating a project like KYTES this is what they had to say:

Jenny: KYTES is not an investment-return type of program. I don't know how KYTES could be evaluated in another way for someone with funding or a politician because, unfortunately, they look at everything by 'How much good is this going to do?' or 'How much money is this going to make?' or 'How useful are these people going to be?'

I wish that there was some way to quantify it for people who need to see those results. I know for me personally and other people that after having been in KYTES, they're doing a lot better now than they were doing before they got there. The funders are looking for immediate success and success is not measured in the short-term and that's what is misunderstood.

Justin: Say you talked with your mother when you were 15 and she gave you some advice and it was like, 'Yeah, whatever.' And then you're 25 and it finally kicks in and you go, 'I finally realize what she was trying to tell me.' KYTES is same sort of thing.

Anna: KYTES seems like a faith project. You can't measure it. I think you believe in something and you go out on a limb and it really sucks that there's a government that doesn't have faith.

Adam: Anyone who felt it was worth their big wad of cash would not be afraid to get down and dirty and actually see what the project was doing and meet the people before and meet them after and actually care, have a real passion for what was happening. The things that are important to the people who are sitting up there are really the last thing on anyone's mind sitting within the troupe. It's a different world.

Robert: They compare KYTES to all these other programs that really suck. Yeah, they'll help me get a job flipping burgers or working in a Roots factory but they're not going to help me find something that I'm going to want to stay at, to keep doing and get better at. I know lots of people who got jobs out of those programs but not many of them are still doing those jobs.

Loree Lawrence, Presentation at Community Performance conference, June 2004

Study questions

In her analysis of this material, Lawrence argues that a successful evaluation of projects such as KYTES needs to take into account definitions of success as they are employed by the target-group – in KYTES case, the street-involved youths who participated in the projects. Lawrence's qualitative survey provides excellent material to argue such a case.

- Reviewing the quotes she gives, what kind of narratives can you construct about the impact of programs such as KYTES?
- What would be respectful and disrespectful ways of interpreting the data Lawrence provides? What does respectful mean here? What assumptions and stereotypes about street-involved youths could get in the way of communicating their voices? How could one avoid these problems?
- Think about presentation of this material: in what ways could you create a collaborative and public conversation about the project's impact, and about the need to continue funding projects like it? Where would you campaign for these issues? What media would you involve?

78 Reflection exercise

Partnerships and defining success

Read through the statement below by François Matarasso, a writer on participatory arts and culture. Think about the practical and political difficulties of these statements.

Make a list of problematic points from Matarasso's citation, and share them in discussion. Do you agree that it is always inappropriate to seek change without informed consent of those involved? Are there individuals or communities whose ability to participate in 'mainstream' communication practices is impaired? Who would have the right/ability to represent them? Can you work in an open way that doesn't immediately set specific goals, or are goals always implied?

The critical issue in impact assessment is not practical at all, but ethical. In one of the early working papers we set out a number of principles for arts work which had a social purpose:

- Projects intended to produce social benefits should address stated needs or aspirations.
- It is unethical to seek to produce change without the informed consent of those involved.
- The needs and aspirations of individuals or communities are best identified by them, often in partnership with others, such as local authorities, public agencies and arts bodies.
- Partnership requires the agreement of common objectives and commitments (though not all goals need to be shared by all partners).
- Those who have identified a goal are best placed to ascertain when it had been met.
- An arts project may not be the most appropriate means of achieving a given goal.
- A process which involves all the stakeholders in agreeing the objectives of an activity, and how they will be monitored, will produce credible evidence of the impact of the arts. It will probably also change everyone involved.

Matarasso, 1998: 21

Another example of qualitative evaluation is storytelling: asking participants to tell/write/record on audio or video material something about the community arts project that was significant to them. There follows an example of a questionnaire soliciting this kind of information.

This questionnaire can be a good guide for questions an evaluator can ask. But there are problems with in-depth questionnaires. Maybe some of your participants cannot or do not wish to write. Audio recordings, videos, photographs of a group in process etc. can be useful alternative documentation: but again, be aware of power issues. Are people happy to disclose information? Many alternative ways of sharing, via voice or video-tape, are less anonymous than questionnaire or qualitative word-based methods. Are participants happy to be identified personally with a specific issue, for instance, are they outing themselves in any way? Are these issues discussed?

6.4 Creative approaches to documentation and evaluation

Any art work you create in the group can be seen as a creative record of the group process. With the permission of the participants, you can use it in that way. But the framing of this creative 'product' is important, and can have significant effects on how funders and the public see the work. Look at the work produced in the group, and your record of it: is the communal creation aspect of the work visible/experiential? Or does the performance/art work lend itself to be seen like a mainstream art product, with a single author/creator/director? For instance, instead of photographing a large picture by itself, a video that shows many hands working on the picture together might

Sample questionnaire

Case stories (participant story)

This case story will be used to describe how a project participant viewed the project/initiative and what they learnt from it.

Please use the following outline to write your story.

Assume that the reader of your story knows little or nothing about the context of your story and describe:

- How you came to hear about the project
- What attracted you to it
- Who was involved
- How you were involved and what you did.

Explain:

- What you liked about the project
- What you disliked about the project (if anything)
- What benefits the project offered you
- What others in your area thought about the project, or about you doing it.

Offer some reflections on your story about:

- What you felt about the quality of art work produced
- What you felt the project should do differently and why
- What the project would need to achieve this
- Whether the project encouraged you to try anything new
- Whether the project changed your ideas or allowed you to develop new skills
- Whether the project had an impact in your area. If so, how?

REMEMBER: you can't tell the whole story of the project/initiative! Focus on one or two themes, your role and what you did, and most importantly what you learnt from it.

The Health Development Agency, 2000: 67

record the point of the exercise better. It is not always easy to highlight the multi-vocal nature of community performance work when just showing the product.

When you work as a community practitioner, it is also important to make sure that your potential funders are clear about the assessment criteria relevant to this way of working.

Jasper, 1996: 14

Linda Jasper on dance

Most community dance practice is invisible, it only becomes public through performance or the publication of documentation of a project. Performances are therefore often used as a means of assessing the work of the practitioner. Careful consideration needs to be taken, by all parties, to understand the nature of what is being assessed in that context. To state the obvious, practice is not performance; everyone needs to be clear that the assessment criteria employed match the aims of the work.

> ## 79 Reflection exercise
>
> Think of examples where assessment criteria for community-based and individual art can clash. Think about issues such as:
>
> * professionalism;
> * 'polished' nature of performance;
> * 'tight' show;
> * single voices/multi voices, contradiction, single aesthetic.

These issues do not just affect funders and outsiders looking at community performance 'products'. Misunderstanding and the inability to accurately access the emotional content of participant experience can also affect other participants. Although it is often hard or inappropriate to get verbal evaluations, visual cues and 'feeling the vibe' are not always an 'accurate' guide to the inner life and experience of participants. So even within a project, the use of different evaluative forms to allow participants to communicate can be a very useful thing, as the example below shows.

A student in a New Zealand community dance class, working with people with intellectual disabilities, learned about these issues:

Holly

> At the conclusion of our dance session one gentleman stood up and thanked us for the dance experience. He reflected on what he had 'done' and told us what he had enjoyed the most. This gentleman however had barely engaged physically in any of the activities. I had assumed that he had no idea what was going on, and I was convinced that he was not enjoying himself. He had merely shuffled around the room and I had not attempted to interact with him because he presented a facial expression that I read as him not wanting to be there. I was blown away by his concluding speech and I felt disappointed in myself for not attempting to engage with him during the session. This indeed proves the need for a different framework for success as well as the dangers and inadequacy of assumption.

Practice report: working in a hospice

In my own practice, I approach evaluation and documentation as part of the creative project, and due to my focus on community practice as research, I can often argue for alternative forms of sharing value and processes. As part of a six-month Caroline Plummer Fellowship in Community Dance, I worked in a hospice (see Chapter 5). How to evaluate and document were hard questions for me: it was always unclear how much time I could spend with participants, since many of them were moved out of the hospice setting to care homes, other palliative facilities, or passed away during the months I spent there. Some people I saw for two sessions, some for four or six, some I saw for private sessions, and we shared our work with the wider hospice community afterwards, as we sat and shared tea within the whole group. I didn't think it appropriate to ask evaluative questions or solicit formal comments in these intimate sessions – I felt that I would be putting my own needs first if I tried to gather this kind of information in the short time we had. Halfway through my fellowship, I gave a short talk about the projects to the trustees of the fellowship, and I was asked how I planned to document the fellowship work. The resulting discussion was open and friendly. The trustees were open to different models of evaluation.

The first level of documentation of the hospice work, then, became the photos we had created together (see Chapter 5). They speak about intimacy and involvement at least as eloquently as any written or verbal statement. Another level of documentation included interviews with hospice staff (some of whom were involved as participants in the project). I considered interviews with family members of the participants, since many participants had given their photos as mementos to their families – but apart from chance contacts and second-hand information, I discarded that idea as potentially unkind. Audiences, of course, are a participant layer in community performance work, so one level of evaluation took place with various people who saw the final photos and danced in the final sharing in the Public Art Gallery. Many audience members offered comments after the short communal dances, and while watching our dance video installation and photos. Others emailed after the event, moved to speak in more detail about their experiences as witnesses of our work. Finally, I kept a journal of my own experiences throughout the various projects created as part of the fellowship. The final report emerged out of all of these elements, and the trustees accepted this multi-layered report graciously.

Study question

In Chapter 3, you focused on an (imaginary or real) project you would like to facilitate. Remember some of these project ideas now, and create a plan for a final report: what different creative elements could you include? How could you bring voices other than your own into the report?

Documenting witnessing

Devora Neumark is an artist living in Montreal, Canada. Her practice engages issues of witnessing, participating and dwelling – of being with a site and with people, and bringing attention to the parameters of life in the city. One of her projects offers an interesting insight into documentation practices. In *Présence* (1997), Neumark spent eight weeks in the city of Montreal, sitting on a wooden market bench near street corners, crocheting. The thread was traditionally used for the creation of Jewish religious men's head-coverings called Kippot or Yarmulkas. Whenever someone approached her and held a conversation with her, she would change the color of the thread she was working with (from yellow to purple), and recorded the duration of the contact through her needlework. After much time, Neumark had created a bi-colored vessel that visually held traces both of her periods of loneliness on the street, and of the encounters she had. Afterwards, in a gallery setting, Neumark radically undid the 'product', bringing attention to the processes that shaped it: she unraveled the threads, undid the knitting, her fingers and her witnesses in the gallery paying attention to the different moments, sharings and encounters like so many colored pieces of string.

In this project, Neumark's piece can be seen as a form of creative documentation: she doesn't document the content of the conversations and contacts she had, but their presence in time and space. She gives them a length, a duration, a volume, a material trace. Whatever stories were shared remain private as she is witnessing her witnessing, the fact that she was there, and that a contact happened, as a material event in space and time.

---

80 Reflection exercise

Think about Neumark's project as a form of documentation. What does her project say to you about:

- ownership;
- product;
- attention and care;
- personal responsibility;
- dignity and privacy;
- duration and 'being with' as a value;
- street practices, homelessness and poverty;
- self-care;
- intercultural practice;
- accountability.

After thinking through these issues, discuss them with a colleague. Now think about documentation: what kind of information is necessary to hold on to the project? What isn't? Is it important to 'catch' the content of the voices of some of the passers-by/participants in Neumark's project? If yes or no, why?

Figure 6.3 *Présence*, 1997. Devora Neumark and participants. Eight-week durational performance (at various locations around Montreal) as part of Sur l'expérience de la ville: interventions en milieu urbain organized by Optica: A Centre for Contemporary Art.   Photo: Mario Belisle

6.5 Workshop approaches to evaluation

What do funders, social services, service providers or other stakeholders need to know about the project you have been involved in? How can you show (rather than state) some of the effects of arts participation? Sometimes it can be useful (and fun) to give a 'taster' session developed out of your community project to the people who need to know about effects and efficacy.

Taster workshop

In one project I was involved in, users of mental health services were working with me for three years. During this project, we moved from the care institutions where we first worked to a community arts center in the locality. For many participants, this move signified an important step in the development of our project: we claimed an independence, a focus on art practice, and a location within the non-disabled community. As one of our evaluation tools, we staged a workshop performance for the social service providers who helped fund our work (the other main funding body was a local community education provider). These social service providers knew the project participants as 'clients' – as people in need of care and services. When they came to 'our' space, and to the community theatre stage we had been able to get for the day, the service providers first settled into the theatre seats, waiting for our performance to begin. We all got onto the stage. But instead of 'showing' our work to them, we had decided on a different way of showing what we had achieved. We invited the social service worker audience onto the stage. One participant stepped forward, and told the story we would work on together that day. And then we began to teach our audience the steps of a storytelling circle dance we had choreographed specifically for them. Each community participant took a few audience members and taught them, explaining our processes and ways of working while doing so. After runthroughs, we shared a performance on the stage. This was our documentation of the positive effects of our project: our guests had seen us as leaders and teachers. Having seen this, they took enthusiastic reports back to their superiors and decision-makers – they were much more involved than they might have been by us handing over 'verbal evidence' of personal growth.

PRACTICE EXAMPLE

6.6 Other forms of validation

Evaluations can validate projects, chart success (however defined) and make the project available to others after it has passed. But there are many other ways in which validation and documentation can occur, and can lead to positive effects for individuals, communities, collaborating organizations. Academic recognition and peer sharing are two further avenues in which community performance work can be validated. Papers at conferences, workshops at festivals and artists' meetings, research dissemination in journals, articles and pedagogical material such as this book can all be part of the documentation, evaluation and reporting procedure. Community performance work continues to be much less recognized and discussed in academic art circles, and, by extension, funding bodies. Publications and sharing through talks can educate the wider academic public as well as the general public about community performances that are often local and (relatively) small in scope. Since process is often more important than product, descriptions and sharings of work processes can allow more people to access the valuable insights community performance projects can offer. Depending on your professional environment and your comfort zones, consider giving talks about projects you've been involved in at your regional university (art teachers might welcome an offer very much), schools, libraries or art councils.

Lacy, 1994b: 180 | ### Art work in myth and memory

The effects of the work often continue beyond the exhibition or performance or interactive public art, and are magnified in the audience that experiences the work through reports, documentations, or representation. This audience includes people who read about the art work in newspapers, watch it on television, or attended subsequent documentary exhibitions. They expand the reach of the work and are, depending on the artist's intention, more or less integral to the work's construction. At least a part of this audience carries the art work over time as myth and memory. At this level the art work becomes, in the literature of art or in the life of the community, a commonly held possibility.

6.7 Validation – towards what end?

In her research on community-based artists and public art, Susan Monagan makes the following suggestions for the development of community-based art practice in relation to evaluation. After reviewing a number of artists and their practices, she sums up the problems facing community artists, the wider art scene, and the wider field within which artists are embedded. The issues of evaluation, measurement and the negotiation of different languages and values underpin many debates about the use of arts for social change:

Based on the analysis of these artists' experiences, I offer two recommendations:

1   In order to measure effectiveness and learn more about the work, specifically, and the field more generally, the field of community-based art must develop a culture of documentation, and build the means of doing this into project design because, as has been said, the final art-product is hardly an effective or complete testament to a successful project. This process of documentation needs to include follow-up so that impact can be measured and described as the art work interacts with the 'audience of myth and memory.'

2   Testimonials to the work's impact and effectiveness need to come from practitioners of other fields such as planning, community development, and economic development. These co-collaborators need to be educated about the unique properties of community artmaking and its resistance to easy definition along instrumental lines. Language needs to be developed and shared across fields that describes the effectiveness of this work and demands more opportunities to make it.

Without a more rigorous approach to documentation of work and systematic analysis of effectiveness, community based artists will have difficulty withstanding the criticism of Miwon Kwon (as referenced by Patricia Phillips) who wonders if it is possible to,

> . . . break thorough the halo-like armature of social do-goodism that protects [community-based artists] from incisive analysis or criticism.
> (Phillips, 1998, p. 5)

Monagan, 2005: 135

---

81 Reflection exercise

Discuss these conclusions. Do you feel comfortable with them? What are the issues, problems, challenges?

The Monagan statement offers a view of the tension between notions of measurement and 'community artmaking and its resistance to easy definition along instrumental lines'.

What can 'effectiveness' mean in community performance practice? Do different populations (such as artists, sociologists, city planners, project participants) have potential different definitions and stakes in 'effectiveness'? Create a list of potential effective outcomes, and think about how these issues could be measured. What kinds of outcomes do you find easiest/hardest to define/ measure/capture? Why?

Do you agree that analysis and criticism have problems approaching community-based artists? Why is that?

Is the onus of change on critics?

Analysts? Artists? All of the above?

This chapter offered guidance about practical aspects of evaluation, documentation and the sharing of outcomes. In this last section about validation, the wider theoretical underpinnings of evaluation emerge as a contested and problematic field. As the field of community performance finds new ways of integrating into the twin fields of art practice and community development, your practices of documentation, evaluation and critique are core sites for the development of a mature communication about the nature and abilities of community arts. If community performance is about widening the circle, bringing different people into collaborative creative activity, so our critical engagement with each other can mirror this effort towards inclusivity and outreach. But it might be important not to adopt uncritically the languages of non-arts-based research methods, and to attempt to fit art practice into sociological categories. Where is the heart of community performance?

CHAPTER 7

Building sustainability

This chapter looks at ways in which you can sustain your practice, how you can ensure your professional life, development and your connections to other practitioners. Funding is a large part of this, and consequently, this chapter looks at various ways of finding money for community projects. I have included various grants and fellowships as examples, even though they might no longer be available by the time you are reading this. I've selected them because they give an overview of the kind of grants available, and the form of narrative most funders require. The funding environment for community per-formance always changes quickly, and funding sources are different in different countries. When it is time for you to look for funding, you can search for the names of the funding agencies mentioned here on the Internet, or telephone your local arts boards: they will most likely have places they can point you towards.

Beyond funding, though, other issues of sustainability are important to community performance artists as well: building audiences that follow the work of a group, training and professional development, and connecting with other practitioners in order to develop and sustain one's own work.

7.1 Funding, proposals, connections

Community performances can be ongoing events, in particular if they are woven into the cultural cycle of a community: Mardi Gras happen annually, passion plays are put on every year at certain times, Gay and Lesbian Pride Parades are by now firm cultural events in many city calendars. But by definition, performances are also one-offs: they happen, and then they are over, although they might resonate, echo and repeat in many ways over time. For many community performance artists, sustainability is a major issue. For many of the non-traditional community performance artists who work in contemporary art traditions of some sort, little ecological embedment of their practice in the life and thought of their communities is a problem. Traditional community performance artists who work, for instance, with church choirs or in other religious or sacred contexts, often have a recognized value and position within their cultural environment – they usually do not have to explain what they do. Of course, they still face their own set of issues, including lack of funding and lack of recognition by and access to those art scenes and funding schemes that build on Western, modern and secular traditions. But if your practice is not necessarily transparent and clear to audiences, funders and community representatives, how can you intervene?

Here are some of the sustainability questions you might need to address:

- How can you find, nurture and sustain funding sources for your own work, and ensure that funding is a resource available to others as well?
- How can you build audiences for your own and other community performance events? How can you ensure that people do not only wish to come again, but also that they can find out about these events, and venues and locales associated with them?

From these considerations flow your own, personal ones: how can you ensure that you can work in such a way that you are supported, financially or otherwise, recognized in ways that sustain you, and that your performance practice can be a manageable and valuable part of your and other people's lives?

Figure 7.1 The Louies, a gay men's performance group, director Joan Lipkin, from That Uppity Theatre Company, St Louis, USA.
Photo: Joan Lipkin

7.1.1 Finding funders

Many community performance projects fund themselves not only through the money performances bring in, direct high profile sponsorship, or participant fees, but also through grants, development money and other funding sources that stress community integration higher than, or as highly as, aesthetic issues. Here are four examples of very different funding sources and their calls for proposals that give a sense of the different kinds of approaches and objectives that community performance facilitators might work with.

Sample project brief 1

Excerpt from 'Art and Community Landscapes' (ACL)

New England Foundation for the Arts, solicitation of artist's proposals (published with permission of the NEFA)

Allston Brighton Lincoln Street Green Strip
Boston, Massachusetts
Partner: Allston Brighton Community Development Corporation

The Lincoln Street Green Strip is a land parcel that was created in the 1960s, when the construction of the Massachusetts Turnpike through Boston physically divided the city's Allston Brighton neighborhood.

Today, the Green Strip is highly accessible to the public, adjacent to several major arteries used by automobiles, pedestrians, and frequent buses. Hundreds of people pass through the site, which serves as a gateway between a residential neighborhood and retail district. The ACL project will be a part of an overall design plan to improve this neglected piece of land, converting it from a weed and trash-filled lot into an attractive public space that improves the neighborhood's quality of life.

The site's organizational partner is Allston Brighton Community Development Corporation (ABCDC). ABCDC's mission is 'to engage neighborhood residents in an on-going process of shaping and carrying out a common vision of a diverse and stable community through community-led projects that protect and create affordable housing, greenspace, and foster a healthy local economy.' One of the most diverse neighborhoods in the region and where 35% of residents are immigrants, Allston Brighton is home to both college students and generations of families. Involvement of community members of all ages and cultures will be paramount to the ACL project implementation process. The artist will work with ABCDC and the community to creatively and comprehensively re-envision the Green Strip, and to plan and create public art work.

Sample project brief 2 (summary)

Community Dance Wales (CDW)

(Published with permission, distributed in various newsletters for dance artists, including the listserv of the Foundation for Community Dance)

'Spirit of the Valleys' (working title)
Community Dance Wales, the national umbrella body for community dance in Wales, is seeking a Choreographer (based in Wales or regularly working in Wales) for a large-scale Community Commission.

The successful applicant will be responsible for the overall artistic vision and choreography of a Site-specific Inclusive Valleys Dance project, working with local, professional dance practitioners.

The 2 week project will commence on August 22nd 2005 with a series of regular workshops and rehearsals across the area, culminating in an open air performance at Rhondda Heritage Park, September 3rd and 4th 2005.

This project is committed to enabling people of all abilities, aged 14 and over, across the six South-East Wales Valleys, to enjoy and design dance within their own landscapes.

The research and choreography fee is £4000.

All applicants must submit a written proposal to CDW, outlining ideas for a choreographic work.

Sample project (grant) brief 3

Excerpt from Australia Council (material from website)

Community Cultural Development: Grants: New Work (grant criteria and application form questions from 2005 grant round)
Through this category, the Board supports one-off projects, which create new artistic work through community-based arts and cultural activity. It is expected that these projects will have a public outcome. Projects may be initiated by communities or by individual artists and artsworkers working with communities. A project may span more than 12 months.

WHO IS ELIGIBLE TO APPLY?
This category is open to individuals and organisations. To be eligible, you must meet the general eligibility requirements, see *How to Apply* to the right, and provide the necessary support material.

Current recipients of a Fellowship grant from the Community Cultural Development Board are not eligible to apply to this category.

WHAT ARE THE SELECTION CRITERIA?

Applications will be selected that best demonstrate:

- artistic merit and innovation
- the calibre of the artists and facilitators involved
- good planning, effective use of resources and an evaluation plan for the project
- evidence of the advancement of community aspirations and effective community participation in the creative process, direction and management of the project.

Selected questions from application form:

- Describe your project, explaining what you plan to do and how you plan to do it.
- How does the project demonstrate a high level of artistic merit and innovation?
- Describe which community/communities will be involved in the project and how they will effectively participate in the creative process, direction and management of the project?
- Outline your evaluation plan for the project.
- How will you document the project?
- How will you promote your project to the wider public?
- How will you manage issues relating to copyright and community ownership of materials resulting from this project?

Note: A brochure on community copyright issues is available from the Australia Council.

Sample project brief 4

ISEA 2006/ZeroOne San Jose, Calif., USA

(Published on various international listservs connected with electronic media, and on their website)

COMMUNITY DOMAIN CALL FOR PROPOSALS FOR COMMISSIONED WORKS

This is an invitation by the ISEA2006 Symposium and ZeroOne San Jose: A Global Festival of Art on the Edge to groups and individuals to submit proposals for exhibition of interactive art works and projects reflecting on the thematic of Community Domain. Up to three commissions will be awarded, and the results will be shown at the ISEA2006 Symposium and ZeroOne San Jose Festival.

ABOUT THE COMMUNITY DOMAIN COMMISSIONS

Over the next year leading up to August 2006, individuals or groups will be commissioned to work with various San Jose communities combining technologies such as GPS, mobile communications or digital imagery to map their experiences and to tell their stories. These experiences and stories will become part of the fabric of the festival. In this way, the Festival becomes not only a glimpse of the possibilities of art and technology, but using some of those same innovative technologies, it is a celebration of the diversity found in San Jose and a platform for community members to participate.

A wide range of cultural contexts, media, art disciplines and venues are feasible within the definition of 'Community Domain'.

Community Domain

The Community Domain theme stands in relation to contemporary debate about 'Public Domain 2.0' (Kluitenberg, 2003), but emphasizes the idea of domain from a grass roots perspective and the idea of community starting with the individual rather than the demographic.

ISEA2006 and ZeroOne San Jose seek to engage diverse communities– of interest, geography, ethnicity, race, belief. In particular, we seek projects that recognize the hybridity of communities and take transverse routes across communities.

Many of the members of these communities have no specific interest in art or technology or their intersection. Yet they have stories to tell and images of the city to map. ISEA2006 and ZeroOnen San Jose are looking for projects that actively engage these audiences and help build bridges between them in ways that may utilize digital technologies, but which are not about those technologies.

In other words, the goal is not to train people to become artists but to use digital and networked technologies to allow people to participate in the creation of their own stories – to become producers rather than only consumers.

Here are a few illustrations of project designs that could fit this definition:

Silicon Valley's major population of high tech workers from India might be solicited via email for digital self-portraits taken in their workplaces, along with brief descriptions of the transformations in community life that have resulted from their relocation to the Bay Area. A team of writers and media artists might then assemble these materials into a mobile digital kiosk installed at a shopping mall during the course of the Festival.

A choreographer-in-residence might work with a local hip hop ensemble or a Vietnamese lion dance group. During the Festival, the results of this collaboration could be performed and simultaneously broadcast via the Internet to communities of interest throughout the world.

A site-specific installation might be created on the theme of Silicon Valley's legendary cubicle culture following a series of interviews with local workers. During the course of the Festival, this installation could feature a live performer who enacted the daily routine of a cubicle worker. The installation and the performer's movements could be relayed by a webcam to work stations and public venues throughout Silicon Valley.

San Jose has a very diverse and hybrid population, and we are particularly interested in projects that traverse different communities.

Proposals may be submitted by individuals or groups: professional artistic credentials and advanced forms of technology are not required. The proposal narrative should be no more than three pages in length and should cover five topics:

Description of the project: What are the characteristics of the project? In what ways will the project connect to the theme of Community Domain?

Audience: In what fashion will an audience be engaged in this project? In what ways will the project seek to engage audience members of varying cultural backgrounds?

Technology: What types of technology will be incorporated into the project?

Personnel: Please identify the key individuals/groups involved in this project, and their qualifications.

Budget: Please provide a brief explanation of how funds will be used to support this project.

Special Considerations: Projects will be welcome in a variety of traditional or new forms of art, media and physical environments. For example, projects in formal theater or exhibition settings or informal community or outdoor settings will be appropriate. All art forms are welcome including literary, performing, visual, media and multidisciplinary. Appropriate forms of technology include, but are not limited to, mobile communications, Worldwide Web, recorded audio or video, film, robotics and digital imagery.

Projects involving teams and collaboration are encouraged.

All projects should incorporate an element of 'shared space' that will be accessible to persons of varied backgrounds.

These four sample calls for proposals showcase the diversity of briefs and funding options for community performers. In each case, a detailed and well-articulated project proposal opens the way to funding and support. The artist's ability to make connections between different agendas is paramount to securing his or her livelihood. There are, of course, significant problems with this approach as well: a large amount of work goes into the preparation of the application materials, and only a very small percentage of the actual applications gain funding.

Figure 7.2 Image of participatory clown performance preceding a play about breast cancer, by the Los Puentes Project, which offers free after-school theatre programs to Latina/o young people in Humboldt County, CA, USA, 2006.   Photo: Petra Kuppers

82 Reflection exercise

Prepare a short response narrative to two of these four sample calls. After you have created these narratives, think about how else you can use the ideas and concepts you have generated: what else can these be useful for, how could you assemble a similar project based on this narrative if you are not successful in your application to these funding bodies?

Think about what the aims and objectives of the funding bodies are. If you can meet their language and politics creatively, your project has more chance of being funded. Research these bodies, and their embedment in wider structures, if you can. Here Steve Dixon and Lloyd Peters reflect on why a suite of six community performance films created in the 1980s and early 1990s were funded by their local councils:

Dixon and Peters, 2002

> The film projects suited the arts policies and criteria of Labour-controlled authorities during the 1980s. The Greater London Council and the local authorities of Calderdale, Leeds and Manchester where the projects took place were all Labour-controlled and shared many of the values and aims stated in the film project's funding bids. The projects sought to promote positive developments and self-determination within local communities, and had an educational and empowerment mission that was founded on large-scale, collective endeavour. The films were also one-off projects which did not require long-term financial support – at the time, a number of authorities were involved in attempting to extricate themselves from long-term funding commitments.
>
> The projects also promised a high-profile outcome in the form of public screenings of the completed films, which offered back some tangible 'proof' that public monies had been well spent. The films themselves were never overtly political, and answered a relatively common charge from the Right during the 1980s that monies for the arts funded 'loony-left' dogmatism, or products that were 'irrelevant' or 'anti-authoritarian'. Both left and right wing could agree on one issue that suited the ethos of the time: the film projects produced outcomes that were considered 'value for money'.

Learning many different languages and fulfilling the funder's expectations can be a considerable drain on community artists. Cultural critic Arlene Goldbard describes the situation many contemporary workers in the field find themselves in:

Goldbard, 2002

> In the face of such obstacles, artists have been amazingly resourceful. Many of the surviving community-based companies have adapted to a nonprofit economy that requires a huge time investment in grant writing to produce a barely adequate return. The philanthropic culture prizes novelty, endowing funders with the right to determine priorities, chasing fads and trends. This requires organizations to constantly repackage and refocus their work, a costly and time-consuming process. 'Success' can mean carrying several demanding and under-funded projects in order to meet overhead. An artistic director we interviewed for another Rockefeller Foundation study ('Community Cultural Development,' submitted December 14, 1999) had this to say: 'I made the decision to speak in many tongues to get the support we needed. I spoke the professional artistic language and made sure all the artists are on that level. I got a degree in social work to get into the elder facilities, because they'd say we don't want artists; and recently I learned the educational and school-reform language.' Others rely on volunteer time. The rest take advantage of opportunities. Surely the reason so much Boal-influenced work is centered in universities is that the faculty members who promote and direct it are willing to use their sinecures to anchor it, perhaps knowing that unmoored, it would never survive.

7.1.2 Fellowships

Fellowships are common in mainstream/professional art practice. They tend to support long-term projects, the development of a significant body of work, or the rigorous application of a new arts research process. Few fellowships exist in the community performance sector, but there are some general fellowships aimed at community engagement. Sometimes, fellowships aimed at mainstream art practice might consider community arts practitioners (although 'considering' them, and making the process accessible to them are two different things). Here is an example of an internationally open and accessible annually awarded fellowship, and of a successful application to it.

Sample excerpts from the application form for the Caroline Plummer Fellowship in Community Dance follow.

The Caroline Plummer Dance Fellowship

New Zealand's premier community dance residency
The Caroline Plummer Memorial Trust and the University of Otago are pleased to offer this fellowship to promote, encourage and enable community dance practice through research, teaching and community service.

1 Background
Caroline Plummer (1978–2003) was a student at the University of Otago, graduating with a Bachelor of Arts in Anthropology and a Diploma for Graduates in Dance, and a recipient of the University of Otago Prestige Scholarship in Arts. The Caroline Plummer Dance Fellowship has been established to commemorate and continue Caroline's passion and vision for dance in the community. Caroline believed in the power of dance in respect to healing, education, cultural understanding and artistic expression. Her holistic view of dance was self developed from her life experiences and her passion for dance. As Caroline wrote, 'When we dance it is one of those rare times that our mind, body, emotions and also our spirits are working as one – consciously directed towards the same intention.'

The Fellowship aims to remember and extend Caroline's belief that dance provides a unique means of celebrating and improving humanity. In Caroline's words: 'I can only hope dance can be utilised in more and more positive ways to help us embrace the diversity and difference that makes our world so fantastic.'

[. . .]

2 Who may apply for the Fellowship?
Applications are invited from New Zealand and international community dance practitioners, teachers and researchers.

Applicants for the Fellowship need not possess a university degree or diploma or any other educational or professional qualification nor belong to any association or organisation of dancers.

[. . .]

4 Tenure of the Fellowship

The tenure of the Fellowship is a consecutive six month period. In exceptional circumstances it may be awarded for a shorter or longer period with the approval of the Caroline Plummer Fellowship Advisory Board (the Advisory Board). The Fellowship will normally commence between 1 February and 1 July each year.

[. . .]

5 The Fellowship stipend

The stipend of the Fellowship will be not less than the minimum salary for a full time university lecturer over a six-month period.

[. . .]

9 Fellowship duties and requirements

The Fellow is required to:

a   work fulltime at their particular community dance project during the tenure of the Fellowship;

b   liaise with the Head of Dance Programme or Dean, School of Physical Education, and contribute to the Dance Studies programme. Such contribution may be in the form of some teaching, a staff seminar or presentation, research mentorship, staff professional development, research supervision, or other, as agreed to by the Fellow and the Head of Dance or Dean;

c   participate in or with Dunedin or other New Zealand based community dance events/community organisations, as appropriate. For example, contribute to the Otago Arts festival; present work, talk, or lend support during Cancer Awareness week; work with specific school communities; run workshops for disadvantaged youths, the elderly, people with disabilities, etc.;

d   submit a written report to the Advisory Board no later than three months after the completion of the six month Fellowship;

e   acknowledge the assistance of the Fellowship when publishing or presenting any work developed during their tenure;

f   agree to the use by the University of his or her name, photograph and details in advertising or publicity; and,

g   agree to reasonable requests from the University to participate in interviews and promotional activities.

10 Selection of Fellow

The Fellowship is awarded by the University Council by delegation to the Vice-Chancellor on the recommendation of the Advisory Board.

The successful applicant will be the candidate who, in the opinion of the Advisory Board, best meets the following criteria:

•   the applicant has proposed an exciting programme of activity, or a project, that furthers Caroline Plummer's belief in, and aspirations for, community dance in New Zealand;

- the applicant has demonstrated a commitment to and understanding of community dance, as evidenced by local, national or international experience.

   [. . .]

12 How to apply

Applications for the Fellowship must be made in writing.

   Applicants must submit:

1   A covering letter that contains the names, addresses and contact phone numbers and/or email addresses of two referees who can speak to the applicant's work.
2   A clear outline of a proposed project, including; objectives, a description of the activity, outcomes, timeframes, and budgets. The proposal should also include a statement describing the contribution that the project/activity will make to the community at large or a specific community and provide evidence that the project/activity will respect and respond to the needs of the community.
3   A curriculum vitae which should include evidence of prior community-based dance experience, and an outline of personal qualifications and skills that will support the completion of the Fellowship project.

Applicants are welcome to send photographic or video examples of their work. Please ensure any material submitted is well labeled.

Caroline Plummer Fellowship, Publicity Materials

83 Reflection exercise

Design a sample project for this fellowship, covering all the aspects asked for in 'How to Apply', section 12. Share the project description with a partner and discuss what is or is not clear.

Figure 7.3 Working with performers of Talking Bodies Company, Cardiff, Wales, 2003.   Photo: Petra Kuppers

New Zealand community dance proposal: *Mapping*

Petra Kuppers

Mapping engages our bodily skills, it asks us to locate ourselves in relation to the land and to others. Where am I? What do I move from? What are the forces that make my move possible? Who has moved here before, how did their movement affect this land, my future?

Gravity	Mythology
History	Sand
Concrete	Grass
Water	Bones
Skin	Blood
Kinesthesia	Exploration
Critique	Celebration
Emotion	Motion

Using movement work, dance technology, small temporal earth sculptures, creative writing and photography, *Mapping* will chart the energy of dance by disabled and non-disabled dancers. Together, we'll see how we all fit on the same page, on the same or different maps, or explore the borderlines of different map-legends. We'll see how we can map each other's movement onto our different bodies. Different cultures, different origins, different (body) languages: these will provide the vocabulary out of which we will choreograph and create.

   With this attention to ourselves, our cultures, and to the land and its histories, we will create a site-specific project series, with workshops both at the University and beyond, culminating in two performances (one at the University, one in an outdoor location), a digital video, and a CD ROM.

   [. . .]

84 Reflection exercise

a   What exactly does this proposal communicate to you? In what ways is it specific, in what ways is it not?

b   In what ways is this proposal specifically aimed at community arts practice? How does it differ from what you understand a mainstream/single-artist project to be?

7.1.3 Getting involved in projects with specific agendas

If you can share the aims and ideas of a specifically commissioned art work, a community artist can be a valuable addition to a team of public artists (who might use consultation and art workshops as part of their process of generating a public art work, but who do not necessarily identify as community artists). You might find employment as part of an already existing project, or you might be able to identify future collaborators and funders through careful attention to calls for proposals and design briefs, even if they do not fit your own practice specifically.

The patient journey in radiotherapy

Once a patient is referred to Radiology for outpatient treatment, his/her journey through the department is likely to take the following route:

The patient will arrive at the Southampton Oncology Centre and after notifying the receptionist will wait in the reception/ waiting area on level A. Waiting times may vary from a few minutes to an hour or more.

The patient moves from the waiting area to a sub-wait, which is close to the treatment area/ bunker called a LINAC – linear accelerator. From here s/he is escorted into the treatment area and set up for positioning which will have been calculated through the planning and simulation stages. It is important for patients to keep very still and every encouragement is used to help people to relax.

Visual therapy ceiling panels have been installed above the treatment beds in the existing LINACs and a further three sets of panels are due to be commissioned for the new LINACs. Visual therapy ceiling panels are specially commissioned backlit images, which are designed for use in treatment and other areas. The images selected are photographs of treetops and skies, photographed and subsequently viewed from the lying position, to avoid visual imbalance and aid relaxation.

THE ART WORK

Aims and objectives

The artist will be required to create an original sculpture that is robust, secure, weatherproof and easily cleaned/maintained. The courtyard will not be under cover and will be exposed to all weather conditions. Power for lighting will be provided to illuminate the work. There will be no water supply and the sculpture should not incorporate a bowl/basin for standing water as this can pose difficulties with maintenance and Health & Safety.

The courtyard will be accessible during the day to users of the Oncology Centre as well as general site visitors.

The sculpture/art work will need to be designed and fabricated to respond to the users of the space who will mainly consist of day case and in-patients and their friends/families attending radiotherapy (and specifically sat in the sub-wait area adjacent to the courtyard), staff, inpatients and visitors in wards and day rooms on level C, Southampton Oncology Centre. Therefore, the art works will need to be:

- welcoming, uplifting, positive
- able to be viewed from different horizontal and vertical planes

The artist will need to liaise with the landscape designer to ensure co-ordination of location, lighting, furniture, as well as the hard and soft landscaping, plus installation.

Theme

The underlying theme for the art work is to be based on nature/ the natural landscape. Further development of this theme will be carried out through consultation/discussion and design approval.

Southampton University Hospitals NHS Trust, 2005

Consider the excerpts on p. 211 from a design brief given by a cancer treatment centre in the UK. It provided this beautifully detailed brief to find a sculptor. How can you use this information to create a community arts project you could offer to the centre? Keep in mind that grant money at the center might be clearly regulated, so funding for a non-solicited project might need to be found in other ways – but it might be possible to create a joint funding application to the regional Arts Council, for instance.

---

85 Reflection exercise

Create a proposal for a community performance project that you can see fitting into the processes and locations of the health care center. Working communally can be very tricky in situation like this, given staff time, patient privacy, and the stigma that affects cancer survivors. Think about small interventions you could offer to the center, small, portable moments of encounter and participation. How can you explore sound-generation, small gestural work, relaxation exercises, for instance? What would be your motivation? Why would you work in this setting, given that you are not a health professional or a councilor? What other function can your project employ – a community link, a sharing of energy, a record of experience? Think through the implications. The object of this exercise is not necessarily to come up with a working idea, but to stretch yourself.

7.1.4 Expanding impact

Chapter 4 introduced the X-Ray Factory as a sample architecture regeneration project. The project promoted an interesting form of community embedment for participating artists, and for the conceptualization of labor and space. Here is the brief they offered to artists, detailing benefits of the newly reclaimed industrial space (a disused heavy machinery factory, historically used to create X-Ray machines), and offering mutually beneficial connections.

Figure 7.4 Motionhouse Dance Theatre, *The Road to the Beach*, June 2004. A performance project in partnership with The Works, Creative Parterships Cornwall and the Extreme Academy. Culminating in 'The Edge' performed by a cast of 700 with school children dancing alongside professionals along the length of Watergate Bay in Cornwall, UK.
Photo: Steve Tanner

It will be what we make it . . .

FACILITIES

- varied gallery spaces.
- a large events area with stage & sound amplification.
- a video, film & interactive-media projection area.
- cafe & meeting area.
- shop – clothing, postcards, art, catalogues, and merchandise.
- computers & net area – one PC, one Mac. Photoshop, etc.
- web-site, with curated photo gallery & weblog.
- a space about the building's history & the area's industrial heritage.
- transport of large items can be arranged at a modest cost.
- basic services: loos, water, electric, etc.

PUBLIC FUNDING

The Sozo Collective will be in receipt of funding from The Public (formerly Jubilee Arts), through funds distributed by Arts Council England.

This public funding is allocated mainly to the materials & labour associated with converting the factory to a suitable temporary arts venue, with a small amount also available for artists' commissions or expenses.

In addition, some participants have attracted sponsorship or funding for their own projects. These will be staged under the umbrella of the *re:*location event.

'I'M AN ARTIST – LET ME IN!'

We intend to make this as easy as possible. You should make your initial approach verbally to Dave Pollard – pitch him your idea or proposal. You should have already thought about . . . 1) the materials & space you might need, 2) your ability to set aside time to realise your work, and 3) whether you are, or hope to be, in receipt of sufficient funding to cover your materials and costs – and if the cheque will be cashed within the *re:*location timetable.

ARTISTS' FUNDING

Where you require funding to achieve your project, there are four possible sources of assistance:

- Some large projects by individuals may be funded up to a maximum of £5,000 by Arts Council England.
- The Public will be commissioning a number of artists on this project.
- Sozo Collective – we hope to employ a number of artists to work with other groups on site during the weeks running up to the show.
- Private and/or business sponsorship. This option is entirely down to you. There are many large industrial businesses in the area, who may be able to offer free materials, transport or production facilities, or even some cash funding. But it's entirely up to you to judge if you have the right project and the personal professionalism to approach them yourself. Please be tactful & polite. Please avoid contacting Avery & GKN since we are already in contact with them.

ARTIST'S AGREEMENT

*Re:*location will only happen if we all commit a significant amount of time & effort to the process. Artists taking part will be expected to sign an agreement, committing themselves to sharing the burden of staging the show through one or more of the following duties:

- General building and labouring work
- Painting & clearing up
- Catering
- Invigilating the show and associated events
- Sharing any useful specialist skills (e.g. plumbing)
- Staffing the 'shop'
- Marketing & distribution of promotional material
- Web-site design and maintenance

In return we hope all of our work will be seen by large numbers of art lovers in the region and beyond, and we are planning for significant exposure in arts and general publications, on the net, and on radio and TV. A number of international artists will be taking part and the networking possibilities are considerable.

Artists will also be required to receive a health & safety briefing.

Quoted from www.re-location.org.uk/about.html

86 Reflection exercise

How can you make this brief work for you as a community performance practitioner? What specific issues arise for you, for your space requirements?

Think about similar projects in your region: is this a useful model for artists/ activists seeking to regenerate under-used post-industrial spaces? What opportunities can arise, what problems can you foresee? Create a fantasy proposal for the regeneration of a site in your region, and building community arts issues into the project brief.

7.1.5 Working with existing groups

One of the main employment opportunities available to community performers who want to work in a group structure is as an education/community arts officer to an existing performance group.

Here is information from StopGAP dance company's website, an integrated UK-based performance group. This is an advertising tool that informs about the company's repertoire, and the website is designed to open up collaborative/performance opportunities.

Orbit

Choreographed by Becky Edmunds
No. of Dancers: 2 (Dan & Laura)
Music: Composed by Scott Smith and Barnaby O'Rourke
Duration: 10 minutes

Beautiful and sensual – very simply, music interpreted by pure movement.

Audience appeal:
A short movement piece without a scripted story, Orbit has an open appeal to everyone.

Idea behind the piece:
Taking the abstract idea of the orbits that happen in atoms and planets, the choreographer explores the paths the dancers make in space and the reaction those pathways and meetings cause to their movement.

Venues performed in:
Day centres, primary schools, secondary schools and community events.

www.stopgap.uk.com/html/orbit.html

87 Reflection exercise

If you had to apply for a community outreach officer position for this company, you might be asked to develop a workshop idea that could accompany this performance piece into its performance venue. Create an exercise that would fit this requirement, and find arguments which you can use to convince an employment board that your ideas will link well with the target audiences/participants (as stated under 'venues').

7.1.6 Raising funds locally

One important source of funds for community performance work is the group you work in, as well as the wider community within which it is embedded. You can fundraise by visiting local business, selling advertising space in your program. This kind of activity can even be part of the project itself: talking about the project with potential local funders already impacts the local site, and enlarges your audience.

There might be people, groups or industry in your environment that sponsor community work: speak with them, their agents or representatives, and you might find that a new sustainable partnership can be built. At the same time, make sure that you and the group are happy with the kind of mutual obligation that comes with sponsorship: are your goals and politics compatible?

You can also use subscription: members of the group pay a small amount (towards materials, hall rental etc.). If you choose this route, though, you have to be clear and transparent about how the group handles issues of non-payment – what do you do when someone just cannot (or will not) pay?

7.2 Finding and keeping audiences

In Chapter 3, I discussed how to find people to work with, and how to find participants. Many of the same avenues will be useful in finding and expanding audiences. Beyond announcing your workshops and sharings in the local media, you can also target audiences specifically by asking organizations to include the information in their newsletters, or to announce it at meetings.

There are also a number of specific techniques that can be useful in keeping audiences, and, with them, future participants. For example, at workshops and sharings, you can prepare lists of names, addresses, email, phone numbers and other contacts that allow you to stay in contact with participants (and, for recurring groups, photocopies of these lists can help participants to connect up again). You can file these names for your own announcements, and, with the permission of the participants, you can share the lists with other local community artists or umbrella organizations.

---

88 Reflection exercise

Using any of the project proposals you worked on in this chapter, draw up a list of ways of enlarging the audience for the project. What specific target groups might be interested in the work? What is the best way of reaching them? Is there a way you can get the audience 'hooked' into the project, making them part of it?

7.2.1 Linking projects/collaboration

One wonderful way of expanding your participant groups, audiences and fields of impact is through collaboration: your network meets someone else's network, and all benefit from the expanded circle. In addition, your skills will be enhanced as you learn about new ways of doing things, and as you teach your own methods to your colleagues.

In this practice example, the meeting of Australian and New Zealand artists means that cultural visitors respond to challenges.

Spaceshifting/shapeshifing

Waderbirds – Odyssey of the Wetlands

An international environmental arts project celebrating the migratory flights of the Eastern Curlew

One of the first creative problems the project team solved together was this one: When we are welcomed to New Zealand by Maori people in a time honoured and beautiful ceremony involved speeches, singing and dancing and we are asked to respond in kind – what shall we flat-footed pakeha do?

   My part of the answer to this question was a simple gesture-based movement phrase to be performed both with and without the following words:

   My heart and my voice I open to you
   I come from this place to that place over the waves
   I come for the birds, the birds, the birds.
   Together we can make a flame with the warmth of our union.

   This movement phrase was to become an emblem for the project, as strongly identified as part of Waderbirds as the giant flying bird image which was the central player in the Waderbirds story. The phrase opened the Melbourne performance in a magical way. As dusk gathered, the audience gathered on a circle of grass between two hills. Fires were lit and drums took up a rhythm as one by one dancers appeared over the crest of each hill, some fifty people, dancing the sinuous, opening, reaching, shifting movements of the phrase.

   Many hundreds of people performed the phrase as part of the Waderbirds performances. It was danced throughout the journey in the ceremonies and rituals which were part of our connection with Maori, Aboriginal and Ainu people. People close to the project used the phrase as a personal or group meditation and as a welcome and farewell. A variation even became part of that year's Stations of the Cross ceremony in Broome, performed by the whole congregation, an extraordinary mix of cultures and ages.

   . . . Is this a process of community choreography? I had always thought that choreography in the community mainly meant communities making their own movement. This process, of people taking a potent fragment of movement and deciding when, where and what to do with it was community creativity working differently.

Shelton, 1997: 24–5

7.3 Reflexive practice: taking care of yourself

If you work as an animator, community dance artist, theatre workshop leader, choral leader, or as an individual artist who supplements her practice with work in community settings, you might face certain problems and difficulties as part of your job:

- burn-out;
- energy loss;
- isolation;
- loneliness;
- lack of professional development;
- financial difficulties;
- stressful interpersonal relations.

The final part of this chapter discusses some of the strategies and ways of thinking and being that have helped community performance practitioners to maintain their practice.

---

89 Reflection exercise

a   Look at the list of potential needs or problems above. Do any of these impact on your life? Could they be part of your future?

b   Focus on one of the areas of difficulty, and think about ways in which this difficulty could be alleviated for you. Ask yourself questions such as: where to go (physically or emotionally)

- for support?
- for understanding?
- for healing?
- for creativity?
- for advice/mentoring?
- for financial/structural support?

c   In Chapter 3, you created network maps. In this map, can you see places, people, organizations, environments that could offer support for you of some kind or another? By now, can you expand/change the map? Can you add on-line, international, national or cross-regional supports or networks?

7.3.1 Practitioner networks

Networks are one of the most sustaining supports for many community performance practitioners. They alleviate a major problem facing people working in the field: isolation. While many of us are helping to build communities, sustain them and develop them, ironically isolation is something many seem to live with. Isolation is not in itself a negative experience, and many of us might search it out in geographic or aesthetic terms. But professional development, skill building and information sharing are needs for many community practitioners. Networks address these issues. There follow some examples of community performance-focused networks.

Foundation for Community Dance (journals and web-based, UK-focused, but with international contributions)

From Introduction screen of webpage, www.community dance.org.uk

The Foundation for Community Dance is the national development agency for community dance. At the centre of the national network for community dance, we represent the diversity of dance in the UK. Established in 1986 by dance artists to raise the profile and be the national voice for community dance, we work for the development of dance for all.

We campaign, take action and represent the concerns, interests and practice of community dance at all levels, acting as a catalyst for the development of partnerships between dance and communities.

Our network of members includes: dancers, animateurs, artists and dance teachers; choreographers and dancemakers; dance companies, organisations, agencies and venues; colleges, universities and training establishments; funding bodies and local authorities.

Through events, conferences, seminars, an advice service and two regular journals, we offer up-to-the-minute information, debate and dialogue about current issues in dance and the arts.

Community Arts Network (web-based, US-focused, but with international contributions)

From Welcoming Page of website, www.community arts.net

The Community Arts Network (CAN) supports the belief that the arts are an integral part of a healthy culture, providing both intellectual nourishment and social benefit, and that community-based arts provide significant value both to communities and artists.

CAN's Web site is an international resource focusing on the work of artists and their community partners – projects and programs that actively promote the arts as part of education, political life, health recovery, prisoner rehabilitation, environmental protection, community regeneration, electronic communication, and more. Here you will find a wealth of data, documentation and criticism about art that is doing important work: improving students' test scores, reducing prison violence and recidivism, reaching across racial and class barriers, bringing generations together, preserving history and culture that will otherwise be lost.

What Is community art?

CAN's *founders* chose to identify this work as 'community arts' for several reasons. Practically speaking, our Internet audience locates us through search engines, which best respond to the least common denominator. Also, the term 'community,' though widely overused in a variety of contexts, is the only one broad enough to provide an umbrella for the territory we cover. For us, 'community' means any community, whether it's defined by geography (a little town in Tennessee, a campus in Ohio, a suburb of Phoenix, a village in Brazil) or tradition (the African-American tradition, the Chicano tradition, the farming tradition) or spirit (the gay/lesbian movement, the labor movement, the Farm Workers movement).

Our definition of the term is reflected in our databases, from the narrowest view of community art as art for social change (activist art that intends to cure social ills) to the broadest view that includes public art (art installed outdoors that intersects with daily community life) and public arts policy (from arts funding to political involvement).

From 'about
ccd-net page',
all at www.ccd.net

ccd.net – a website that brings community cultural development practitioners in contact with one another, promotes projects, and provides information, Australia

Community cultural development does not have a formally agreed theory or code of practice, but is based on a framework of understanding that is loosely agreed on by those working in and with the sector. While these ideas are not overtly stated or even acknowledged, it can be argued that they still operate to shape the work of ccd.

Community development principles are a useful starting point for understanding ccd, however, ccd is more than community development + art. It is a unique practice that works creatively with communities on their own ground, on their own issues, through cultural practice.

Key features of ccd.net
Self-publishing

Publish via your web browser to ccd.net news & events, document ccd projects (current & completed) to a directory and enter your ccd-related organisation to a ccd directory. If you're brave you can put your project into the forum for comments and discussion.

ccd projects are searchable by location, art form, nature of community and include issues-based metadata for projects which address issues such as mental health or drug rehabilitation.

All Talk
online forums

Participate in web, email and live chat topical discussion forums.

Members can even use the ccd.net forum tools to create their own online network.

'Send a postcard'
Promote ccd.net practice for upcoming launches, events.

ccd E-zine
A regular edited ccd e-zine of topical issues, projects and practice.

ccd resources & more
A clearinghouse for all things ccd – web links, publications, theory & research, training & much more, with voices ranging from the seriously intellectual to the totally irreverent!

An example of a regionally-based community performance organization follows.

Community Dance Wales – history and aims

Committee for Culture, Welsh Language and Sport, Policy Review – Dance in Wales

The community dance movement in Wales has a history spanning a quarter of a century. For over twenty years a small, dedicated group of community dance practitioners worked together to support each other and share ideas. In 1989 the group was formalised as Community Dance Wales. Community Dance Wales is the national umbrella body supporting and developing best practice in community dance in Wales and receives revenue funding from ACW. It is a membership organisation, constituted as a company limited by guarantee and a registered charity.

Community Dance is for everyone – it brings people together to celebrate, to share and to dance together on an equal basis.

Aims

- lead community dance development and good practice in Wales
- promote awareness and understanding of community dance activities throughout Wales
- advocate for recognition of and increased support for community dance across Wales

Main areas of work

- organises training events
- produces regular news bulletins
- offers advice, support and consultancy
- lobbies local authorities and arts funders
- plays a role in decision and policy making
- provides opportunities for meeting and sharing

7.3.2 Personal development

One significant area of personal sustainability is training. How can you update your skills, hone your abilities? Training courses can be very useful places to meet like-minded artists, network, make new contacts for collaborations, and generally have some fun as someone other than you leads the art practice. Many community performance training institutions know that their clientele might need to find ways of making their time pay, and some might therefore offer funded places, or even payment for participating in the development sessions.

Some samples of training offers follow.

Community Music Training for World Musicians, UK

The community music course aims to help musicians from Britain's ethnic minority communities as well as people recently arrived, to learn skills in running workshops and encouraging young people to get involved in new kinds of music. The course will cover workshop leading, communication skills, networking to find work, and placements with more experienced community musicians. It runs on Wednesday evenings from October 22 to January 14.

There is high demand for world music activities and a shortage of experienced and trained musicians to lead them. People completing the course will join databases and networks of community music and arts organizations that can put them in touch with work opportunities.

The course leader is Duncan Chapman, an internationally renowned musician, trainer and project leader for all kinds of cross-cultural musical projects around the world. Other experienced musicians from a range of traditions, including Afro-Caribbean, Asian and African will also be visiting to share their experience.

This World Music course is part of 'Generation', a training program run by Sound it Out Community Music and the three Youth Music Action Zones in the region: Shropshire/Herefordshire, Staffordshire/Stoke and Birmingham.

Two other courses for musicians with more experience of community work are also running this autumn: Early Years, and Youth Offending – also areas where there is high demand for music activities and a shortage of experienced and trained musicians to lead them.

Cornerstone Institute Summer Residency Program, US (July 9–August 6, 2006)

The Cornerstone Institute Summer Residency Program offers a unique, hands-on collaborative experience creating theater and exploring strategies for community engagement while living with and within a small, diverse community. Students learn both through classroom training and hands-on creation of community-specific productions, which combine their own artistry with that of experienced professionals and community collaborators. Classroom training and production experience will combine to provide a thorough understanding of the community collaboration process, from beginning to end.

Who should apply?

Institute students are individuals seeking to study and collaborate with professionals who are well-versed in ensemble, community-based theater. Theater experience is helpful but not required. Students must be 18 or older and can be at any stage of their education or career. Applicants may include theater artists of any discipline (performers, writers, directors, designers, administrators, etc.) as well as educators, community organizers, activists, or anyone else interested in the intersection of theater and community. Past participants have ranged in age from 18 to 59, and have included undergraduate and graduate students (in disciplines of theater, education, sociology and anthropology), filmmakers, teachers, playwrights, musicians and clergy.

Each student will fulfill specific positions in the production process – performing, building, painting, assisting with dramaturgy, designing, community relations, creating music, public relations, working with local youths, etc. Since the whole endeavor is collaborative, individuals will share many practical and creative responsibilities.

Who is the community?
Cornerstone seeks to create theater with interesting and interested communities. A community can be defined by geography, occupation, circumstance or culture. We ask the community to support the production with time, energy and sharing of their stories and experiences. We do not ask for money, but we do seek assistance with housing for the incoming artists (faculty and students) who will reside in the community for 4 to 6 weeks. Housing solutions have included residing in school buildings, vacant houses and apartments, and empty restaurants.

Curriculum
The Institute offers hands-on participation, mentorship and course curriculum in Cornerstone's unique methodology to gain an understanding of the community collaboration process from beginning to end.

Topics of study include: Cornerstone's own history of creating community-based theater in rural and urban America, working as an ensemble, dialogue/communication and decision-making techniques, identifying a community and community partners, story circles and play adaptation techniques, practical production needs specific to community-based theater, ongoing relationships with community artists, and concepts in collaboration.

Material from website, www.cornerstonetheater.org

Laban Guild Community Dance Leaders Course, UK (material published with permission)

Initiated in 1981, the Laban Guild Community Dance Leaders course is now a well established course, accepted by professional bodies and eligible for funding from the Regional Sports and Regional Arts Councils. It has been employed by Education Authorities and Dance Animateurs. Courses have run in such places as Suffolk, Somerset, Nottingham, Essex, Wiltshire, Powys, Belfast, Dublin and Kildare. The N. Wales Access and Credit Consortium have validated this course for recognition by the Open College Network.

The pool of highly qualified and experienced tutors within the Guild ensures that each module of the course is taught by specialists in that area.

The course attracts participants from many different backgrounds and experiences including teaching, physiotherapy, social work, therapy, choreography, youth work and the arts.

Aims
To train leaders for community dance groups.
To develop in them a practical knowledge of Laban's analysis of movement.
To stimulate in them an ambition to further this knowledge at a higher level.

Entry requirements

Some experience of Community Dance plus a recommendation from a group leader

> or

Experience of teaching dance

> or

Experience of leading a dance group.

A selection procedure will be employed and two references will be required with the application form.

Course structure

The course extends over two years and includes:

10 weekends of practical and theoretical study, (Sat am to Sun pm) approximately 120 hours.

Attendance at 2 Laban Guild AGMs.

Attendance at a recognised Summer Course (1 week of full time study).

Assignments to be completed at home.

Assessment weekend. This is offered to those completing the course, subject to

> recommendation by course tutors.

Content

The course is designed in three modules:

Three weekends of Laban Fundamentals of Movement.

Three weekends of Anatomy, Teaching Skills and the preparation of Community Dance

> sessions.

Four weekends of Ideas for Dance and Dance Making.

Each weekend will focus on particular areas of Laban based study; covering concepts of body awareness, quality of movement, spatial orientation and relationships.

Attention is given to composition work and the teaching of movement and dance with special reference to the needs of community dance groups.

Various teaching styles and methods useful in presenting material to community groups are introduced and practised.

A well designed input on basic anatomy and physiology, with particular emphasis on common injuries and their prevention, will be an integral part of the course.

Starting points and accompaniments for community dance sessions will be covered.

Such topics as running a group, finding members, venues, finances, publicity etc. will also be included.

Requirements of the course

Each course member will undertake to:

Attend each of the 10 weekends and participate fully in them. If prevented by illness from

> participating in all or part of a weekend, a course member may be required to complete an
> additional assignment set by the course tutor.

Keep a coursework file/journal, containing notes on the practical and theoretical sessions of the weekends with personal comments and evaluations.

Keep a diary of community dance work done between course weekends.

Complete various written and practical assignments involving reading, observation, collection of resources and the preparation and presentation of teaching sessions.

Practical work, course work files and assignments will be assessed by course tutors and a panel of external assessors, overseen by an external moderator.

Those members presenting themselves for Certificate Assessment will have to show evidence of the knowledge and skills gained and be able to demonstrate these in preparing and leading a practical session.

Successful candidates

Will be placed on the Guild Register of qualified teachers and be eligible for full insurance cover.

Will be deemed eligible for certain Further Education courses, such as City and Guilds Acset for the teaching of adults.

Will have the opportunity for further development by attending more advanced Laban Guild courses including the C.D.T. Stage II course.

Laban Guild, publicity material

7.3.3 Artists' residencies

One wonderful personal development opportunity for artists is artists' communities. Even though your main practice might be in working with other people, time out to develop new skills or to reflect on past or future projects can be very valuable. Many organizations in different countries all over the world offer artists a room to stay, and often a studio. Some residencies pay artists a modest fee to cover board and travel, others require a (usually small) weekly fee for their offers. Most artists' communities work as not-for-profits, and all exist to make creative inquiry possible. Community artists are often in a strange position in regard to application procedures: if you do not put your personal signature to the art making you facilitate, how can you present yourself in an art work that tends to value the individual artist, working by her- or himself, and creating recognizable products? While translating your practice for application forms can be daunting, it is useful to remember that most of these organizations are run by artists, or by people well aware of the complex and multifaceted nature of contemporary art practice. You can always phone or email the organizers, and ask them for advice on how to present your application. Given the hundreds of artists' residences, colonies, retreats etc., you are likely to find some that are sympathetic to your practice and your needs.

Resources for artist's residencies:

www.artistcommunities.org
www.resartis.org

7.3.4 Local networks

Another excellent source of support is your local network. When we set up a regional community performance professional development network in Rhode Island in 2004, many different people found their way to us, mainly through word of mouth, but also through our advertising in local free listings. The group met about every three to four weeks, had lunch together, and exchanged notes from our work life, information, and set up training opportunities. As part of our skill development, members gave short, fifteen-minute talks to each other: they introduced their own practice. We also organized performance picnics in local parks and a community performance sharing in a local theatre as ways of raising our profile, educating critics and funders about the nature of our work, and having fun together. One recurrent theme in our discussions was an in-depth analysis of what we understood the term 'community performance' to mean. We refused to accept any one definition, and this openness at the heart of our assembly provided a useful motor for us.

This chapter presented multiple ideas of ensuring sustainability of your practice: from finding funds or projects to link into, to ways of keeping yourself skilled, engaged and informed. Ultimately, though, I have always found that the key to my own sustained practice is working with others. The energy of projects and participants feeds my practice, and helps me to find my way, in touch with others. If your life and circumstances do not allow you to work all the time in fully developed workshops, just try to find other ways of hooking into the energies community practice offers: get some friends together on a beach, in a forest, in a car park, in a city park, in a home, and try out project ideas.

> 90 Reflection exercise
>
> Given the nature of your locality, how can you access other practitioners who might be interested in community performance? Are there community theatre or community dance classes run by your local training providers, and students or trainees that you could contact?

Figure 7.5 *(Facing page)* Community performance picnic. Networking, sharing and celebrating what we do, learning from each other: as part of this open day of music, performances, workshops and food in a Providence park, Carol Anne Buckley teaches Hawaiian hula, Amy Lynn Budd presents belly dancing, Shanthi and Pavitra Muthu perform and then teach Indian dance forms, Susan Masket presents her waste-art and leads us in making music with instruments created out of trash. The event was part of the closing of a year-long professional development series, 2005.   Photos: Petra Kuppers

Epilogue

In the introductory chapters, I invited you to begin a map of community performance definitions. By now, you will probably have amassed a wealth of information, insights, practice ideas and concepts.

You will have some of your own ideas about the histories that make up the legacy of community performance, you will have familiarized yourself with some of the issues you face as you set up and run a group, you will have many session ideas, and you will have encountered issues of documentation, evaluation and professional development. Through quotes, images and your own research, you will also have encountered many different kinds of community performance praxis.

Your map and all this explanatory material can only ever be tools to help you as you actually engage the territory of community performance. Your main source of inspiration, knowledge and insight will be your own experience, and the generosity of the people you work with. And value your experience: share it, talk and write about your group's work in your networks, so that our resource box of inspirations and exercises grows heavier and fuller.

Have fun, challenge yourself and, communally, change the world.

Bibliography

Abdu, Sulaiman. 2003. 'Theatre For Development and its Challenges in Eritrea', KIT Special on Theatre for Development, theatre for development resources webpage.

Abrams, David. 1996. *The Spell of the Sensuous: Perception and Language in a More-Than-Human World*. New York: Vintage.

Anderson, Benedict. 1991. *Imagined Communities: Reflections on the Origin and Spread of Nationalism*. London and New York: Verso.

Anger, Katherine. 2001. 'Beyond the Barricade'. *New Internationalist*, 338, September 2001.

Angharad, Jen. 2004. 'Welsh through the Medium of Dance'. *Animated*, Summer 2004.

Annabelle Jackson Associates. 2004. *Evaluation Toolkit for the Voluntary and Community Arts in Northern Ireland*. Report for the Arts Council of Northern Ireland, Bath.

Arguilles, Lavernia, Emman Carmona, Emma Davies-Webb *et al.* 1998. *Dagyaw: A Manual to Help Groups Use Popular Theatre to Explore, Analyze and Take Action on Local and Global Environmental Issues*. Footprints Ensemble.

Artaud, Antonin. 1970. 'Seraphim's Theatre', in *The Theatre and its Double*, trans. Victor Corti. London: Calder and Boyars.

Bakhtin, Mikhail. 1968. *Rabelais and His World*. Cambridge, MA: MIT Press.

Barnes, James. 2004. *Sea Songs. Reader's Theatre from the Pacific*. Portsmouth, NH: Heinemann.

Barrios, Joi. 1998. 'The Taumbayan as Epic Hero, the Audience as Community', in Jan Cohen-Cruz (ed.) *Radical Street Performance: An International Anthology*. London: Routledge: 255–61.

Beatson, Peter and Dianne Beatson. 1994. *The Arts in Aotearoa New Zealand: Themes and Issues*. Palmerston North: Massey University.

Benjamin, Adam. 2001. *Making an Entrance. Theory and Practice for Disabled and Non-disabled Dancers*. London and New York: Routledge.

Berrigan, F. 1974. *'Animation' Projects in the UK. Aspects of Socio-Cultural Community Development*. Leicester: National Youth Bureau.

Bharucha, Rustom. 2000. *The Politics of Cultural Practice: Thinking Theatre in an Age of Globalization*. London: Athlone Press.

Block, Erika. 2005. 'The Walking Project: Desire Lines, Walking and Mapping Across Continents', Community Arts Network website.

Boal, Augusto. 1992. *Games for Actors and Non-Actors*, trans. Adrian Jackson. London and New York: Routledge.

Bourriaud, Nicolas. 1998. *Relational Aesthetics*. Paris: Presses du Réel.

Brecht, Bertolt. 1964. *Brecht on Theatre*, trans. John Willett. London: Methuen.

Byram, M and Ross Kidd. 1976. 'The Performing Arts and Development: A Botswana Experiment in a New Approach to Rural Education', *Proceedings of the AFRO Workshop on Rural Environment and Development Planning in Southern Africa*. Gaborone: University College of Botswana: 85–95.

Cameron, Ronaldo. 1997. 'Ronaldo Cameron, Edited and Introduced by Nicola Cameron', in Helen Poynor and Jacqueline Simmonds (eds) *Dancers and Communities: A Collection of Writings About Dance as a Community Art*. Walsh Bay: Ausdance: 4–11.

Casey, Edward S. 2002. *Representing Place: Landscape Painting and Maps*. Minneapolis, MN: University of Minnesota Press.

Cohen-Cruz, Jan. 2005. *Local Acts: Community-Based Performance in the United States*. New Brunswick, NJ: Rutgers University Press.

de Certeau, Michel. 1988. *The Practice of Everyday Life*. Berkeley, CA: University of California Press.

Dixon, Steve and Lloyd Peters. 2002. 'Big is Beautiful'. Salford: University of Salford (www.smmp. salford.ac.uk/research/performance/bib/funding.html).

Driskill, Qwo-Li. 2003. 'Mothertongue: Incorporating Theatre of the Oppressed into Language Restoration Movements', in Jon Reyhner, Octaviana V. Trujillo, Roberto Luis Carrasco and Louise Lockard (eds) *Nurturing Native Languages*. Flagstaff, AZ: Northern Arizona University: 155–63.

Eames, Penny. 2003. *Creative Solutions and Social Inclusion: Culture and the Community*. Wellington: Arts Across Aotearoa.

Eldredge, Sears A. 1996. *Mask Improvisation for Actor Training and Performance: The Compelling Image*. Evanston, IL: Northwestern University Press.

von Emmel, T. 2005. 'Somatic Performance: Relational Practices and Knowledge Activism of Bodies Improvising', unpublished dissertation, Human and Organization Development. Santa Barbara, CA: Fielding Graduate University.

Fensham, Rachel. 1997. 'Dance and the Problems of Community', in Helen Poynor and Jacqueline Simmonds (eds) *Dancers and Communities: A Collection of Writings about Dance as a Community Art*. Walsh Bay: Ausdance: 14–19.

Filewood, Alan and David Watt. 2001. *Worker's Playtime: Theatre and the Labor Movement Since 1970*. Sydney: Currency Press.

Finnan, Kevin. 2003. 'Holding the Balance'. *Animated*, Summer, 2003.

Fisher, Amanda Stuart. 2004. 'The Playwright in Residence: A Community's Storyteller', *TDR*, 48 (3): 135–49.

Fletcher, John. 2003. 'Identity and Agonism: Tim Miller, Cornerstone, and the Politics of Community-Based Theatre', *Theatre Topics*, 13 (2): 189–203.

Fox, John. 1991. *A Plea for Poetry*. National Arts and Media Strategy Unit, Welfare State International website.

Fox, Jonathan (ed.). 1987. *The Essential Moreno: Writings on Psychodrama, Group Method, and Spontaneity by J.L. Moreno*. New York: Springer.

Francis, Fi. 1999. 'Increasing Visibility', *Animated*, Summer 1999.

Frazer, James Gordon. 1922. *The Golden Bough*. New York: Macmillan.

Freire, Paulo. 1983. *Trans. Myra Bergman Ramos: Pedagogy of the Oppressed*. New York: Continuum.

—— 1998. 'Cultural Action and Conscientization', *Harvard Educational Review*, 68 (4): 502.

Gablik, Suzi. 1991. *The Reenchantment of Art*. New York: Thames & Hudson.

Garavelli, Maria Elena. 2004. 'Ethics, Aesthetics and Politics: A New Involvement in the Community', first published in *Interplay*, *Journal of the International Playback Theatre Network*.

Garfinkel, Harold. 1967. *Studies in Ethnomethodology*. Englewood Cliffs, NJ: Prentice-Hall.

Goffman, Erving. 1959. *The Presentation of Self in Everyday Life*. London: Penguin.

—— 1963. *Stigma: Notes on the Management of Spoiled Identity*. New York: Simon & Schuster.

Goldbard, Arlene. 2002. 'Memory, Money, and Persistence: Theater of Social Change in Context', *Theater*, 31 (3).

Gomez-Pena, Guillermo. 1991. 'A Bi-National Performance Pilgrimage', *TDR*, 35 (3): 22–45, 22–3.

Grantham, Barry. 2000. *Playing Commedia. A Training Guide to Commedia Techniques*. Portsmouth, NH: Heinemann.

Haedicke, Susan C. 1998. 'Dramaturgy in Community-Based Theatre', *Journal of Dramatic Theory and Criticism*, XIII: 1.

—— and Tobin Nellhaus. 2001. 'Introduction', in Susan C. Haedicke and Tobin Nellhaus (eds) *Performing Democracy: International Perspectives on Urban Community-Based Performance*. Ann Arbor, MI: Michigan University Press: 1–23.

Hawkins, Gay. 1993. *From Nimbin to Mardi Gras: Constructing Community Arts*. Sydney: Allen & Unwin.

The Health Development Agency. 2000. *Art for Health: A Review of Good Practice in Community-based Arts Projects and Initiatives which Impact on Health and Wellbeing*. London.

Hobsbawm, Eric. and T. Ranger (eds) 1983. *The Invention of Tradition*. Cambridge: Cambridge University Press.

hooks, bell. 2003. *Teaching Community: A Pedagogy of Hope*. London and New York: Routledge.

Horwitz, Tony. 1998. *Confederates in the Attic: Dispatches from the Unfinished Civil War*. New York: Vintage.

Hyman, Colette. 1997. *Staging Strikes: Worker's Theater and the American Labor Movement*. Philadelphia, PA: Temple University Press.

Illich, Ivan. 1981. *Shadow Works*. London: Marion Boyars.

Jasper, Linda. 1996. 'Community Dance and Education', *Thinking Aloud. In Search of a Framework for Community Dance*. Leicester: The Foundation for Community Dance: 11–14.

Jellicoe, Ann. 1987. *Community Plays: How To Put Them On.* London: Methuen.

Jung, Carl. 1973. *Mandala Symbolism*. Princeton, NJ: Princeton University Press.

Kaplan, Rachel (ed.). 1995. *Ann Halperin. Moving towards Life. Five Decades of Transformational Dance*. Hanover and London: Wesleyan University Press.

Kaprow, Allan. 1966. *Assemblages, Environments, and Happenings*. New York: Abrams.

Kast, Maggie. 2000. 'Dance-Camp for Grown-Ups', *Contact Quarterly*, 22: 4.

Katz, Elias. 2002. *Arts Centers for Adults with Disabilities*. Community Arts Network website.

Kaufman, Moisés and the Members of the Tectonic Theatre Project. 2001. *The Laramie Project*. New York: Vintage.

Kerr, D. 1995. *African Popular Theatre*. London: James Currey.

Kershaw, Baz. 1978, 'Theatre Art and Community Action', *Theatre Quarterly*, VIII: 30.

—— 1997. *The Politics of Performance: Radical Theatre as Cultural Intervention*. London and New York: Routledge.

Kuftinec, Sonia. 1997. '*Odakle Ste?* (Where Are You From?): Active Learning and Community-Based Theatre in Former Yugoslavia and the US', *Theatre Topics*, 7 (2): 171–86.

—— 2003. *Staging America: Cornerstone and Community-Based Theatre*. Carbondale, IL: Southern Illinois Press.

Kuoni, Carin (ed.). 1990. *Energy Plan for the Western Man: Joseph Beuys in America*. New York: Four Walls Eight Windows.

Kuppers, Petra. 2003. *Disability and Contemporary Performance: Bodies on Edge*. London and New York: Routledge.

—— 2005. 'Dancing Dolphins: Approaches to Eco-Arts and Community Dance', Arts Culture Nature newsletter.

—— and Robertson, Gwen (eds). 2007. *Community Performance Reader*. London: Routledge.

Kwon, Miwon. 2002. *One Place After Another: Site-Specific Art and Locational Identity*. Cambridge, MA: MIT.

Lacy, Suzanne (ed.). 1991. 'Saving the World: A Dialogue between Susanne Lacy and Rachel Rosenthal', *Artweek*, September 12 (1): 14–16.

—— 1994a. *Mapping the Terrain: New Genre Public Art*. Seattle, WA: Bay Press.

—— 1994b. 'Debated Territory: Toward a Critical Language for Public Art', in Suzanne Lacy (ed.) *Mapping the Terrain. New Genre Public Art*, Seattle, WA: Bay Press: 171–85.

Lazarus, Joan. 2004. *Signs of Change: New Directions in Secondary Theatre Education*. Portsmouth, NH: Heinemann.

Lefebvre, Henri. 1991. *The Production of Space*. Oxford: Blackwell.

Lev-Aladgem, Shulamith. 2004. 'Whose Play Is It? The Issue of Authorship/Ownership in Israeli Community-Based Theatre', *The Drama Review*, 48 (3): 117–34.

Lomas, Christine. 1998. 'Art and the Community: Breaking the Aesthetic of Disempowement', in Sherry Shapiro (ed.) *Dance, Power and Difference: Critical and Feminist Perspectives on Dance Education*. Champaign, IL: Human Kinetics: 149–69.

Lorde, Audre. 1984. *Sister Outsider*. Freedom, CA: Crossing.

Magill, Tom. n.d. Interview with Augusto Boal, Northern Vision Media Center (www.northernvisions.org).

Martin, John. 2004. *Intercultural Performance Handbook*. London and New York: Routledge.

Mason, Bim. 1992. *Street Theatre and Other Outdoor Performances*. London: Routledge.

Matarasso, François. 1998. 'Valuing Dance', *Animated*, Summer: 20–1.

Mendel, Tessa. 2003. 'Introduction', in *Women's Voices and African Theatre: Case Studies from Kenya, Mali, The Democratic Republic of Congo and Zimbabwe*, Article 19: 1–9.

Merleau-Ponty, Maurice. 1962. *Phenomenology of Perception*. London: Routledge & Kegan Paul, 1962.

Miles, Dillwyn. 1992. *The Secret of the Bards of the Isle of Britain*. Llandybie: Gwasg Dinefwr Press.

Monagan, Susan. 2005. 'The Artmaker as Active Agent: Six Portrait', unpublished Master's thesis, Cornell University.

Nalungiaq. 1983. 'Interview by Knud Rasmussen', trans. Edward Field, in Jerome and Diane Rothenberg (eds) *Symposium of the Whole*. Berkeley, CA: University of California Press: 3.

Olsen, Andrea. 2002. *Body and Earth. An Experiential Guide*. Middlebury, VT: Middlebury College Press.

Paterson, Douglas. 1996. 'A Brief Introduction to Augusto Boal', *High Performance*, 72, Summer 1996, republished on the Community Arts Network website.

Paxton, Steve. 1978. *Contact Quarterly*, III: 1.

Peppiatt, Anthony. 1996. 'What is a Framework and Why Does it Matter', *Thinking Aloud. In Search of a Framework for Community Dance*. Leicester: The Foundation for Community Dance: 2–3.

Perlstein, Susan. 2002. 'Arts and Creative Aging Across America', published on the Community Arts Network website, October.

Phillips, Charles. 1999. 'Questions of Heaven', in Tony Allan and Charles Philip (eds) *Land of the Dragon: Chinese Myth*. London: Duncan Baird Publishers: 28–49.

Pond, Wendy. 1995. 'Wry Comments from the Outback: Songs of Protest from the Niua Island', in Ruth Finnegan and Margaret Orbell (eds) *South Pacific Oral Traditions*. Bloomington, IN: Indiana University Press: 49–6.

Pratte, Richard. 1979. *Pluralism in Education*, Springfield, IL: Charles C. Thomas.

Prentki, Tim and Jan Selman. 2000. *Popular Theatre in Political Culture. Britain and Canada in Focus*. Bristol: Intellect.

Rhodes, Colin. 2000. *Outsider Art, Spontaneous Alternatives*. London: Thames & Hudson.

Ricoeur, Paul. 1996. 'Reflections on a New Ethos for Europe', in Richard Kearney (ed.) *Paul Ricoeur: The Hermeneutics of Action*. London: Sage Publications.

Roach, Joseph. 1996. *Cities of the Dead. Circumatlantic Performance*. New York: Columbia University Press.

Rogers, Dave. 1997. 'Banner Theatre: What Kind of Theatre', Banner Theatre website.

Sainer, Arthur. 1997. *The New Radical Theatre Notebook*. London and New York: Applause.

Schechner, Richard. 1994. *Environmental Theatre. Expanded Edition*. London and New York: Applause.

Schutzman, Mady. 1994. 'Brechtian Shamanism', in Mady Schutzman and Jan Cohen-Cruz (eds) *Playing Boal: Theatre, Therapy, Activism*, New York: Routledge: 137–55.

—— and Jan Cohen-Cruz (eds). 1994. *Playing Boal: Theatre, Therapy, Activism*. London and New York: Routledge.

Shelton, Beth. 1997. 'Change through Human Motion: Reflections on Choreography in Community', in Helen Poynor and Jacqueline Simmonds (eds) *Dancers and Communities: A Collection of Writings about Dance as a Community Art*. Walsh Bay: Ausdance: 24–8.

Smith, Ron. 2005. 'Magical Realism and Theatre of the Oppressed in Taiwan: Rectifying Unbalanced Realities with Chung Chiao's Assignment Theatre', *Asian Theatre Journal*, 22 (1): 107–21.

Southampton University Hospitals NHS Trust. 2005. Partnerships for Arts in Healthcare. Southampton Oncology Center Phase 2A. Artists' Brief – 3D Art/Sculpture for Courtyard – Level A. Commission No.: SOC2ACOURTYARD, published by the Southampton University Hospitals NHS Trust.

Stewart, James T. 1968. 'The Development of the Black Revolutionary Artist', in LeRoi Jones and Larry Neal (eds) *Black Fire: An Anthology of Afro-American Writing*. New York: William Morrow.

Stock, Cheryl. 1997. 'Meet Me at Kissing Point', in Helen Poynor and Jacqueline Simmonds (eds) *Dancers and Communities: A Collection of Writings about Dance as a Community Art*. Walsh Bay: Ausdance: 121–7.

Sullivan, John. 2005. *El Teatro Lucha de Salud del Barrio: Theater and Environmental Health in Texas*. Community Arts Network website.

Tauroa, Hiwi and Pat. 1986. *Te Marae. A Guide to Customs and Protocol*. Auckland: Heinemann Reed.

Te Maire Tau. 2003. 'Te-Puna-o-Wai-whetu', *Te Puàwai o Ngāi Tahu: 12 Contemporary Ngāi Tahu Artists*. Christchurch: Christchurch Art Gallery: 10–14.

Thiong'o, N'Gugi Wa. 1998. *Penpoints, Gunpoints and Dreams: Towards a Critical Theory of the Arts and the State in Africa*. Oxford: Oxford University Press.

Turner, Victor. 1982. *From Ritual to Theater: The Human Seriousness of Play*. New York: Performing Arts Journal Publications.

Unit for the Arts and Offenders. 2002. *Getting Our Act Together. Literacy through Drama in Prisons*. Unit for the Arts and Offenders.

Van Erven, Eugene. 2001. *Community Theatre: Global Perspectives*. London and New York: Routledge.

Wetland Care Australia. 2000. *Living with Wetlands – A Community Guide*. Ballina: Wetland Care Australia.

Williams, Raymond. 1973. *Keywords*. New York: Oxford University Press.

Young, Iris Marion. 1990. 'The Ideal of Community and the Politics of Difference', in Linda J. Nicholson (ed.) *Feminism/Postmodernism*. New York and London: Routledge: 300–23.

Index

Related titles from Routledge

Disability and Contemporary Performance
Bodies on Edge

Petra Kuppers

Disability and Contemporary Performance presents a remarkable challenge to existing assumptions about disability and artistic practice. In particular, it explores where cultural knowledge about disability leaves off, and the lived experience of difference begins. Petra Kuppers, herself an award-winning artist and theorist, investigates the ways in which disabled performers challenge, change and work with current stereotypes through their work. She explores freak show fantasies and 'medical theatre' as well as live art, webwork, theatre, dance, photography and installations, to cast an entirely new light on contemporary identity politics and aesthetics.

This is an outstanding exploration of some of the most pressing issues in performance, cultural and disability studies today, written by a leading practitioner and critic.

ISBN13: 978–0–415–30238–8 (hbk)
ISBN13: 978–0–415–30239–5 (pbk)

Available at all good bookshops
For ordering and further information please visit:
www.routledge.com

Community Theatre
Global perspectives

Eugene van Eerven

Community theatre is an important device for communities to collectively share stories, to participate in political dialogue, and to break down the increasing exclusion of marginalised groups of citizens. It is practised all over the world by growing numbers of people.

Community Theatre: Global perspectives is a unique record of these theatre groups in action. Based on Eugene van Erven's own travels and experiences working with community theatre groups in six very different countries, this is the first study of their work and the methodological traditions which have developed around the world.

ISBN13: 978–0–415–19034–3 (hbk)
ISBN13: 978–0–415–19031–2 (pbk)

The Aesthetics
of the Oppressed

Augusto Boal

'We must all do theatre – to find out who we are, and to discover who we could become.'

Augusto Boal – legendary Brazilian theatre director and creator of *Theatre of the Oppressed* – is back, with a stunning new collection of essays and stories.

Boal's vision of the transformative power of theatre reaches new heights with this latest polemic against globalisation and the sedative effects of Hollywood and television.

The Aesthetics of the Oppressed describes the basis of a practical theatre project which enables individuals to reclaim themselves as subjects. Its central message is that we can discover Art by discovering our own creativity, and by discovering our creativity we discover ourselves.

In this latest despatch, Boal communicates his inspirational vision – articulating and expanding upon the practical and theoretical foundations of the work which over the last thirty years has become a vibrant international theatre movement.

ISBN13: 978–0–415–37176–6 (hbk)
ISBN13: 978–0–415–37177–3 (pbk)

Performance Studies
An Introduction

2nd Edition

Richard Schechner

Praise for the first edition
'An appropriately broad-ranging, challenging, and provocative introduction, equally important for practicing artists as for students and scholars of the performing arts.'

Phillip Zarrilli, *University of Exeter*

Fully revised and updated in light of recent world events, this important new edition of a key introductory textbook by a prime mover in the field provides a lively and accessible overview of the full range of performance.

Performance Studies includes discussion of the performing arts and popular entertainments, rituals, play and games as well as the performances of every day life. Supporting examples and ideas are drawn from the performing arts, anthropology, post-structuralism, ritual theory, ethology, philosophy and aesthetics.

The text has been fully revised, with input from leading teachers and trialled with students. User-friendly, with a special text design, it also includes:

- new examples, biographies, source material and photographs
- numerous extracts from primary sources giving alternative voices and viewpoints
- biographies of key thinkers
- activities to stimulate fieldwork, classroom exercises and discussion
- key readings for each chapter
- twenty line drawings and 202 photographs drawn from private and public collections around the world.

For undergraduates at all levels and beginning graduate students in performance studies, theatre, performing arts and cultural studies, this is the must-have book in the field.

ISBN13: 978–0–415–37245–9 (hbk)
ISBN13: 978–0–415–37246–6 (pbk)

Available at all good bookshops
For ordering and further information please visit:
www.routledge.com

eBooks – at www.eBookstore.tandf.co.uk

A library at your fingertips!

eBooks are electronic versions of printed books. You can store them on your PC/laptop or browse them online.

They have advantages for anyone needing rapid access to a wide variety of published, copyright information.

eBooks can help your research by enabling you to bookmark chapters, annotate text and use instant searches to find specific words or phrases. Several eBook files would fit on even a small laptop or PDA.

NEW: Save money by eSubscribing: cheap, online access to any eBook for as long as you need it.

Annual subscription packages

We now offer special low-cost bulk subscriptions to packages of eBooks in certain subject areas. These are available to libraries or to individuals.

For more information please contact webmaster.ebooks@tandf.co.uk

We're continually developing the eBook concept, so keep up to date by visiting the website.

www.eBookstore.tandf.co.uk